The Master Trend

How the
Baby Boom Generation
Is Remaking America

The Master Trend

How the Baby Boom Generation Is Remaking America

Cheryl Russell

PLENUM PRESS • NEW YORK AND LONDON

Library of Congress Cataloging-in-Publication Data

Russell, Cheryl, 1953–
    The master trend : how the baby boom generation is remaking
America / Cheryl Russell.
        p.   cm.
    Includes bibliographical references and index.
    ISBN 0-306-44507-7
    1. United States--Social conditions--1945-   2. Baby boom
generation--United States.   3. Social problems--United States.
4. Individualism--United States.   I. Title.
HN57.R79   1993
306'.0973--dc20   93-11511,
                                                                  CIP

ISBN 0-306-44507-7

© 1993 Cheryl Russell
Plenum Press is a division of Plenum Publishing Corporation
233 Spring Street, New York, N.Y. 10013

Printed in the United States of America

For Sky and Julie,
free agents

Preface

Something is terribly wrong in our country. As Americans, we hear this message all the time. There is too much divorce, there is urban violence, and there is drug abuse. Our public schools are failing, our citizens are apathetic, poverty rates are rising, health care costs are soaring. The list of our ills is a long one.

But why? No one is able to explain *why* things seem to have taken such a turn for the worse. They know *when* things started to go bad—the social fabric started to fray about thirty years ago. They can recite *what* is wrong—divorce, crime, drug abuse, materialism, a lack of duty and commitment, and an unwillingness to sacrifice. But no one can explain why American society seems to be unraveling.

As a member of the baby boom generation, and as someone who has studied the generation for many years, I believe I have the answer. My career has been devoted to tracking the trajectory of the baby boom through the American economy and culture. This demographic perspective answers the question of why. The explanation for the upheaval in American society lies in the baby boom generation itself. The attitudes and values of baby boomers are profoundly different from those of older Americans. These different attitudes and values have permanently changed our culture. That is why things started "going downhill" about thirty years ago—when the oldest baby boomers began to come of age. That is why our lives continue to change, as baby boomers replace older generations of Americans. The baby boom is remaking American society because it is the first generation of "free agents."

Americans too often focus on bad news and ignore the good. In fact, the coming of age of the baby boom generation has been good for our society in many ways. This book explores both the good and bad consequences of Americans' new attitudes and values. It also describes what we can expect in the future. Much of what will unfold is still up to us. Our society could provide a better life for many more people depending on the decisions we make now, once we know *why* things have changed.

More than two years of research and writing went into this book. None of it would have been possible without the support of my family, friends, and colleagues. First, I want to thank my editor, Linda Regan, who convinced me that I had another book to write. Many thanks go to my friends and colleagues Margaret Ambry, Penelope Wickham, and Doris Walsh for their ideas and for putting up with "the book." Thanks to Cally Arthur for her common sense and critical eye. Thanks to Mike Edmondson for unearthing his Curt Flood baseball card and introducing me to the world's first free agent. Thanks to Susan Mitchell for her editing skills. Thanks to Lisa Genovese, Lindsay Waldrop, Cathy Mac-Caskill, Kay Eckstrom, Jennifer Dowd, Stahl Caso, and Cally Arthur for tending baby Julie while Mom worked. I thank my husband, Rick Eckstrom, for gracefully surviving another book. Finally, I want to thank my parents, Dave and Penny Russell, who raised me to be a free agent.

CHERYL RUSSELL

Contents

VI. FREE AGENTS AND THE 21ST CENTURY

VII. FREE AGENTS, FOR BETTER OR WORSE?

Introduction

It is common practice to mark the passage of time in ten-year intervals. It is also common to assign those intervals a distinct identity as succeeding generations of Americans define who they are. A decade's image becomes its personality, a generalization that sums up the mood and events of the time. The personalities of decades are difficult to define in words, but the feeling is easy to evoke simply by saying the words *fifties*, *sixties*, *seventies*, or *eighties*.

A decade is usually assigned its identity after the fact. Looking back, the media pronounces a decade as conservative (1950s) or rebellious (1960s) or confused (1970s) or glamorous and greedy (1980s). The 1990s are different because Americans assigned them an identity before the fact, as if they could foresee the recession, the urban unrest, and the handwringing that lay ahead. In the late 1980s, *New York* magazine labeled the coming decade "the nervous nineties." This label and others like it stuck because they rang true. Americans are indeed anxious in the 1990s. The reasons are both external and internal—a rapidly changing economy along with psychological conflicts pulling millions of people apart.

The psychological conflicts are striking the enormous middle-aged population of Americans, commonly known as the baby boom generation. If the middle-aged population were not so large and growing so fast, the 1990s might feel very different. But because the baby boom dominates the demographic landscape, its mood becomes the mood of the times.

The chances are nearly fifty-fifty that an American adult belongs to the baby boom generation, born between 1946 and 1964. Even those born before or after these dates are buffeted by the obsessions of the baby boom. The baby boom's experiences determine the trends, what's in and what's out, their spending habits drive the nation's economy, through bad times as well as boom times. The baby boom's sense of well-being dictates the nation's mood, and today, the baby boom's mood is one of dismay and anxiety as it navigates midlife.

The oldest baby boomers are now approaching 50 years of age. The youngest are almost 30 years old. As the generation passes through the middle years of life, the next two decades will be marked by the conflicts occurring within the boomers themselves. As millions of baby boomers attempt to resolve their anxieties or escape from them, they will make the United States a different country from the one their parents or grandparents knew.

The emotional turmoil of the baby boom could be called a midlife crisis, but in reality, it is more than that. Every generation hits the wall of middle age, where youthful dreams give way to mundane realities. But the baby boom is struggling with a much bigger problem, a conflict between its strong sense of individuality, a trait unique to the baby boom and younger generations of Americans, and the communal demands of midlife—family, work, and community obligations.

Baby boomers will shape the American future as their sense of individualism pulls them one way and their need for community pulls them another. This book describes the future that will result from the baby boom's struggle, a future that now fills Americans with apprehension.

In 1941, on the eve of America's entry into World War II, most Americans believed the world held less opportunity for their children than it did for them. Today, once again, a plurality of Americans feels the same way. In 1941, the United States was on the brink of the political, social, and economic upheaval brought about by World War II. Today, the country is also on the brink of revolutionary change as individualistic baby boomers take the reins of a new economy. On the eve of sweeping social change, when all the old rules have been called into question, it is difficult for people to envision a future that works. Instead, they see only the breakdown of the world they once knew.

Fortunately, the future holds more promise than many people now believe, and this book describes that future. The book is for parents who want to know more about the world their children will inherit, for workers who want to know how to make more money, for employers who want to know how to make their workers more productive, for reporters who want to know how trends will evolve, for businesses tracking consumer change, for politicians looking for answers to pressing social problems. It is for those who still harbor a hope that the future—a different world from the one they have known—just might work.

This book explores the conflicts facing the baby boom in midlife and how those conflicts will reshape American society. At the most intimate level, the individualism of the baby boom generation is on a collision course with family life. Baby boomers are fiercely independent, but so far they have been slow to integrate their independence with their need for others. As this integration takes place, a new kind of family will form the foundation of the future.

At the professional level, baby boomers face a conflict between their need to work and their love of leisure. Unlike previous generations, baby boomers value free time more than time on the job. Yet they're still searching for a workable compromise in managing both. The result is too much scheduling and too little pleasure. In the future, the boundary between work and leisure will blur.

At the public level, baby boomers are hesitant to participate in civic duties, just when the country needs their commitment to solve its problems. The result is voter apathy and political gridlock. But a new political coalition will emerge to carry Americans into the future.

The final conflict is physical. The baby boom is battling impending old age. Aging challenges the boomers in both physical and financial terms. So far they have avoided confronting their impending vulnerability. One consequence of this attitude is uncertainty about the future, which feeds the anxieties of advancing middle age.

This book is about a future that millions of Americans cannot now foresee. One day their pessimism may seem as naive as the pessimism of Americans in 1941, before the invention of pantyhose, credit cards, photocopying machines, microwavable popcorn, and computers, before the discovery of DNA, before the development of the polio vaccine, and before the birth of the baby boom itself.

❖ I ❖

THE MASTER TREND

❖ 1 ❖

The Thrill Is Gone

In the minds of most Americans, the 1980s were the "yuppie" years, a decade of greed and glamour, a time when people pursued selfish interests with abandon. Materialism became a virtue as a millionaire movie star moved into the White House. The stock market reached record highs as the economy boomed. Many felt rich as housing values soared and incomes rose. People banked on the expanding economy, borrowing money to buy cars, televisions, microwaves, boats, and other big-ticket items.

Also in the minds of most Americans, the bills of the 1980s are coming due in the 1990s. The economy is sluggish while poverty rates climb. Health care costs are soaring, while millions are uninsured. The high schools churn out graduates who can't read. Local taxes are rising as the federal government curtails handouts. Jobs are disappearing, families are breaking apart. By the early 1990s, over 80 percent of Americans said they were unhappy with the way things were going in the country, up from 26 percent in 1986. The 1992 presidential election provided temporary relief from this anxiety and pessimism. The percentage of people believing the country was on the wrong track edged downwards after the election. But the undercurrent of anxiety remains, because most Americans fear that no president can right the many things that seem so wrong.

What caused Americans to change their minds about the future, from optimism in the 1980s to pessimism in the 1990s? Although the recession of the early 1990s is partly to blame for the nation's ugly mood, the answer lies beyond gross national product

(GNP) growth, bank failures, interest levels, poverty rates, unemployment claims, or other current events. There were many troubling trends in the United States in the 1980s, just as there are today. There are many promising trends today, just as there were in the 1980s. But the cup that seemed half full a few years ago now seems half empty. The bad news makes headlines while the good news—and there is good news—gets buried. Infant mortality rates are at a record low; the proportion of students graduating from high school is at a record high; and a near-record share of households have affluent incomes. These successes are ignored in favor of the prevailing wisdom that somehow the United States veered onto the wrong track. Many Americans fear that their children will not live as well as they themselves do today.

The American attitude toward the future has taken a turn for the worse. Behind this change is the mind-set of a huge segment of the population—the baby boom generation. Baby boomers are Americans born between 1946 and 1964, now accounting for 42 percent of the adult population. Seventy-eight million strong, they share many experiences, setting the pace in the consumer marketplace and influencing the nation's psyche.

Ever since baby boomers gained a measure of independence from their parents, predicting national trends has been a simple task, requiring only a glance at population figures. Whatever age group happens to be expanding with baby boomers determines the mood of the times. Some may scoff at the notion that any one generation directs the emotional ups and downs of a country. But a generation the size of the baby boom—accounting for nearly half of all adults—has been driving national trends for over three decades. Teenaged boomers made the 1960s rebellious. Young adult boomers made the 1970s directionless, and maturing boomers gave the 1980s a selfish edge.

During the 1960s, baby boomers inflated the number of teenagers by the millions, with the oldest boomers starting the decade at age 14 and ending it at age 24. At these ages people typically question parental authority and the assumptions of the society in which they find themselves. The social upheaval of the 1960s was partly a consequence of the baby boom's passage through its teens.

During the 1970s, millions of boomers entered their twenties, with the oldest aged 24 in 1970 and 34 in 1980. At these ages people search for direction, hopping from job to job, school to school, and bed to bed. As baby boomers shuffled about searching for identity, the 1970s appeared to be a decade with little identity. Looking back, the 1970s—sometimes called the "me" decade—are often viewed with derision for their lack of a well-defined theme.

During the 1980s, baby boomers grew up. The number of Americans in their thirties exploded. The oldest boomers were 34 in 1980 and 44 in 1990. At this time of life, people establish their life-styles, pursuing careers, relationships, and possessions (cars, houses, espresso makers, and the like) with gusto. Some predicted that the 1980s would be the "we" decade, to make up for the "me" decade of the 1970s. But this was not in the cards as millions of thirtysomethings instead pursued personal goals.

From 1990 to 2000, the oldest boomers will age from 44 to 54. The number of Americans in their forties will expand by one-third. Most Americans think middle age begins when people are in their forties. Stereotypically, midlife is thought to be accompanied by a midlife crisis. So far, few baby boomers have experienced such a crisis—only 20 percent claim to have already had one. But *midlife crisis* is too personal a term to describe what the middle aging of the baby boom means to the 1990s.

Middle-aging boomers are turning the 1990s into a time of uncertainty. The confusion felt by the generation has polarized the public on a variety of issues in an array of settings. Locked in their positions, prochoice and antiabortion factions seem unable to resolve the abortion issue. Businesses flipflop between layoffs and worker empowerment to increase productivity and boost profits. Parents shower their children with gifts, but are stingy with time. Communities struggle with shrinking budgets and voter backlash.

Adding fuel to these conflicts is the emotional turmoil within each baby boomer. As boomers enter middle age, they are pulled in two directions. On the one hand, they insist on the primacy of the individual—the right to do what they want when they want. On the other hand, the demands made on them by the communities in which they live—their families, their careers, their localities—are growing as they reach middle age. Increasingly, the baby boom's strong sense of individuality is at odds with the community's need for supportive parents, willing volunteers, informed citizens, and productive workers. The tension between these two forces—individual rights and community responsibilities—prevents Americans from resolving many troubling issues—such as abortion rights, the federal deficit, the condition of the inner cities, health care, education, and environmental protection. When politicians and special interest groups align themselves on opposite sides of the spectrum, they play out the internal conflicts within each baby boomer.

❖ 2 ❖

The Birth of the Baby Boom

To understand how and why the baby boom's psyche wields so much power and what it will mean for the 1990s, it is necessary to examine where the baby boom came from and how it has already transformed American society.

The baby boom began immediately following World War II. From 1946 through 1964, about 20 million more people were born than would have been born had young women followed the family traditions of their mothers. But the mothers of the boomers broke with tradition because World War II turned their world upside down. When the soldiers returned from Europe and Asia in 1945 and early 1946, a wave of euphoria swept the country. This feeling of triumph drove social and economic trends in the United States for the following two decades.

In June of 1946, about nine months after the first soldiers returned from Europe, American women began producing babies in record number. By the end of 1946, women were having 100,000 more babies each month than in the same month a year earlier. That was only the beginning of a nineteen-year wave of births that created the baby boom generation.

A million more babies were born in 1947 than in 1946. This spike in births has scratched its way through the American culture ever since. The spike turned 40 in 1987—a year marked by the stock market crash and hence the psychological end of the profligate 1980s. It was more than coincidence that the 1980s came to a symbolic end in the same year that the first massive wave of baby boomers turned 40. The pursuit of possessions, a characteristic of people in their thirties, gave way to the more reflective mood of people in their forties.

Wave after wave of babies followed the spike of 1947. For the next 17 years, birth remained at record levels, peaking in the late 1950s with more than 4 million births a year.

The birth boom of the late 1940s took the nation's demographers by surprise. They predicted its end within a year or two. But as the babies kept coming, the demographers then began to predict they would never stop, that the United States had entered a new era of large families. But the boom come to a halt nineteen years after it began. The publication of *The Feminine Mystique*, the introduction of the birth control pill, and the year 1964 nearly coincided. In 1965, births plummeted, women joined the work force, and the baby boom generation was now fully formed.

During the peak years of the baby boom, the typical family had four children in quick succession. Researchers still do not know why the young women of that era had so many children, breaking a centuries-long pattern of ever-smaller families. About one-fifth of the babies born from 1946 through 1964 would not have been born if the women of the 1950s had had children at the same rate as their mothers. Interestingly, women of that time reported that about one in five pregnancies was accidental rather than planned.

Accidental pregnancies may explain the unprecedented rise in births, but they leave one question unanswered: Why did young women of the postwar era have so many unplanned pregnancies when birth control was more socially acceptable and more widely available to them than to their mothers?

Most likely, the answer lies in the tenor of the times. Following the trauma and dislocations of the Depression and World War II, Americans embraced domesticity. With stability finally at hand, no one wanted to upset the status quo. It was as though the entire nation was holding its breath, hoping nothing would disturb the unfolding good fortunes of so many families. Conformity became of paramount importance, since it was a way to maintain stability and keep the good times rolling.

The code word for conformity was *maturity*, says social commentator Barbara Ehrenreich. Maturity was a significant, even heroic goal for adults of the 1950s, according to Ehrenreich. At the time, psychologists believed people achieved maturity by accomplishing a series of life tasks, including marrying, having children, managing a home, working, and participating in public life.

The first task of maturity was selecting a mate. Marriage was so highly valued by Americans of the 1950s that most believed those who chose not to marry were immoral or mentally ill. Thus, nearly half of women married by the age of 20. Teenaged brides were the norm, rather than the exception.

Divorce was a sign of immaturity. To avoid divorce, husbands and wives had to learn to live together, for better or worse. Baby boomers did things differently. As of 1990, more than one-third of the first marriages of the oldest baby boomers had already ended in divorce.

One of the most important tasks of maturity was having children. Women of the 1950s did a superb job of fulfilling this duty, creating the baby boom generation. Americans' enthusiasm for big families peaked in 1959, when 81 percent thought the ideal family had at least three children. Today the proportion favoring large families has fallen to 29 percent.

Maturity also required managing a home. The baby boom's parents embraced this task with enthusiasm, building the nation's suburbs in the 1950s and 1960s. Homeownership rates rose to historic highs and continued to climb until the 1980s.

Having a career was central to maturity. For women, only one career was acceptable: housewife. Men had more occupational choices, as long as they chose to be the breadwinner.

Taking on civic responsibility was also required of the mature adult. Voting rates reached record highs by the 1960s. But this postwar patriotism went too far, culminating in witch hunts for Communists. During the 1950s, Senator Joseph McCarthy ranked among the top ten most admired men.

The mature adult was also expected to find a congenial social group. Church memberships grew and social clubs blossomed.

But the clubbiness of the 1950s had its dark side. Only certain people were allowed to join the club, while others were kept out. Racial prejudice was the norm in the 1950s. Most Americans favored laws against interracial marriage. Most thought whites should have the first chance at jobs. Most thought whites had a right to keep blacks out of their neighborhoods.

The postwar rules of life were taken very seriously by the parents of the baby boom. The young adults of the 1950s embraced this sober life-style—women wore hats and gloves, men wore suits and ties. Ironically, these pillars of the status quo spawned the rebellious baby boom generation.

❖ 3 ❖

The Baby Boom Breaks the Rules

Most baby boomers have mixed feelings about their membership in the most infamous of generations. On the one hand, they like being part of a powerful generation. On the other hand, they wince when reminded of the well-known antics of their youth. Though the baby boom is associated with the drug-loving counter-culture of the 1960s, in fact only about half of boomers admit they indulged in drugs, according to a Gallup survey. Perhaps, like President Clinton, the rest just didn't inhale. Only about one-third say they were hippies. Only one in four say they joined protest marches against the Vietnam War. A majority now say they had little in common with the people who went to Woodstock.

In the 1980s, baby boomers were associated with "yuppies" (or young urban professionals). Yuppies, according to popular opinion, were rich, spoiled, and selfish. But in fact, only a tiny minority of baby boomers had the right jobs, incomes, and attitudes to qualify as yuppies.

Whether boomers identify with the commonly held images of their generation does not matter. The power of the baby boom does not stem from a conscious generational identity, but from numbers alone. Baby boomers dominate the demographic landscape. This makes them a prime target for businesses and a mass audience for the entertainment industry. Consequently, American culture bends to their will, reflecting their prejudices and passions.

15

No one could accuse youthful baby boomers of taking life too seriously. Proving their maturity was never an issue for "baby" boomers, members of the "youth" culture, the "new" generation. In their youth, baby boomers united to break the rules of their parents' world. They questioned every value their parents held. But they had a lot of help in doing so. American business was fully behind them as it outfitted them with the tools of rebellion—cars, clothes, and music.

The baby boomers turned the norms of the 1950s upside down. They did not select a mate; they mated. The sexual revolution started in the late 1960s with heavy petting. It hit with full fury in the early 1970s when women started saying yes more often than no. A glimpse into these facts of life is recorded for posterity in a twenty-year study of the sexual behavior of students at an unnamed southern college. The proportion of women students who had ever engaged in "heavy petting" rose from a minority of 34 percent in 1965 to a majority of 60 percent just five years later in 1970. The proportion who had experienced premarital sex rose from a minority of 37 percent in 1970 to a majority of 57 percent in 1975, a jump of 20 percentage points in five years. Most men had been enjoying these sexual preoccupations all along. The percentage of men who engaged in heavy petting rose from 71 to 79 percent in the late 1960s, and those experiencing premarital sex rose from 65 to 74 percent in the early 1970s.

Society is still reeling from this rejection of traditional morality. Americans now in their forties have had an average of ten sexual partners, more than any other age group. People now in their sixties and seventies, who have had two or three additional decades to accumulate bed partners, have been intimate with only four or five people, on average.

Unlike their parents, baby boomers were slow to marry. They were too busy doing their own thing—going to school and selecting bed partners—to worry about a lifelong commitment to just one person. Only 28 percent of women aged 20 to 24 were single in 1960. By 1980 the proportion had increased to 50 percent and continues to rise to this day. Instead of marrying, many baby boomers set up house without a marriage license. Nearly half of women now in their thirties have at one time or another lived with a man outside of marriage.

When boomers did commit to marriage, they did not necessarily commit for life. When confronted with adversity, they split apart from their spouses at a record rate.

Baby boomers were also slow to start families. Millions of boomers decided that raising children called for more responsibility than they could handle. They felt that bringing children into the world really did require maturity. Thus, they managed better than their parents to avoid accidental pregnancies. But when sex did lead to an unplanned pregnancy, the 1973 Supreme Court decision legalizing abortion prevented unwanted children from intruding on their lives. Today, of course, baby boomers feel differently about children, accepting the tasks of parenthood with the zealotry of the newly converted.

Baby boomers embraced home ownership, but not as a symbol of maturity. Boomers knew a bargain when they saw one. The oldest members of the generation bought homes at rock-bottom prices in the 1970s. The younger baby boomers had to take what they could get, or afford, in the 1980s. People who bought homes in the mid-1970s, for example, took on a mortgage payment of just over $300 a month, or 24 percent of their monthly income. Those buying homes in the late 1980s were strapped with a mortgage payment of over $1000 a month, amounting to one-third of their monthly income. Though housing prices and mortgage interest rates fell in the early 1990s, baby boomers who bought homes before 1980 still got the better bargain.

Baby boomers depended on debt instead of savings to buy what they wanted, while businesses, spotting a profitable opportunity, readily assisted them in this endeavor. Credit cards became the boomer savings account and consumer debt soared. Savings levels dropped to historic lows by the 1980s.

Baby boom men and women also rebelled against their parents' idea of work. Among baby boom women, only one in five is a housewife. Older baby boom men rejected the primacy of career and the necessity to make money. Among college freshmen of the late 1960s and early 1970s, finding a meaningful philosophy of life was much more important than making money. While younger baby boom men took the career track more seriously because they faced greater job competition, both younger and older boomers rated leisure as more important than work.

Baby boomers also avoided civic duty. Baby boom men went to college in record proportions to avoid the draft. President Clinton's draft status was an issue in the 1992 Presidential campaign, but he was just one of millions of men who used their educational status to avoid going to Vietnam. In fact, men born in 1946—the year President Clinton was born—are the most highly educated of all Americans, thanks in large part to the Vietnam war.

Baby boomers also avoided other civic duties, such as the duty to vote. Baby boomers and younger Americans are less likely than older Americans to regard voting as a duty. Among people aged 65 or older, fully 77 percent "agree completely" that it is their duty as a citizen to vote. Among boomers aged 30 to 34, only 61 percent completely agree that voting is a duty. When the baby boom came of age, voting rates began to fall, skidding to just 50 percent of the voting-age population in the 1988 Presidential election. While 55 percent of Americans voted in the 1992 Presidential election, this rate is still far lower than the record of 63 percent set in 1960. The widespread political alienation felt by Americans today is partly a consequence of the maturing baby boom's disinterest in public life.

Finally, baby boomers rejected the clubhouse mentality of the 1950s. They fought the exclusivity of the middle-class world of their parents, demanding equal opportunity for blacks, women, and other long-excluded groups. Civil rights became a central concern, and racial tolerance rose dramatically as the baby boom heralded the growing diversity of American society.

The boomers succeeded in changing society because of the power of numbers. They discovered early on that they could get what they wanted when they wanted it. They needed schools, and their communities built schools. More elementary schools were built in 1957 than in any other year before or since. Ten years later, in 1967, more colleges opened than in any year before or since. Baby boomers needed cars, and cars were built just for them— small, inexpensive, and foreign. Baby boomers needed houses, and housing starts rose to record levels during the 1970s. Baby boomers needed jobs, and jobs were created by the millions.

Of course there have been setbacks along the way. When so many people fight for jobs, as they did in the 1970s, pay levels fall; with so many people trying to buy houses, prices rise; during recessions, jobs disappear. These setbacks occurred like clock-work about once a decade, in the early 1970s, 1980s, and 1990s. But following each recession, new jobs emerged as the economy grew again.

All in all, baby boomers have succeeded in getting almost everything they wanted out of life—so far. They can credit this success to their parents, who taught them to think for and of themselves, thus raising the first generation of individualists. The rising affluence of the 1950s allowed the parents of the baby boom to give in to their children's demands, indulging the younger generation as never before. They made sure their children were not deprived as they themselves had been during the Depression and World War II. They invested in their children's skills by financing their college educations. They encouraged their children to succeed in an economy that increasingly rewards individual skills.

The individualistic spirit of baby boomers first surfaced in their battle against authority. They refused to be like their parents, fighting the conformity of the 1950s on many fronts. This rebellion temporarily united the generation. Baby boomers shocked the older generation by growing their hair, wearing blue jeans, indulging in drugs, spurning marriage, and marching for peace. But the glue of rebellion that held the generation together began to dissolve by the early 1970s, as the counterculture overdosed on drugs and as the Vietnam war ended. It was only after these unifying forces disappeared that baby boomers began to distance themselves from one another. As the diversity within the baby boom generation grew, their strong sense of individualism emerged.

The wheels of this diversity were greased by money. As baby boomers joined the work force and earned a paycheck in the 1970s, astute businesspeople saw opportunity in the numbers. There were profits in giving millions of young people what they wanted. Businesses offered individualistic baby boomers a growing array of customized products and services. In turn, these products and services allowed baby boomers to customize their lives. The houses, cars, furniture, appliances, clothes, vacations, jobs, leisure time, and even beliefs of the boomers became increasingly unique, shared by fewer and fewer others. Individualism became the dominant social and economic force in American society. Now, in the 1990s, the baby boom's strong sense of individualism has run head on into the communal demands of middle age. The baby boom has hit the wall.

❖ 4 ❖

The Baby Boom Hits the Wall

During the 1990s, the number of people in midlife, stretching roughly from ages 35 to 54, will grow four times faster than the population as a whole. The rapid expansion of the number of people in their forties has already catapulted middle-aged concerns to the top of the national agenda. These concerns include family issues, health care, tax rates, crime prevention, and community standards. But how to resolve these issues remains up in the air. Until now, baby boomers have gotten what they wanted out of life by demanding their right to do as they please. Now, treading the unfamiliar territory of middle-aged responsibilities, they aren't sure how to proceed.

Baby boomers have discovered what every generation discovers upon reaching its thirties and forties: Most of society's responsibilities rest on the shoulders of the middle aged. The middle aged are the nation's CEOs, its scientists, its judges, and its politicians. The middle aged earn and spend most of the nation's money; they are the driving force behind the economy. The middle aged raise the nation's children, discipline its teenagers, employ its young people, pay college tuitions, and imprison criminals. The middle aged link younger generations to older ones, hosting family reunions and holiday gatherings. They care for the nation's old people and bury the nation's dead. Many baby boomers feel overwhelmed by the multiple roles of middle age, but the baby boom is not the first generation to feel these pressures.

21

What is new for baby boomers is the need to integrate the values of middle age with their prevailing sense of individualism, for it is individualism that is the trend behind the trends. It is breaking families apart, it is changing the way businesses do business, it is creating a new kind of worker, it is the reason for political alienation. These lesser trends make the headlines while their common cause is rarely addressed. That common cause is the belief in the primacy of the individual at the expense of the community. This belief is at the core of baby boomers' world view and that of younger generations of Americans.

Many social observers decry the importance of individualism in today's society, demanding that people show more concern for community needs. But individualism is not something that can be turned on and off like a faucet. It is not a perspective that younger generations of Americans choose, like a new pair of jeans. It is the way they see and relate to the world. For better and for worse, individualism is here to stay, the master trend of modern times.

The term *individualism* is too general to accurately describe how this perspective shapes people's attitudes and behavior. The individuality of Americans under the age of 50 is more accurately described by the term *free agent*. In baseball, basketball, and football, free agents are players who negotiate their contracts as individuals rather than as part of a team. Today there are more free agents off the playing fields than on them. Most Americans under the age of 50 are free agents, negotiating their way through life.

As free agents, baby boomers created a customized culture. They ignored the rules that guided their parents and placed their families, jobs, and country at the mercy of their personal desires. Only now are they beginning to reap what they have sown. A generation that puts personal interests and goals ahead of community needs must watch in dismay as communities disintegrate, families break apart, school budgets shrink, inner cities decay, and budget deficits grow.

The middle aging of the baby boom generation was inevitable. So was the growing conflict between individual rights and community responsibilities. This conflict must be resolved or American society will remain paralyzed with anxiety for the foreseeable future, because baby boomers are only the first generation of free agents. The generations that follow the baby boom are even more individualistic than the baby boom generation itself.

❖ II ❖

THE FIRST FREE AGENTS

❖ 5 ❖

The First Free Agent

Curt Flood is hardly a household word. Baseball fans are the only ones who remember him or know why he's important. But Flood's story is the story of the first free agent.

Curt Flood had no inkling that he was playing a bit part in the unfolding of a master trend when in 1969 he declared himself a free agent—the first free agent in the history of baseball. Before Flood's refusal to play the game, the sport of baseball was run by its teams. But when the St. Louis Cardinals traded Flood to the Philadelphia Phillies, Flood was a no-show. Instead of fielding fly balls, he filed an antitrust suit claiming players had the right to play for whatever team they chose.

Though Flood lost his suit, other players soon demanded freedom of choice. In 1975 an arbitrator ruled in favor of free agency. In 1976, free agency became a part of baseball, allowing the best players to sell themselves to the highest bidder. Basketball players earned the right to become free agents in 1988, while football players gained this right in 1993. Now these sports are run by the players as much as the team owners, with far-reaching consequences. Since free agency became the norm in baseball, the game has never been more competitive. In the sixteen seasons between 1976 and 1991, twelve different teams claimed the World Series title.

Flood was the first free agent in baseball, but he was one of millions of free agents in the world at large. Free agents are individualists. For them, the interests of the individual take prece-dence over the needs of the family, the rights of an organization, or the power of the state. This perspective is more emotional than intellectual, more psychological than political. It is not a conscious belief, but an unconscious force, shaping the relationships between free agents and their families, friends, neighbors, employers, and the community at large. Free agents' sense of individualism is at the core of their personality, the basis from which they make decisions, from the mundane (how to spend their paychecks) to the profound (whether to have children).

Sociologists define individualism as the tendency to withdraw from social institutions and groups—including families, local communities, political parties, churches, and the nation. Individualists favor their own personal needs over community needs. They make commitments for personal gain rather than for moral reasons. As individualistic baby boomers came of age over the past thirty years, they withdrew from the institutions of American society. With the maturing of the baby boom, voting rates fell, a rising share of Americans said they had no religion, divorce became not just acceptable but the norm, privacy became a right, and Americans began to prefer leisure to work.

Trends usually produce countertrends, and the long-term trend toward individualism is no exception. The "communitarian" movement, led by George Washington University sociologist Amitai Etzioni, preaches the complement to individual rights, which is individual responsibility. Communitarians want people to take more responsibility for their communities. They want two-parent families to stage a comeback. They want children to be taught the virtues of citizenship. But free agency has fractured traditional families and other social institutions. They cannot be patched together again by preachers, sociologists, or politicians. The communitarian movement may succeed in calling for a debate over individual rights versus responsibilities, but it will not turn free agents into dutiful citizens.

Individualism's permanent place in modern society is anchored by two strong roots. First, it is a result of modern technology. Personal computers, instant communication, and worldwide

information networks bring millions of people together in anonymity—a fertile environment for the rise of individualism.

The other root of individualism is the relationships between
parents and children. The social norms and values people learn in
childhood shape them for life. The baby boom's parents raised
their children to be free agents, and baby boomers are raising their
children to be even more ardent free agents than are the boomers
themselves. The question, then, is not how to turn back the clock,
but how to move forward. Americans must find a way to endow
free agents with a willingness to solve community problems.

✣ 6 ✣

Technology and Individualism

Today's generations of free agents are the direct result of the technology that drives society. In today's economy, competition rather than cooperation is the key to success, and this fosters individualism. The reasons become clear in a comparison of farm life in the past with the new economy of today.

For better and worse, the farm economies of the past tied people to their families and local communities. Relationships with family, friends, and neighbors lasted a lifetime. People rarely moved, either from village to village or up the socioeconomic ladder. In this kind of economy, dependent on trading food and other hand-crafted products rather than money, good long-term relationships with other community members were critical for each person's economic well-being. When people traded with one another, it was important for both parties to be satisfied with the exchange so that both were willing and eager to trade again. People who refused to act cooperatively, who pursued the best deal for themselves at the expense of others, were cut off from the communal economy. The dependence of neighbor upon neighbor made cooperation the key to success in the premarket economy, creating a communal orientation in society, according to sociologist Margaret Mooney Marini. In this type of society, parents taught their children to obey communal norms and values, to succeed through cooperation. Children learned that success depended upon meeting their community's needs. This type of society, says Marini, spawned the moral tenets of the Judeo-

Christian religions—do unto others as you would have them do unto you.

With the rise of factories and mass-produced goods in the nineteenth century, economies shifted from agrarian to industrial. Money and the market economy replaced barter and personal relationships in economic transactions. Villages grew into cities as people sought a more efficient way to exchange goods. In the cities, hundreds of thousands and sometimes millions of people crowded together. The few long-term economic relationships of farm societies gave way to numerous and fleeting monetary transactions between strangers. The anonymity of modern economies makes it possible for people to pursue their own interests at the expense of others. The satisfaction of the other party in an exchange is much less important because buyer and seller are not likely to meet again.

In this environment, those who act cooperatively, in the common spirit of the past, are at the mercy of those out to get the best deal for themselves. The meek will be pushed to the end of the line, whether they're trying to get a good job, decent pay, or a nice house. They will lose social and economic status to those who are more competitive. In this kind of society, parents teach their children to think for themselves and to compete with others. As their children grow up, the social norms and values of society shift away from communalism toward individualism, away from cooperation toward competition.

Modern technology allows individualism to be taken to its extreme. In the information age, people can substitute computers, modems, telephones, faxes, and answering machines for face-to-face contact with others. They can work and play in anonymity. Individualism is the master trend of our time, feeding on the anonymity of the information age. This master trend is much too powerful to be stopped by anything short of a world-wide nuclear war. Instead of trying to return to a more cooperative time (and a more communal economy), a society of free agents must put the power of individualism to work for the common good.

❖ 7 ❖

The First Generation of
Free Agents

The baby boom is the first generation of free agents—the first to see and relate to the world as individuals rather than as family or community members. While this individualistic perspective has been gaining strength for generations, it is only within the past few decades that it has become pervasive. The rise of this individualistic perspective is recorded in a series of personality tests administered by the Mayo Clinic. In 1940, only 11 percent of women and 20 percent of men agreed with the statement, "I am an important person." By 1990, both women and men thought differently: fully 66 percent of women and 62 percent of men believed that they were important people.

The responses to this one survey question clearly show the changes in the attitudes of Americans since World War II. They explain the transformation of American society over the past few decades, describing the demise of communal values and the rise of individualism. They also reveal the marked similarity in the perspectives of men and women today.

Communal values surrendered to individualism as baby boomers came of age because baby boom women are as individualistic as baby boom men. Their adoption of individualistic values left no one looking out for society's communal needs, setting the United States on its current course of conflict and confusion.

Men had long been more individualistic than women. Men left farms for factories; women stayed home. Men competed for jobs; women managed the family. Men spent their days apart from their wives and children; women held communities together. But with the coming of age of baby boom women, the communal glue finally gave way.

This watershed occurred in the 1970s and is documented in annual surveys of the nation's college freshmen taken by UCLA for the past three decades. In the 1960s, when the first baby boom women entered college, most expressed a strong communal orientation. Eighty percent of women college freshmen in 1966 said that "helping others in difficulty" (a communal value) was a "very important" goal. In contrast, "making a lot of money" (an individualistic value) was "very important" to only 32 percent—nearly 50 percentage points less than the communal value. Among men, these two goals were neck and neck in the 1960s, at 59 and 54 percent, respectively.

By the early 1980s, when the last baby boom women were in college, 65 percent of women said they wanted to make a lot of money, nearly equal to the 69 percent who wanted to help others in difficulty. Among men, those citing money making as an important goal stood at 73 percent. While women were still more concerned with the community than men, they were almost equally individualistic in their pursuit of personal goals. For men, and particularly for women, the individualistic perspective had grown sharply in less than two decades.

Behind these changing attitudes are the norms and values baby boomers learned in childhood. For the parents of the baby boom, the ever-present instruction manual for bringing up baby was *Dr. Spock's Baby and Child Care*, with its emphasis on raising children to be independent. In fact, independence was the single most important quality parents of the 1950s wanted to nurture in their children. This is in stark contrast to the way parents raised their children a century ago. In 1890, just 16 percent of parents thought independence was one of the most important characteristics to nurture in their children. But 64 percent thought obedience was one of the most important characteristics. Communal society demands obedience, while modern society demands independence.

The perception that independence was a desirable trait grew slowly over the decades. By 1924, about one in four parents thought it was important to raise a child to be indepe dent. One-third gave it top priority in 1945. After World War II, the value of independence boomed with the economy. By the late 1970s, three out of four parents put independence at the top of their list.

As might be predicted, teaching children to be obedient plummeted in importance. From 64 percent in 1890, the percentage of parents who cited obedience as one of the three most important characteristics in childrearing fell to 45 percent in 1924 and remained there through 1945. By 1978, obedience was thought to be most important by only 17 percent of parents.

The baby boom's parents raised their children to be independent because independent thinking is necessary for success in a rapidly changing and diversifying economy. Jobs requiring little more than nimble fingers and obedient minds were growing slowly during the 1960s and 1970s. At the same time, the big paychecks were going to those who could think on their feet, who could manage others, who could adapt to changing business needs. To succeed financially, people needed to think for themselves rather than obey orders. The parents of 1958 scored "to think for themselves" a 4.1 on a scale of 1 to 5 among traits to be nurtured in their children.

While baby boomers may be the first generation of free agents, they aren't the last. Individualism is growing in strength as each generation raises the next. Younger generations are even more committed to individualism than the baby boomers themselves. Again, the evidence for this is in surveys of college freshmen.

Today's college students are much more self-confident and goal-oriented than baby boomers ever were. In 1990, 51 percent of college freshmen rated themselves above average as leaders. This generation knows how important it is to be out in front. In comparison, only 38 percent of the first wave of baby boomers in 1966 thought they were above-average leaders. Forty-eight percent of today's college freshmen say they are confident in their intellectual abilities. Only 36 percent of baby boomers felt so self-assured in 1966. Seventy-three percent of 1990 college freshmen said they were going to college in order to make more money, up from 50 percent in 1971. The proportion of freshmen who think that the ability to make more money is the chief benefit of a college education has increased from 56 percent in 1967 to 71 percent in 1990. The share whose major goal in life is to be very well off financially skyrocketed from 44 to 74 percent.

Belonging to the team is even less important to today's young adults than it is to baby boomers. The proportion of college freshmen who plan on joining a fraternity, sorority, or other club while in school fell from 31 percent in 1967 to 17 percent in 1990. The proportion who want to keep up with political affairs fell from 51 to 42 percent. And the share who plan on marrying in college or within a year of graduation fell from 31 to 20 percent. Well over half of today's young adults have a hero, but they cannot agree on who it is. No one person is mentioned by more than 10 percent of young adults.

Today's college students are adopting the principles of free agency with an enthusiasm that chills even the most hardened of baby boomers. They are investing in themselves, pursuing the fast track of free agency. Just as Curt Flood could not market himself to the highest bidder unless he could offer superb skills as a baseball player, so too free agents in the work force must offer superb skills to their potential employers, in the expectation that they will be duly rewarded.

The financial rewards for such an investment are real. Though today's college graduates are having trouble finding jobs as the economy limps out of recession, government statistics show that a college degree pays off in the long run. Americans with college degrees make twice as much, on average, as those who went no farther than high school, according to the Census Bureau. Those with professional degrees make almost five times as much as high school graduates. The incomes of the college-educated have been rising faster than inflation, while those of high school graduates have barely kept up with the cost of living.

Younger generations of Americans have responded to these facts of life. They are much more educated than their parents or grandparents. One in four men and women under the age of 45 has been to college for at least four years. Among those now in their twenties, the proportion of men and women with a college degree is virtually identical as women pursue economic success as seriously as men. This marks the first time in history that men and women have been educated on equal terms.

❖ 8 ❖

The Next Generation of Free Agents

Today's parents rate raising children to think for themselves a 4.4 on a scale of 1 to 5. Independent thinking ranks far higher than raising children to work hard (3.2), help others (3.2), obey (2.8), or be well liked (1.4). Apparently, popularity is not viewed as an avenue to success.

The children of baby boomers are destined to be much more independent than the boomers themselves. Not only do boomer parents consciously promote independence in their children, but the baby boom life-style encourages children to be independent. Most of the baby boom's children spend their days apart from their parents, while most baby boomers spent their days with their mothers in the typical nuclear family of the 1950s. Many of the baby boom's families include stepchildren who already have an established set of family relationships distinct from their relationships with step siblings. In contrast, baby boomers shared their family relationships with their many brothers and sisters.

Since both parents work in most of today's two-parent families, each family member's day has become unique. Children begin in infancy to live apart from their parents. They sleep at home at night, but during the day they live a separate existence.

Contrast today's independent childhood with farm life several centuries ago. Back then, fathers, mothers, and children spent the day together, working and living on the farm. Family members saw one another throughout the day, sharing activities. This sharing came to an end during the nineteenth century when men gave up their plowshares and headed for factories. But mothers and children continued to spend their days together, at least until the children were old enough to go to school.

Now entire families spend most of the day apart from one another and away from home. Mothers and fathers race to the office, and very young children head to the local day-care center or baby-sitter. Homes have been replaced by centers, mothers have been replaced by providers, childhood friends have been replaced by "playdates."

Over half of new mothers today are back at work before their children celebrate their first birthday. Sixty-three percent of children under the age of 5 whose mothers work are cared for in a day-care center or another home. Most baby boomers, men and women alike, must work to support their families. Most have no choice but to give their children a hug and drive off into the sunrise. Today's child-care books even advise parents on how to say goodbye at a day-care center, letting their children know they enjoy going to work. In this way, the books help parents reinforce the individuality of their children, raising them to be free agents.

Because of divorce and remarriage, families are becoming much more diverse. Only 61 percent of children today live in traditional families—meaning they live with their biological parents. Eighteen percent live in single-parent families, while another 20 percent live in blended families—meaning they include stepparents, stepchildren, or some other combination of relatives. The children in blended families have unique relationships with other family members outside the blended family. They do not share the same parents within the blended family. They may have brothers and sisters living elsewhere. They may share their bedrooms with half-brothers or half-sisters. They may have a different set of grandparents, aunts, and uncles than other children in the family. They may spend their weekends, holidays, and vacations apart, visiting a father not shared by other children in the family.

The independence of today's children is also evident in family eating patterns. Family members today often eat separately. With parents and children rushing to get to work or school, few families have the time to eat breakfast together. With everyone away from home most of the day, many families find it impossible to eat lunch together. With parents and children arriving home at different times, often with evening activities on their schedules, many families find it hard to sit down together for dinner. Of the twenty-one meals people eat each week—three meals a day, seven days a week—families eat only nine of them together (one in three breakfasts, one in five lunches, and three out of four dinners).

As children become more independent, they also gain more control over money. It is no coincidence that the first estimates of children's spending power were published in 1968, when millions of baby boomers were children. Today, children aged 4 to 12 have an income of $14 billion a year, most of it from allowances. They spend $3.2 billion a year on food, and another $2.6 billion on toys. As they spend, they learn how to navigate the market economy and get the best deal for themselves—in other words, they learn how to shop. No wonder shopping malls are one of the most respected institutions of American society. They foster the kind of independence parents want to encourage in their children. By the age of 7, most children shop regularly for themselves, spending their allowance on toys, candy, and clothes.

Today's teenagers also have more money and more freedom than those of previous generations. Teenagers are more likely than their baby boom parents were to own cars, stereos, TV sets, and telephones. Parents encourage their teenaged children to buy cars so that they won't have to chauffeur them around. Owning a car, in turn, gives teens mobility, widening their circle of friends, job opportunities, and shopping alternatives, all of which foster greater independence.

The consequences of raising children to be so independent are still to be seen. But observing today's young adults indicates that there may be surprises in store. It seems, paradoxically, that the more independent children become, the longer it takes them to leave home. Today's young adults live at home longer than young adults of the 1960s and 1970s. More than half of 18- to 24-year-olds still live with their parents.

The seeming contradiction between the independence of today's young adults and their decision to continue to live with their parents makes sense when examined more closely. First, it is in the interest of youthful free agents to live with their parents and enjoy a more affluent life-style for as long as possible. In fact, those most likely to continue to live at home are young adults whose families have the highest incomes. Another reason young people are increasingly likely to live with their parents is that they face so many choices. Often, the smartest move they can make is to experiment before they commit themselves to any one person, life-style, or career. As they dabble in life, trying one thing after another, they return home to recoup when things don't work out.

The years between 18 and 24 are increasingly a testing ground where young adults learn how to compete. As competition in the world outside the family intensifies with growing individualism, the learning process lengthens. It now takes young people longer to graduate from both high school and college than it once did. A growing share of students is remaining in high school for more than four years. College students are taking more time to get their bachelor's degree because they're going to school part-time or dropping out of school for a while to work. On average, it takes today's college graduates 6.2 years to earn a degree, up from 4.5 years for college graduates in 1972.

For the parents of the baby boom, the route to adulthood was marriage; for baby boomers, the route was college. Now there is no dominant route as younger generations test the waters, exploring the diversity of economic opportunities and life-styles permitted by free agency. Demographers report that there is so much diversity in how young adults go about their lives that no one life-style characterizes those in their early twenties. Some go to college while others go to work. Some marry while others stay single. Many live with their parents, some live with housemates, and others live alone. Demographers report that the single most common life-style shared by young adults, living with housemates, is experienced by only one-third of them.

As one generation of free agents raises another, baby boomers may find their relationships with their children smoother than their relationships with their parents. Teenaged baby boomers embraced free agency while their parents clung to communal values, creating friction between the generations. This friction still surfaces at family gatherings, with 40-year-olds bristling at the rigidity of their 60-something parents. In contrast, the children of baby boomers are also free agents, agreeing with their parents about many things. Surveys show that tensions between parents and teenagers have declined over the past two decades. A majority of high school seniors agree with their parents about most issues, including what to do with their life. The percentage of high school seniors agreeing with their parents is higher today than in 1975 on issues ranging from what is permitted on a date to the value of an education, the role of women, and race relations.

One area in which there is less agreement than in 1975, however, is how to spend money. Today's teenagers are far more materialistic than baby boomers were as teenagers, which may cause friction between the generations on the issue of money.

The baby boom's children will adopt values and life-styles very similar to those of the baby boom. Like third-generation immigrants, they are fully assimilated into the culture of individualism. In contrast, the baby boom's parents are like first-generation immigrants, still longing for the old country and speaking the language of communal values, such as life-time marriage, sacrificing for the family, and duty before pleasure.

As the second generation in the middle, baby boomers can speak the language of the old country, but only haltingly. They're fluent individualists, but they worry about a world controlled by free agents. Their children do not share their concerns. They don't speak the language of the old world at all.

❖ 9 ❖

Free Agents around the World

The United States is not the only country in which younger generations are embracing individualism. In most developed countries, free agency has been enthusiastically adopted by younger generations for the same reason it has been adopted here. In modern economies, people get ahead through competition. Investing in individual skills is the best way to compete. Parents raise their children for this competition. In Germany, Great Britain, and Italy, parents rate thinking for oneself as the most important concept to be taught by the schools, according to cross-national studies of childrearing. In contrast, the importance of teaching respect has plummeted among modern European parents.

The coming of age of younger generations of free agents is one factor turning dictatorships into democracies. The breakup of the Soviet Union, the end of authoritarian rule in Eastern Europe, and the dismantling of the Berlin Wall are the consequences of the coming of age of the individualistic postwar generations. As free agency grew in the West, the Communist regimes (which are, by definition, communal societies) in the USSR and Eastern Europe fell behind economically, unable to compete with the rapid technological change characteristic of economies run by free agents. Faced with economic ruin, these regimes had two options: They could prevent their citizenry from finding out how much better life was elsewhere, or they could give up. Global communication networks and the instantaneous flow of information make it almost impossible to keep a citizenry in the dark for long. To do so requires governments to become increasingly oppressive, an unstable situation that eventually leads to collapse. The people rebel, and they replace the government with one that allows free agency to develop.

The nations already dominated by free agents can be identified by two necessary and sufficient factors: one, a majority of women must work, and two, the population must devote a relatively large amount of money to entertainment and recreation. When women work and earn their own paychecks, both men and women are freed from their economic ties to the family, laying the foundation for the independent thinking of free agents. Spending on leisure is the mark of a materialistic population intent on personal enjoyment, the central characteristic of free agents.

Three out of four women under the age of 50 work in the United States. The proportion is similar in most of Western Europe. European women work for the same reasons American women work—they need the money, and they want independence and personal fulfillment. Surveys in Italy, the United Kingdom, and West Germany show that most working women would continue to work, even if they had enough money to live comfortably without working. In a British survey, fully 60 percent of respondents agreed that "having a job is the best way for a woman to be an independent person."

Women's labor force participation rates by themselves do not signal a country dominated by free agents. Countries where women's labor force participation rates are high, but leisure spending is low, tend to be totalitarian regimes where the independence of the population is suppressed by the government. Women participated in the labor force at extremely high rates in Eastern Europe when it was controlled by the Communists because women were required to work. But the people of Eastern Europe had little money to spend on entertainment or recreation, the second factor that signals a country dominated by free agents.

Leisure spending by itself does not mark a country as dominated by free agents. Countries where women's labor force participation rates are low but leisure spending is high (such as Italy and Spain) tend to be communal societies where free agency is just beginning to develop.

Leisure spending is the ultimate materialistic pursuit. It is a measure of the attitudes of a population. For free agents everywhere, spending on leisure is a priority. In the United States, spending on leisure ranks sixth as a share of all spending, after housing, food, medical care, transportation, and personal business. Americans now spend more on having a good time than they do on clothing. The same pattern is true in many European countries as well. In Switzerland, households spend 14 percent of their budgets on leisure, 19 percent on food, and 16 percent on housing. In the United Kingdom, 10 percent of the household budget goes for leisure, another 10 percent is devoted to housing, and 13 percent to food.

Together, these two indicators—the percentage of women participating in the labor force and the percentage of income spent on leisure—reveal the countries where individualism is the dominant value. Nine Western European countries fit this definition. They are, in order of their per capita spending on leisure: Switzerland, Denmark, Finland, Norway, Sweden, Belgium, the United Kingdom, Germany, and France. In the decades ahead, other countries will join this elite club as younger generations of free agents mature and take over the reins of power.

The passing of the torch from older, communal generations to individualistic, younger people does not always proceed smoothly. While the transition has been relatively peaceful in the United States, in other countries, it will be deadly. The civil wars of the future are likely to occur in countries where younger generations of free agents face unyielding, traditional-minded older generations. China is a good example of a country already besieged by such a conflict. More often than not, the wars of the future will be fought between countries ruled by free agents and those still controlled by communally oriented populations.

The tension between individualism and communalism is one factor creating friction between Western nations and some of the Islamic countries of the Middle East. This friction is not likely to ease until the countries of the Middle East are also controlled by free agents, an event that is not likely to occur in the baby boom's lifetime.

❖ 10 ❖

On a Collision Course

In the United States, the greatest battle of the 1990s will take place inside the minds of middle-aged Americans. This battle could have been foreseen many years ago, a consequence of the middle aging of the first generation of free agents.

In the 1970s, when free agents became a fact of life for baseball owners, the oldest baby boomers were in their twenties. Today, those same baby boomers are almost 50 years old. It's easy to be a free agent at age 20 or 24, but much harder at age 50. As teens and young adults, baby boomers nurtured their independent impulses because youthful values and the values of free agents are one and the same. The young are independent and self-centered, and so are free agents. The young are impulsive and demanding, and so are free agents. As the first generation of free agents entered their twenties, the most independent stage of life, age and attitude converged with the enormous size of the baby boom generation to bring about the rapid spread of individualistic life-styles.

For Americans long stifled by the rigid rules of the 1950s this change was liberating. Husbands and wives who had silently suffered through unhappy marriages could divorce. Divorce rates more than doubled between the 1960s and the 1970s. Minorities gained power as younger generations demanded civil rights for long-excluded Americans. Women went to work as their choices expanded. People fulfilled their fantasies as prohibitions against sex and drugs fell by the wayside. But new problems emerged: Broken homes, latchkey children, drug addiction, violent crime, and sexually transmitted diseases are some of the unforeseen problems created by errant individualism.

Individualism also unleashed an explosion of choices. As baby boomers became increasingly diverse, businesses abandoned their mass-market approach to profits. Instead, they divided the population into ever smaller market segments, producing a greater variety of products, from espresso coffee makers to pump toothpaste. With the increasing variety of products and services available to them, baby boomers could customize their life-styles. Though choice is often liberating, too much choice is stressful. Increasingly, the choices available to people today are overwhelming, making people feel pressured for time because they face so many decisions. The average person is exposed to thousands of advertisements each day: twenty-four-hour shopping is as close as a telephone. The average supermarket carries four times as many products as it did in 1950, and hundreds of new products line supermarket shelves every week.

Choosing among competing products can be time consuming. Choosing among competing life-styles can be deeply disturbing. Americans face more choice today than any previous generation in history, from types of mustards in the grocery store to varieties of telephone sex. The thrill of having so much choice wears thin after three or four decades of decision making.

For many fortysomething baby boomers, telephone sex is not the kind of choice they readily support. The values of middle age are often at odds with the values of free agents. The anything goes attitude of individualists conflicts with the more responsible mind-set of middle age.

And yet, most baby boomers would not welcome a return to the values of the 1950s. No matter how disturbed they are with the unhappy consequences of free agency, the generations of Americans under the age of 50 are unwilling to be boxed in by someone else's idea of right and wrong. This ambivalence resounded in the "family values" debate of the 1992 Presidential election. The judgmental attitude toward family values coming from the Republican convention turned off younger Americans. The Democrats, in contrast, were more inclusive, with candidate Clinton calling for more responsibility at the same time that the Democratic platform upheld a broad spectrum of individual rights. Baby boomers supported the ticket that offered them more choice. They want their options, whether they're choosing an automobile or an abortion. As one Planned Parenthood spokesperson once put it, most Americans favor abortion in only three circumstances: rape, incest, or their own unwanted pregnancy.

Because baby boomers don't want to be boxed in by rules, they face a moral dilemma each time a community need conflicts with a personal need. Divorce is an example of such a conflict. Most people today think it's worse to stay married to someone they no longer love than to divorce—even if children are involved. Fully 82 percent of mothers think unhappy spouses should split up rather than stay together for the sake of the children. But most Americans also think divorce hurts children. It's a moral stand-off: divorce is both good and bad, right and wrong. For free agents, divorce is entirely acceptable. But middle-aged baby boomers, many of whom have been through a divorce, aren't so sure.

Choices can be costly. Sometimes these costs are spelled out, as they are when buying a new car. Other times choices have a hidden price, like the emotional cost of divorce for husbands, wives, and children. Divorced couples pay a price for wavering on their marriage vows, including financial hardship, bewildered children, and personal unhappiness.

The choices that thrilled baby boomers in their youth can create unhappiness in midlife. In their teens and twenties, baby boomers did not worry about marriage or divorce. Some of them denounced marriage altogether, and most postponed it. Now in their thirties and forties, baby boomers long for meaningful, long-term relationships. Americans rank having a happy marriage as one of the most important ingredients of the "good life." At the same time, a shrinking proportion of husbands and wives report that their marriages are happy. The reason for this paradox, according to sociologists, is too much choice. Couples know they have the option of divorce, and this makes marriage more tenuous. Without a life-long commitment, husbands and wives do not work as hard at pleasing one another, and marriages become less satisfying. Free agents may demand choice, but they can't demand happy marriages.

Middle-aged baby boomers are searching for values, but as free agents, they're not sure they can live with them. Their ambivalence puts American society on a collision course between individual rights and responsibilities. For the next twenty years, the conflicts between rights and responsibilities will eat away at the baby boom's peace of mind. The conflicts will change families, alter careers, and determine the personal well-being of Americans for decades to come. The resolution of these conflicts will decide the future direction of America as a nation.

Americans cannot avoid the conflicts that lie ahead. But by understanding what causes them, they may find a way to reach a compromise between individual rights and community responsibility, a compromise that could lift the country out of the muck of indecision and inaction and set it on a course for the twenty-first century.

❖ **III** ❖

FREE AGENTS AND THE
PERSONALIZED ECONOMY

✤ 11 ✤

The Personalized Economy

The first generation of free agents, now approaching the age of 50, must cope with a world dramatically different from the one in which they grew up. Luckily for them, their parents must have sensed the coming technological revolution as they watched the first black-and-white televisions. They also sensed the coming social revolution in women's roles, encouraging their daughters to prepare themselves for the work force in case they needed to earn a living, never dreaming that most of them would. Parents of the 1950s taught their children to think for themselves and encouraged them to invest in their skills. But at midcentury, few could visualize the reality that would confront their children today—the hotly competitive, fast-paced, and technologically sophisticated economy of the 1990s.

Free agents were raised to cope with this economic reality, instilled with values that help them cope. Free agents value speed because speed gives them an edge in the competition. They value leisure because of the pressure from the fast pace of life. They value money and material goods as highly as they do family and friends. Behind the new values of free agents, and behind the harsh environment in which they live, is the personalized economy.

Never has so much technological change occurred in so short a span of time as in the past several decades. The changing technologies have created a new type of economy. This personalized economy is as different from the industrial economy of the recent past as the industrial economy was from the agricultural economy of the distant past. The agricultural economy was based on the production and distribution of food and hand-crafted products. The industrial economy was based on the production of mass-produced products. The personalized economy is based on the production of customized products for individualistic consumers. This new economy demands a new way of life.

In an agricultural economy, people's roles are unchanging. Their position in life, both socially and geographically, is determined by their family circumstances. Their success depends entirely on their skill at getting along with others.

In an industrial economy, people's position in life is less static, but they're trapped in elaborate social and economic bureaucracies, which are a byproduct of the massive production and distribution systems of industrial society. While people can better themselves, to do so means following the bureaucratic rules. They have to attend the right schools, wear the right clothes, work for the right company, go to the right meetings, marry the right person, and live in the right neighborhood.

In the personalized economy, customized goods, designed for individualistic consumers, are the basis of the economy. This makes information about customers and their needs the key resource of the personalized economy. Because of rapid technological advances in computing and communications technologies over the past twenty years, the information that forms the basis of the personalized economy is inexpensive and readily available to those with the skills to use it. With the building blocks of the economy at hand, people can escape the bureaucracies. They become much more anonymous and independent. This is an environment where entrepreneurs can quickly become multi-millionaires, like Steve Jobs (Apple Computer) and Bill Gates (Microsoft). As increasing numbers of people operate independently of one another, the bureaucracies of industrial society break down, economic transactions speed up, and the pace of life increases in exponential terms.

Success in the personalized economy demands different strategies than success in the industrial economy. The personalized economy rewards innovation more than loyalty, instant action more than careful analysis, and short-term gains more than long-term goals. These new economic strategies created free agents, who in turn became the eager market for the personalized economy, creating a personalized culture in the process.

The culture of the personalized economy is already pervasive: public faxes, automatic teller machines, cellular phone companies, video outlets, computer stores, fast-food restaurants, and twenty-four-hour supermarkets line the highways of urban and suburban America. The contrast between the culture of free agents and the communal culture of the 1950s could not be greater: microwaves versus ovens; fast-food restaurants versus family dinners; fax machines or telephones versus letters; televisions versus newspapers; computer networks versus libraries; videos versus books; credit cards versus savings accounts; twenty-four-hour shopping versus banker's hours. While many older Americans still cling to the communal culture of midcentury, most of those under 50— particularly Americans who must work for a living—belong to the culture of free agents, if not out of choice then out of necessity.

The culture of free agents is fast and personal. Speed is the competitive edge in the personalized economy, giving rise to one-hour film processing, walk-in medical clinics, 30-minute pizza delivery, and one-minute managers. The ultimate consequence of the fast-paced culture of free agents is "real time" products and services. These are products and services delivered at the instant someone demands them. The telephone, an instrument of "real time" communication, is more popular than the mail. The fax is displacing overnight delivery. Television itself offers an increasing amount of real-time information through twenty-four-hour news networks and live reporting.

The technology of the personalized economy gives free agents greater control over their environment. The more control they have, the more they want. Businesses have responded to this demand with a multitude of products that offer ever greater control. The VCR gives people control of television schedules. Notebook computers give people control of information no matter where they are. Cellular telephones let people talk to one another anytime and anywhere, from the seaside to the roadside. Even the automobile has become an instrument of personal control over the past four decades. Once owned by families, cars are now more often owned by individuals. Only six out of ten households owned a car in 1950. Today, the average American household is home to 1.9 adults and 2.0 cars.

Customization—or the design, manufacture, and marketing of products and services to suit individual tastes—is the way businesses sell to individualistic consumers, and it is one far-reaching consequence of the demand for personal control. As businesses have become increasingly customized over the past thirty years, manufacturing, marketing, and retailing have been transformed. There is no better example of this than the evolution of food shopping. At mid century, the average grocery store carried only 3,750 items. Today, the average supermarket carries 16,500 items as manufacturers target a multitude of consumer segments. Many products now sold in supermarkets were unknown to most Americans in the 1950s: yogurt, tabouli, tofu, Belgian endive, kiwis, flavored waters, gourmet sodas, and salsas—to name just a few. The services in today's supermarkets are those once offered by the entire main street in small cities: bakeries, delis, salads, fish markets, cheese shops, butchers, hot entrees, and ice-cream bars. The simple meat and potatoes that filled shopping carts of the 1950s have had to make room for the customized products and services demanded by individualistic free agents.

The fast pace and individuality of the personalized economy have already created scores of technological marvels, and many more will be forthcoming with the ongoing integration of computing and communications devices. But no new technology so far has affected the average American as much as television, to which much of the blame and credit for the personalized economy can be traced.

Television is the door into the personalized economy. First marketed for family entertainment, TVs are now personal appliances like so many other technologies. The average American home has 2.6 people and 2.0 television sets.

As the first generation raised on television, it is no coincidence that baby boomers are also the first generation of free agents. Video technology nurtures free agents by linking them anonymously to the world, allowing them to monitor events from the sanctity of their homes. Free agents use television differently than older generations of Americans. For free agents, television is a way to stay in touch with the world; for older Americans, it's entertainment. Fifty percent of baby boomers are "reflexive" television viewers—they turn on the TV before they decide what program to watch. In contrast, most older viewers decide on a program before turning on the set. Baby boomers and younger Americans also are more likely than older people to leave the TV on as "background" entertainment, even when they're not watching it. As free agents matured and became a larger share of adults, the proportion of Americans who watch television reflexively jumped from 29 percent in 1979 to 43 percent by the end of the 1980s. The share who usually have the TV on in the background grew from 25 to 39 percent.

The importance of television is best revealed by its power over one of the most finite of resources—time. Television changed the way people spend their time more than any other technology including the automobile, according to sociologist and time-use researcher John P. Robinson of the University of Maryland. While cars changed the American landscape, creating suburban development and superhighways, they did not significantly change the amount of time people spend commuting or traveling, says Robinson. In contrast, television now commands 38 percent of the free time of Americans—hours people once spent reading, visiting with friends and relatives, listening to the radio, or enjoying hobbies. With the advent of "real-time" reporting, television is becoming even more compelling. People can watch events on television as they happen, from hurricanes to Supreme Court decisions. Television coverage of the Persian Gulf War in early 1991 caused retail sales to plummet as Americans sat glued to the tube.

Americans admit that watching television is one of the most satisfying things they do, according to the Roper Organization. Forty-six percent say watching television gives them greater satisfaction than any other daily activity. Only spending time with the family was mentioned by a larger proportion of people (71 percent).

As television becomes more interactive in the future, giving people greater control over what they see (such as the ability to choose camera angles in sports events, to view products up close while catalog shopping, or to order from a multitude of pay-per-view movies) it will dominate people's time even more than it does today. As the number of television channels increases by tenfold in the near future, as some predict, it is likely that the pace and pressure of modern life will grow beyond the nearly intolerable level of today. Television is the Pandora's box of options.

Television turned on the flow of information. Free agents are reluctant to turn it off, afraid of what they will miss. Consequently, free agents are overwhelmed by the volume of information—some relevant but most of it irrelevant—generated by the personalized economy. Only a few of the thousands of advertising messages people see daily are useful to them, for example. Yet they must cope with them all. For free agents, the result is the feeling that they're constantly under the gun.

The baby boom is not the first generation to feel overwhelmed at life's midpoint. But its plight is more difficult than that of any previous generation because free agents must cope with so much more. In life's performance, baby boomers play all the roles, from breadwinners to homemakers. At the same time, they must cope with the extraordinary volume of information unleashed by television and the multitude of options of the personalized economy.

Over 40 percent of baby boomers feel as if they can't slow down. Most feel they have less free time than they once did. In fact, baby boomers do have less free time than they did several decades ago when they were in their teens and twenties, because the middle aged have less free time than any other age group. This statement is easily proved by comparing the daily routines of someone in middle age with those of someone twenty years younger, in college or working at an entry-level job. Few 20-year-olds have children. At the end of the day, most can leave their job or college classes behind and join their friends for a good time. In contrast, the middle aged have children and spouses who need their attention at the end of the day. In essence, they work a "second shift."

The feeling of being pressed for time, however, is due to more than just middle age. It is the consequence of all the options available to free agents. In fact, baby boomers have more free time than people their age did two decades ago. Their fathers spent more time working than they do. Their mothers spent more time taking care of children, cooking, and cleaning house than they do.

Determining how much free time Americans have is a difficult task, because the answer depends on how researchers ask the question. In one recent survey, researchers from the Louis Harris Organization asked Americans how much free time they had in an average week: the answer was seventeen hours. In a similar survey done by the same organization two decades ago, the answer was twenty-seven hours. From these surveys the notion arose that Americans' free time was shrinking—dropping by a full ten hours a week in the past two decades.

But when researchers ask people to measure their free time in a more detailed way, the answer is quite different. When researchers from the Roper Organization asked Americans how much free time they had on Monday, Tuesday, and every other day of the week, then added up the answers, the result was 37 hours of free time a week, nearly double what the Harris survey revealed. The Roper results are close to those reported in time-use studies, where people continuously record their activities in diaries over a period of several days. Diary surveys are considered the most accurate measure of time use, and they show that Americans have about forty hours of free time each week. Men have about the same amount of free time as they did in the mid-1960s, while women have five hours more free time than women did two decades ago.

Free agents may find it hard to believe that free time has expanded over the past few decades because they feel so pressed for time. But the reason they feel so busy is that their options are overwhelming them. No matter how many activities people cram into a day, they are bound to miss something. While their choices have expanded, their ability to manage them has not.

The clutter and urgency of modern life is revealed in a comparison of life now with life on a farm centuries ago. When darkness fell two hundred years ago, there was little to do but go to bed. There were no electric lights or television. Candles lit the interior of homes, but only dimly. Acres of farmland separated families from one another. Miles of dirt road separated farm families from the nearest town. Farm life operated from dawn to dusk. People rarely missed anything by turning in early. Even if they wanted to go out in the evening, there was nowhere to go and no way to get there.

In contrast, today's society operates twenty-four hours a day. After dark there are an infinite number of things to do, whether people go out or stay home. Unlike their counterparts two centuries ago, when people go to bed early today, they will miss something. In fact, they will miss many, many things.

With over thirty television channels to choose from in most homes today, people are bound to miss something they would enjoy watching on television. With hundreds of new magazines on the newsstand each year, they're likely to have a stack of unread magazines piling up on the coffee table if not strewn about the house. With thousands of new books being published each year, they're behind in their reading. And with dozens of new movies being released each season, they're missing several they meant to see, including those that have just hit the cable stations.

Beyond the home, other temptations beckon: restaurants, night clubs, health clubs, shopping malls. Dozens of stores are open twenty-four hours a day within a few miles of most homes. Grocery shopping is a possibility at 1:00 A.M. Catalog shopping can be done at 3:00 A.M. The personalized economy never shuts down, never even pauses. The feeling that they're always missing something may be why one-fifth of Americans say they're too busy to have fun, and why 69 percent want to slow down and live a more relaxed life. For free agents, a leisurely life-style is appealing but increasingly elusive, because they must earn a living.

❖ 12 ❖

A Preference for Leisure

It takes more work to maintain a middle-class life-style in the personalized economy than it did in the industrial economy. As businesses compete furiously with one another for ever smaller groups of customers, profit margins have been shaved razor thin, and salaries, too, have suffered. Consequently, more Americans are at work than ever before. Sixty-six percent of the population aged 16 or older is now in the labor force, up from 59 percent in the 1950s. As men's salaries stagnated over the past quarter-century, women poured into the labor force to make up the difference.

Perhaps because of the growing necessity to work, Americans now regard leisure time as more meaningful than their time on the job, according to a Roper Poll. Thirty-six percent of Americans say leisure is more important than work, larger than the 30 percent who say work is more important than leisure. Sixty-eight percent of workers say they enjoy their leisure time more than they enjoy their time on the job, up from 49 percent in 1955. The rising importance of leisure among Americans signals the growing dominance of free agents over traditional-minded older generations. Most Americans now believe that a reasonable amount of leisure time is a right, not a privilege, up from a minority who held this belief just a few years ago.

The conflict between work and leisure is another of the central conflicts in the lives of middle-aging free agents. More than nine out of ten men, and more than seven out of ten women aged 25 to 54 are in the labor force. Nearly all working men and three out of four working women work full-time. But because free agents find their leisure time more meaningful than their time on the job, job satisfaction is down. According to a Roper Poll, the proportion of Americans "completely satisfied" with the personal satisfaction they get from their work recently hit a record low, falling from 46 percent in the mid-1970s to 36 percent in 1992. Free agents—Americans younger than age 50—are far less satisfied with their jobs than older people. Just 36 percent of 30 to 49 year olds are "completely" satisfied with their jobs, versus a 55 percent majority of older workers. These older workers are the same ones who, in the mid-1950s, said they enjoyed their jobs more than their leisure time. Clearly, baby boomers have a different attitude toward work than older generations of Americans.

The conflict between the need to work and the longing for leisure is likely to grow through the 1990s and into the next century. Early retirement will be far less common for baby boom men and women than it was for their fathers, as employers limit early retirement plans. The fathers of the baby boom generation eagerly accepted the opportunity to retire early, a trend that began in the 1960s and accelerated in the 1970s. It is unlikely that baby boomers will get the same opportunity.

After nearly two decades of throwing themselves into their careers, free agents are realizing that at least two more decades of work lie ahead. They have little enthusiasm left for employers, work schedules, business travel, and rushed vacations. As baby boomers have children, they are gaining new priorities, say social historians Barbara Dafoe Whitehead and Ralph Whitehead, Jr. Work seems far less significant than it once did. It no longer defines the lives of free agents. Rather, family life and leisure pursuits are far more meaningful to baby boomers in midlife. As work diminishes in importance, baby boom parents are withdrawing from the workplace psychologically, say the Whiteheads. Consequently, society is experiencing a massive psychological shift away from the work-centered values of the past two decades.

The Whiteheads' observations are supported by survey results showing that free agents would like to work less than they do. But given the economic realities of their lives, few will find a way to do so. The proportion of women who say they would rather stay home than go to work stood at 53 percent in 1992, up from 43 percent in 1985, a reversal of the downward trend in this statistic since the early 1970s. Two out of ten men also say they would prefer homemaking to the career track.

The shift in attitudes toward work is occurring at the same time births are peaking and more Americans are having their second and third children. It was a predictable shift, based on the steady rise in women's labor force participation and in births. Behind the shift is the stress felt by free agents as they juggle work and family schedules. Sixty percent of mothers say the conflicting demands of work and family put them under a lot of stress, according to a Roper poll. Half of working mothers and 40 percent of working fathers have considered cutting back their hours or quitting their jobs altogether to spend more time with their families.

That's the fantasy, but it is unlikely to become a reality. Women's incomes are essential to today's families, and given the choice, few women would permanently retreat to home and hearth. A rising proportion of women regard their work as a career rather than just a job. In 1990, this proportion reached 45 percent, up from 41 percent in 1985. Among men, 57 percent regard their work as a career, the same proportion as in 1985. In an ideal world, men and women might choose to work part-time rather than full time. But in the real world, part-time work doesn't pay the bills.

There is another reason women can't go home again. As free agents, they won't risk the dependency of homemaking. Baby boom women know their chances of divorce are greater than their chances of celebrating a fiftieth wedding anniversary. They need the economic independence of a job. Among all women, 58 percent are in the labor force, up from 43 percent in 1970. Among women aged 25 to 44, 75 percent are in the labor force, up from 48 percent in 1970. The most rapid climb in labor force participation rates has been among mothers with infants. Over half of married women giving birth in 1990 were back at work before their baby celebrated its first birthday, up from fewer than one-third in 1976.

In the personalized economy, women must be breadwinners, homemakers, and mothers.

Free agents may be loath to go to work each morning, but they long for the money work brings. According to a Gallup poll, a majority of Americans would like to be rich, but only 25 percent are "very" willing to work twelve- to fourteen-hour days, year-round, for guaranteed riches. Free agents value money highly because of the enormous expenses of the personalized economy. They value work primarily as a way to make money. In midlife, free agents face a multitude of financial demands. Many have big mortgage payments, equally large day-care costs, and an urgent need to save for college and retirement. Millions of boomers are in a financial squeeze that will keep them from feeling affluent in the decade ahead, though many may qualify for affluence on paper.

Despite the financial demands of the personalized economy, Americans spend a larger share of their incomes on recreation and entertainment than ever before, revealing just how important leisure is to free agents. If the amount of money people spend on having a good time is evidence of the status of leisure, then leisure has become a necessity of life. As the baby boom matured, spending on entertainment and recreation grew rapidly. Since 1987, Americans spend more on having a good time than they do on clothes. With most of Americans' basic needs met, they have devoted an increasing share of their spending to having fun.

Americans spent $290 billion on recreation and entertainment in 1991, two-thirds as much as they spent on transportation and nearly half as much as they spent on food or medical care. Even in the midst of recession, spending on recreation grew steadily through the early 1990s, after adjusting for inflation, while spending on food (including eating out), clothing, household operations, and transportation fell.

A closer look at how people spend their recreational dollars reveals even more about how free agents like to have fun. One of the most rapidly growing single categories of recreation spending is something called "commercial participant amusements," rising from $2 billion in 1970 to $23 billion in 1991. A bowling tournament, an all-day pass to Disney World, ski-lift tickets, casino gambling, a swim at the local pool, a round of golf, a sightseeing tour of the Rockies—all fall into this category of spending. These experiences ranked seventh among categories of recreation spending in 1970. But by 1991, participatory amusements were in fifth place, behind only video and audio equipment, toys, sports equipment, and magazines and newspapers. Spending on participatory recreation far surpasses spending on ball games, movie tickets, or other spectator events.

In the 1990s, the spending habits of free agents are beginning to succumb to middle-aged sensibilities. Free agents are impulse buyers, while the middle aged plan for the future. Free agents are carefree spenders, while the middle aged are cautious. The economy is reeling as the spending patterns of its largest consumer segment shift from carefree to careful.

During the past thirty years, the free-spending free agents of the baby boom generation made the youth market an economic powerhouse. Unfortunately, many businesses came to believe that young adults controlled the consumer marketplace. Whole industries arose to serve youth.

As the baby boom's spending priorities began to shift in the late 1980s, many businesses ignored the change. Their sales fell, finally propelling the economy into recession. Though many businesses blame the limp recovery for their economic woes and anticipate a return to boom times, in fact there will be no return to the heady days of conspicuous consumption in the 1980s.

In their teens and twenties, people spend money on themselves. In middle age, people must spend money on their families. The spending priorities of the baby boom shifted from "me" to "we" during the past decade, an entirely predictable event if anyone had stopped counting the cash long enough to look ahead.

For decades, businesses reaped the benefits of the baby boom's postponed responsibilities, creating the youth market. The baby boom's parents married as teenagers; the baby boom boosted the median age of first marriage up to a historic high. The baby boom's fathers were responsible for supporting a family before they reached the age of 25; many baby boomers delayed having families until they were in their thirties. Compared to their parents, then, baby boomers enjoyed an extra ten or fifteen years of spending on themselves. The consequence was the youth market of the 1960s and 1970s and the yuppie market of the 1980s.

All this came to an abrupt end when free agents had children. For the first time in their lives, they had other people to support and future expenses to plan. Businesses wondering where their customers went need look no further than maternity wards, playgrounds, and PTA meetings. Retail sales of infant, toddler, and preschool products rose at a healthy clip throughout the recession of the early 1990s.

This shift in spending priorities does not mean boomers have stopped spending. On the contrary, households headed by people aged 35 to 54 spend more than those headed by younger or older people. Few businesses are aware of the spending power of the middle aged, however, because for the past two decades the middle aged were vastly outnumbered by the burgeoning young adult population. Now that the number of middle-aged Americans is growing rapidly, the spending of the middle aged will power the economy for the foreseeable future. But the middle aged spend money differently from young adults. Beer, rent, and coin-operated laundromats are some of the few things young adults spend more on than the middle aged. Doctors, hospitals, and heating oil are some of the few things older people (those 55 or older) spend more on than the middle aged. People aged 35 to 54 spend more than younger or older householders on just about everything else, including shoes, cars, televisions, furniture, restaurant meals, and motels. As the huge baby boom generation moves into this middle-aged group, it will control a growing share of the market for most products and services. By 2000, people aged 35 to 54 will control 54 percent of all household spending in the United States. For many categories of products and services, such as clothing, entertainment, and education, they will control an even higher share of the market.

This spending is good news for the American economy, but it

presents baby boomers with a dilemma. Because so many waited so long to have children, many will be nearing retirement about the time their children head off to college. These two factors, children and retirement, make boomers much more budget conscious. As baby boomers face these realities, the share of American families who do not budget their expenses is falling, from 42 percent in the late 1970s to 25 percent today, according to the Roper Organization. Half of Americans now say they are strict financial planners, up from 36 percent in the late 1970s.

To pay for the huge expenses to come, free agents have three choices. They can spend their money differently, avoiding expensive restaurants and fancy clothes, and investing instead in their children and in retirement accounts. They can try to earn more money by working more, or they can borrow more.

In the long run, borrowing will not work, especially for those trying to build a nest egg for retirement. Baby boomers are beginning to get the message. Americans are finally paying off their debts. Consumer installment debt, such as credit card balances and car loans, fell in 1991 for the first time in thirty-three years. Now that baby boomers are paying off their debts, it is not likely that they will dig themselves into the hole all over again.

It is also unlikely that more hours on the job will be popular among free agents who prize leisure time. And while there is a good chance baby boomers will make more money on the job in the years ahead, rising paychecks alone won't cover all their expenses. Something else had to change, and beginning in the late 1980s there were major cutbacks in spending on such luxuries as $100 restaurant meals and $500 suits, expensive cars and champagne brunches, diamond earrings and designer briefcases, power boats and European vacations. Businesses built on the impulsive spending of free agents are folding as middle-aged baby boomers spend instead on mutual funds, back-to-school supplies, and baby formula. Spending on an array of luxuries began to fall in the late 1980s as baby boomers indulged less and devoted more of their dollars to their children.

Most baby boomers find it difficult to save. Some may ask

their children to pay college bills themselves, rationalizing their inability to save by questioning the value of a college degree. In the competitive personalized economy, their children will be doomed to downward mobility. Other baby boomers are biting the bullet and saving for the first time in their lives. Currently, 58 percent of baby boomers are saving money. Among the savers, 38 percent are saving for retirement while 35 percent are saving for their children's college education, according to a Merrill Lynch survey. As they save, their net worth is inching upwards.

The net worth of households headed by 35- to 44-year-olds rose by 6 percent between 1983 and 1989, after adjusting for inflation, according to the Federal Reserve's Survey of Consumer Finances. While this gain was less than the 10.5 percent rise in the net worth of all American households, the baby boom managed to accumulate slightly more assets than the average household ($52,800 versus $47,200). Most of the baby boom's wealth is in its homes. Sixty-six percent of 35- to 44-year-olds owned a home in 1989, and it was worth a median of $80,000. Forty-four percent had a retirement account, but it was worth just $8,000.

Ninety percent of baby boomers are in debt, but their debts are not as overwhelming as many proclaim. Including mortgage debt, boomers aged 35 to 44 owed a median of $31,100 in 1989, up from $25,400 in 1983, after adjusting for inflation. But baby boomers are more likely to be in debt than the average American household (73 percent have debts), and they owe more (the average American household owes just $15,200). Nevertheless, because their assets grew faster than their debts, their net worth rose in the 1980s. No doubt the recession of the early 1990s reduced the baby boom's net worth at least temporarily. Once the recovery is under-way, the net worth of baby boomers is certain to grow again as the perspectives of free agents turn toward the future.

For some baby boomers, the net worth of their parents is of greater interest to them than the value of their own bank accounts. Some studies, well-publicized by the media, predict that the baby boom generation will inherit substantial wealth from its parents. There are several problems with this scenario. First, the baby boom is a big generation. Most boomers have several siblings with whom they will have to share any wealth that comes their way. Second, in a world fueled by self-interest, parents who have learned a bit about self-interest from their children are more likely to spend on themselves and leave less to their brood. Today's elderly sport bumper stickers proclaiming this very fact: "I'm spending my children's inheritance." Those words may carry more truth than baby boomers want to admit. In any event, economists predict that the average baby boomer will inherit no more than $40,000 upon the death of his or her parents. If free agents want all the things money can buy, most will have to work for it, and some will have to work much harder than others.

❖ 13 ❖

The Star System

Free agents need money to be players in the personalized economy. It is no surprise, then, that as free agents matured, the importance of money grew. In the 1980s, baby boomers postponed the emotional attachments of marriage and children to indulge their materialistic whims, which gave rise to yuppies and the spending spree of the 1980s. In the 1990s, Americans are continuing their quest for material goods, though that quest is influenced by the growing importance of families and family life. Sixty-one percent of Americans say materialism is "in," rather than out, according to a Roper survey. At the same time, most also report that marriage and children are in. The pursuit of both material and emotional goals creates yet another conflict in the lives of middle-aging free agents.

Americans are increasingly likely to rate material goods as essential to happiness. A home, a car, and lots of money all rank among the top five ingredients of the good life, according to the Roper Organization. The proportion of Americans citing possessions as essential to the good life grew during the 1980s, with the importance of "lots of money" growing the most. By the end of the 1980s, 62 percent of Americans said having "lots of money" was essential to the good life, a full 19 percentage points more than said so in 1981. In contrast, the proportion of Americans citing family as essential to the good life did not change much. While having a happy marriage ranks second among the necessary ingredients of the good life, the proportion of Americans citing this as essential to the good life actually fell by 2 percentage points since the early 1980s. Having children was up by 3 percentage points to 72 percent. That figure is equal to the proportion who think a car is essential to the good life.

While few free agents will ever feel that they have a lot of money (only 4 percent of Americans do), most want the opportunity to reach the top. Americans would rather take their chances than not have a chance at all. A shrinking share of Americans believe in income equality, for example. The percentage of Americans who strongly agree that the government should reduce income differences among people dropped from one-third in 1973 to just one-fifth by the late 1980s.

As materialistic values rise in importance, free agents are becoming increasingly anxious about the economy. Many think the country is on the wrong track, and they wonder how well their children will do. This anxiety began long before the recession of the early 1990s. The first symptom surfaced a decade earlier when Americans began to fret about the disappearance of the middle class, a phenomenon documented by both government and academic researchers. Since over 90 percent of Americans regard themselves as middle class, no matter how wealthy or poor, any threat to the middle class sends a collective shudder through the American psyche.

During the past ten years, a variety of studies have shown that the middle class—defined as households or individuals with incomes in the middle of the income distribution—is indeed shrinking. Census Bureau statistics show that the proportion of households with annual incomes between $25,000 and $50,000 fell from 35 percent in 1980 to 33 percent in 1990, after adjusting for inflation. The proportion of working-age adults with middle-level household incomes, defined in one study as incomes between $18,500 to $55,000, fell from 75 percent in 1977–1978 to 68 percent in 1985–1986, according to an analysis of the longitudinal Panel Study of Income Dynamics by researchers Greg J. Duncan, Timothy M. Smeeding, and Willard Rodgers. The share of income accruing to households with incomes in the middle of the income distribution fell from 52 percent in 1980 to 50 percent in 1990, according to the Census Bureau.

Only now are researchers beginning to discover that the cause of the shrinking middle class lies in the growing diversity of American workers and wages, which results in increasing income polarization. In other words, the extremes are growing at the expense of the middle. Several decades ago, the majority of Americans shared a similar life-style (nuclear family) and income level (middle). But this similarity ended when free agents came of age. The life-styles of free agents range from those living alone to nuclear families. Their educational levels range from high school dropouts to Ph.Ds. While these extremes also existed among older generations, among free agents the extremes are not tiny minorities but sizable portions of an enormous generation.

As baby boomers matured beyond young adulthood in the late 1970s and 1980s, the diversity of their life-styles began to affect income statistics. As a rule, single-parent families do not earn as much as dual-career couples. As both types of families became more numerous, incomes polarized. Typically, high school graduates do not earn as much as college graduates (although there are some exceptions, such as plumbers and other skilled blue-collar workers). As the proportion of householders with a college degree began to equal the proportion who went no further than high school, incomes polarized. As incomes polarized, the middle class shrank, and Americans quaked with fear.

With incomes polarizing, Americans sense that the future will be unlike the past. They feel increasingly insecure about the economy. This kind of insecurity has been documented one other time in American history—on the brink of U.S. involvement in World War II. Then, as now, the American social and economic systems were about to undergo enormous change; Americans had little feel for the future; and many people feared their children would not live as well as they did.

Despite these generalized fears about the nation's future, most Americans today, including baby boomers, are optimistic about their personal futures. This optimism may stem from the fact that growing affluence, rather than growing poverty, accounts for much of the decline in the middle class. The proportion of households with incomes above $50,000 reached a record high in 1989 before declining slightly in the recession of the early 1990s. The proportion of working-age adults living in households with incomes above $55,000 grew by five percentage points, from 8 to 13 percent between 1979–1980 and 1985–1986, according to the Duncan, Smeeding, and Rodgers study. Over half of baby boomers say they are better off than their parents were during the last few years they lived at home, reports the Conference Board. Two-thirds of men and three-fourths of women aged 35 to 44 believe they have more opportunities than their parents did. And despite their apprehension about their children's future, most think their children eventually will attain a higher standard of living than they themselves now have.

But as some people pull ahead, others are left behind. Income polarization is a fact of life in the personalized economy. A growing number of people reap enormous financial rewards and a growing number lose out as the global economy pulls manufacturing jobs overseas.

Income differences are to be expected in any free market. Few would argue that entry-level workers should earn as much as experienced employees. No one would make the case that dual-earner families, who put in 80-hour work weeks, should earn no more than single-earner families who put in only 40-hour work weeks. Retirees living on pensions and Social Security should not earn as much as workers contributing to the economy. Those who invested in getting an education should earn more than those who did not make the investment.

But income inequality is growing beyond these explanations, because the importance of individual skills has given rise to a new economic order, sometimes called the "star system." In the star system, a few people rise to the top, commanding enormous salaries, and everyone else must make do with the leftovers. In the past, the most successful Americans built their fortunes by manufacturing the products of the industrial era. In the personalized economy, the most successful Americans are those who control the flow of information. The success stories include entrepreneurs who create innovative ways to organize information, intellectuals who come up with new theories to explain information, entertainers who capture the attention of the television or movie audience, corporate executives who gain a competitive edge with consumer information, and TV news anchors who become stars simply by bringing all this information to the public.

The star system is most obvious in sports. The average salary for NBA or major league baseball players is already close to $1 million a season. Proven performers make much more than that, while competition among team owners for the most talented players continues to drive salaries up. Most Americans think the salaries paid to professional athletes are too high, but most actually underestimate the amount of money top sports stars earn.

Paying people millions of dollars to play a game was unthinkable a few years ago, as were multimillion dollar contracts with singers, such as Michael Jackson, Prince, and Madonna. The $10 million advances paid to best-selling authors such as Stephen King or Tom Clancy were unimaginable, as were the $100,000-a-year contracts major magazines pay their top writers, or the millions guaranteed to top movie stars.

The star system is deeply entrenched in the personalized economy, in fields ranging from sports to music to business. Stars rise in any field where information drives profits. There are no stars in the field of plumbing, for example. But there are many business stars including Lee Iacocca, John Sculley, and other corporate leaders who make millions because of their star status. These corporate stars drive up CEO salaries in other major corporations as boards of directors vie for top talent. The average CEO of a major corporation makes eighty-five times more than the average American worker.

Economic researchers describe the star system as "a market in which a handful of participants reap a disproportionate share of the total rewards." This phenomenon became pervasive in the past few decades as the industrial economy evolved into the information-driven personalized economy. The technology of the personalized economy allowed stars to publicize their skills through the media, spurring competition for their services. Consequently, in a variety of fields from tennis to business, the gap between the pay of top performers and average performers is growing. In tennis, the best players are increasingly valuable because they can command a television audience of millions. Meanwhile, average players lose fans as stars grab the spotlight. As top performers become increasingly well known, team owners, motion picture companies, major publishers, boards of directors, and other big organizations compete for their services with big-money offers. This leaves less for everyone else. Publishers pay millions of dollars in advances to best-selling authors, but the average advance for run-of-the-mill authors ranges from $1500 to $2500.

Free agents live and die by the star system because it is the road to riches in the personalized economy. The star system motivates them to go to college, start their own businesses, or write books. The dream of becoming a star drives the multibillion dollar lottery industry. It makes television shows like "Lifestyles of the Rich and Famous," "Entertainment Tonight," and magazines like *People* and *Entertainment Weekly* flourish. The star system is the engine of the economy, an engine fueled by the dreams of free agents. Nearly two out of three Americans under the age of 30 think they have a good chance of becoming rich. Among those aged 30 to 49, one-third believe they have a good shot at wealth.

On a more modest scale, free agents with specialized skills reap disproportionate rewards for their services. The pay of doctors and lawyers, for example, has grown much faster than the pay of average workers during the 1980s because of the competition for the specialized skills of those professionals. The gap in pay between well-educated workers and those who dropped out of high school also has grown substantially during the past few decades as free agents with specialized skills command ever higher rewards, while those with few skills find themselves with little bargaining power.

Though few free agents will achieve star status, the best and the brightest have the opportunity to fight their way to the front of the pack. Left behind are those who never got the opportunity to put up a good fight, the victims of an economy that demands much and forgives little. But many Americans under the age of 50 invested heavily in their personal skills. They will do well in the economic battleground of the 1990s, a decade which is likely to end with record levels of affluence.

Until the recession, American households had already achieved a record level of affluence, but in the early 1990s, household incomes fell. Even so, 26 percent of households had an income of $50,000 or more in 1991, up from 22 percent in 1980, after adjusting for inflation. One in ten had an income of $75,000 or more, up from 7 percent in 1980. As a growing proportion of American households achieved affluence during the 1980s, a shrinking proportion of households remained in the middle and lower ends of the income distribution. The proportion of households with incomes below $25,000 fell from 43 to 42 percent between 1980 and 1991, after adjusting for inflation.

Today's affluence is the consequence of three ongoing trends which will boost incomes during the remainder of the decade: the middle aging of the baby boom generation, the rise of dual-earner couples, and the baby boom's high level of education.

Though businesses have long targeted the "youth" market, in fact the middle aged earn the most money. The low earnings of young adults were partly responsible for the sluggish economy of the 1970s. During that decade, millions of baby boomers were in college or entering the work force and taking on low-paying entry-level jobs, competing with one another for the minimum wage. Median household income peaked in 1973, and did not set a new record until 1986 as the labor force absorbed millions of baby boom workers.

During the 1980s, baby boomers moved from their entry-level positions into better-paying jobs. With more experience, they earned more money, resulting in record levels of affluence by 1989.

During the 1990s, baby boomers will enter their peak earning

years. Workers aged 45 to 54—at the height of their careers—
make more money than younger or older workers. Households
headed by people aged 45 to 54 had a median income of $44,000 in
1991, compared to a median of just $30,000 for the average house-
hold. Forty-six percent of households headed by 45- to 54-year-
olds will have an income of $50,000 or more by 2000, up from 40
percent in 1990, after adjusting for inflation according to projections by The Conference Board. Among all households, 30 percent
will have incomes in the $50,000-plus range, up from 24 percent in
1990, because of the middle aging of the baby boom and the rise of
dual-earner couples.

Most baby boom couples are dual earners. Married couples
are by far the most affluent household type, with a median income
of $41,000 in 1991, $11,000 more than the median income of the
average household. Couples in which both husband and wife
worked full time had a median income of $57,000. More than 80
percent of households in the top income quintile are married
couples, according to Census Bureau statistics. These richest
households received 47 percent of national income in 1991, up from
44 percent in 1980.

The gap between the incomes of dual-earner and single-
earner couples has grown rapidly. The reasons for this growing
gap are the rapidly rising incomes of women and the stagnating
incomes of men. Though men, on average, still earn more than
women, men's incomes barely kept pace with inflation over the
past few decades while women's incomes soared. Consequently,
the incomes of dual-earner couples have been rising faster than
inflation for years, while those of single-earner couples have fallen
behind. Since men are the breadwinners in most single-earner
families, the incomes of single-earner families fell as men's earnings eroded with the loss of high-paying manufacturing jobs. In
1970, the incomes of dual-earner couples were 32 percent greater
than those of single-earner couples. By the early 1990s, the gap
had widened to 60 percent.

The personalized economy is a service economy. The service
industry accounts for a growing share of jobs. According to the

Census Bureau, 42 percent of new workers enter "low-paying" service industries (such as retail trade, personal services, and entertainment and recreation services); 34 percent enter "high-paying" service industries (such as communication, finance, insurance, real estate, professional services, and public administration); while only 24 percent enter goods-producing industries. By 2005, 81 percent of all nonagricultural wage and salary workers will be employed in service-producing industries, according to government projections, up from 71 percent in 1975.

The growing demand for both high- and low-paid service workers means the economy is producing fewer jobs that support a middle-class life-style. In the past, many manufacturing jobs offered high levels of pay, negotiated by powerful unions. But with global competition ending the power of unions, and with manufacturing employment shrinking, an increasing proportion of men make little money. The share of men who work year-round, full-time yet earn too little to lift a family of four out of poverty, climbed from 7 percent in 1974 to 14 percent in 1990, according to the Census Bureau. Among men aged 18 to 24, the proportion with low earnings climbed from 17 to 40 percent.

Those hit the hardest in the personalized economy are workers with little education. Many baby boomers will avoid this fate, since they belong to the most highly educated generation in American history. Half have at least some college experience. With the economic returns to education growing, the affluence of well-educated baby boomers should also grow. While job creation was sluggish during the recession of the early 1990s, once the economy picks up steam, those with the most education are likely to reap the most rewards.

The median income of households headed by college graduates amounted to $52,000 in 1991, much higher than the $30,000 median for the average household. The income gap between the college educated and everyone else began to grow rapidly in the late 1980s after years of little gain. The stagnation in the earnings of college graduates during the 1970s and early 1980s came from the competition among so many well-educated baby boomers, fresh out of college, vying for entry-level jobs. Now that the boomers are entering their peak earning years, the financial returns to a college diploma are becoming abundantly clear. By 1991, the median income of households headed by college graduates was 83 percent greater than that of households headed by high-school graduates.

Married couples aged 45 to 64 with at least four years of college had a median income of over $73,000 in 1990. This is more than twice the median income of the average household. As married and well-educated baby boomers move into this age group, their growing affluence is virtually assured.

But not everyone will enjoy rising affluence. As some become richer, others will find themselves stuck at the lower end of the income distribution. Structural changes in the economy have created a greater diversity of wages, with high-skilled workers rewarded with premium wages and low-skilled workers losing ground to inflation. These facts are revealed in an examination of trends in personal income. Personal income is the money people make from all sources, including their paycheck, dividends or interest, government benefits, and so on.

Personal rather than family income statistics are the best indicator of how incomes are growing because they are unaffected by family change. If all families were headed by single-earner married couples, family income statistics could be reliably compared over time. But as an increasing share of families are headed by dual-earner couples or by single parents, these changes in family composition affect family income statistics. For example, median family income grew from $35,000 in 1980 to $36,000 in 1991, after adjusting for inflation. But this apparent stagnation hides a number of different trends. The median income of dual-earner married couples, for example, rose from $44,000 in 1980 to $48,000 in 1991, after adjusting for inflation. In contrast, the median income of single-earner married couples fell from $31,000 in 1980 to $30,000 in 1991, after adjusting for inflation. The median income of single-parent families headed by women remained stable at about $17,000. In contrast to this complexity, personal income statistics reveal the bottom line changes in the incomes of individual Americans.

On average, the personal incomes of women (including working women and women not in the work force) grew rapidly. The incomes of this group were up by 29 percent between 1980 and 1991, while the personal incomes of men (workers and non-workers) fell by 1 percent, after adjusting for inflation. By age, men younger than 65 saw their incomes fall, while the incomes of men aged 65 or older grew. Personal income grew for women of all ages, the biggest gain being for women aged 35 to 44, the older baby boomers. Their personal incomes rose by 41 percent during the 1980s, after adjusting for inflation.

Despite these gains, there is still a considerable gap between the personal incomes of men and women. Overall, men had a median personal income of $20,000 in 1991, while women's personal income was just $10,000. Much of this gap is due to the fact that a larger proportion of men than women work full time. Narrowing the comparison only to men and women who work full time, men's median personal income amounted to $29,000 versus $21,000 for women. The gap between the incomes of men and women is narrower than in the past, but the gap still remains. The 59 cent dollar (the old ratio of women's earnings to men's) is now a 70 cent dollar.

The personal incomes of free agents with a college degree rose during the 1980s, while the incomes of those who did not go to college fell. Men who went no further than high school saw their personal incomes drop by 26 percent between 1980 and 1990, after adjusting for inflation. In contrast, men with four or more years of college held their ground economically. While women of all educational levels saw their personal incomes rise during the 1980s, the incomes of those with college educations rose by 22 percent, versus a smaller 12 percent increase for those who went no further than high school.

During the recession, nearly everyone lost ground. The income inequality in place before the recession remained virtually unchanged during the recession. Overall, household income fell by 5 percent between 1989 and 1991, after adjusting for inflation. All types of households and people of all ages saw their incomes shrink as unemployment took its toll. The long-awaited recovery is not likely to close the income gap. In order to reduce wage inequality, free agents would have to become more like each other as people were in the 1950s, with similar educational levels, family types, and jobs. This scenario is unlikely. While many Americans will partake of growing affluence in the years ahead, the good times will not be had by all.

Some say this phenomenon means the rich are getting richer and the poor are getting poorer. But the "rich" and "poor" are not an unchanging group of people. They are two populations constantly in flux. Americans move both up and down the income scale, and they always have. Typically, young people start with relatively little money, but their incomes rise as they get older. Typically, older people must live on less when they retire from the work force.

While this ebb and flow among the income classes is natural, recent statistics do indicate that the income gap between the rich and poor is growing. A Census Bureau analysis examining the incomes of Americans revealed that the proportions of people at both the high and low ends of the income scale are growing, while the proportion in the middle is shrinking. The proportion of people with incomes twice the median increased from 11 percent in 1969 to 15 percent in 1989. The proportion with incomes less than half the median also rose during those years, from 18 to 22 percent. At the same time, the proportion with incomes in the middle fell from 71 to 63 percent. Though American incomes have grown over the past few decades, income polarization has also grown. And there is evidence that the increasing diversity of American workers and their economic opportunities is resulting in increasingly unequal earnings over a lifetime.

Unequal incomes are not necessarily bad, as long as there is considerable income mobility. In the United States, income mobility is substantial, but the level of mobility is no greater than it was two decades ago. At the same time, a growing share of people are earning relatively high or relatively low incomes. Consequently, lifetime incomes are becoming more unequal, according to Urban Institute researchers Isabel Sawhill and Mark Condon. Low-skilled workers make less than they did a few decades ago, and they're not any more likely to move out of these jobs and up the economic ladder than similar low-skilled workers in the 1970s. High-skilled workers are making more than they once did, and they're not about to give up their good-paying jobs. With higher wages at the top and lower wages at the bottom, and with no change in mobility, the wage inequities of today are likely to be long-lasting.

As if that is not enough, there is an additional factor driving income inequality. According to an analysis by W. Norton Grubb and Robert H. Wilson of the Bureau of Labor Statistics, structural changes in the economy and demographic differences among people account for only some of the differences in wages. Grubb and Wilson suggest that other hard-to-measure factors are playing an increasingly important role. Individual differences in skills and opportunities are affecting earnings at all levels, they find. While an examination of these differences is yet to come, they could include negotiating skills, the quality of educational training, and even computer skills. According to Alan Krueger of the National Bureau of Economic Research, people who work directly with computers earn 10 to 15 percent more than those who don't. Furthermore, claims Krueger, computer skills accounted for nearly half of the growing gap in pay between college and high school graduates during the 1980s. This is an additional piece of evidence that the personalized economy rewards those best able to manipulate information—in this case, the computer literate.

Clearly, it's harder to make a good living in the personalized economy than in the industrial economy of midcentury. At the very least, a comfortable life-style requires more hours of work per family than it once did. Today's working couples work 80 hours a week in return for middle-class earnings. In contrast, the single-earner families of the 1950s devoted just 40 hours a week to the labor market in return for a middle-class life-style. Success in the personalized economy also demands a higher level of education. College graduates move ahead, while high school graduates lose ground. And success takes a variety of personal skills—the ability to manipulate information, the competitive drive to spot opportunity, and the good sense to seize it quickly. In the era of free agents, prosperity is hard won.

❖ 14 ❖

The Working Family

The families of free agents are diverse. They need different employee benefits and new work schedules to fit their diverse lifestyles. This is why Americans workers are demanding change in the workplace. The proportion of workers who think employers should provide a wide selection of benefit packages to suit individual needs has risen by a full 15 percentage points since 1981, to 69 percent, according to a Roper survey. The proportion who want flexible work hours was up 9 percentage points, to 60 percent. Fully three out of four Americans support the law requiring employers to provide unpaid family leave.

While new ways of working are on the horizon, few have been institutionalized. Today, free agents are caught in a transition between work styles supportive of nuclear families at midcentury and those evolving to meet the needs of the families of free agents. With the baby boom generation beginning to take the reins of political and corporate power, these support networks—family leave, universal health insurance, flextime, part-time options, and cafeteria benefits—will begin to spread through the corporate world.

Emerging trends in the workplace today suggest that the work patterns most supportive of the families of free agents may be those of the distant past, when families worked together at home. Advances in telecommunications and the changing nature of corporate employment may bring work back into the home, or at least closer to home. The technology of the personalized economy makes it possible for people to participate in the personalized economy without commuting to company offices. Portable computers, fax machines, modems, answering machines, electronic mail, and an array of telephone services allow people to conduct business and communicate with colleagues from far-flung locations.

Home is only one of those locations. At least 39 million Americans worked at home in 1992, according to LINK, an organization that tracks the home work market. This figure represents 30 percent of the nation's work force and includes the self-employed as well as employees who bring office work home with them. The fastest growing segment of the home work market is employees working from home during normal business hours. This group grew by 20 percent between 1991 and 1992, to nearly 6.6 million. Half of these "telecommuters" have children under the age of 18 living at home.

Research conducted by GTE Corporation shows that most of those who work at home are baby boomers, and many have young children. They are affluent, well-educated free agents. With businesses looking for ways to cut expenses, encouraging employees to work at home saves the cost of renting office space. It saves employees the time and cost of commuting. The cost advantages for both employers and employees will drive the home work trend in the 1990s.

Working at home has its problems, however, not the least of which is child care. Parents who work at home still need someone to look after their children, particularly parents of preschoolers. But working at home allows parents much more flexibility in their day-care arrangements. School-aged children can come home to Mom and Dad rather than spend their afternoons in after-school care, for example, or baby-sitters can be hired to fill in at certain hours. This flexibility relieves much of the stress of juggling work and family life.

Some experts argue that telecommuting does not necessarily mean working at home. The homes of many people are not suitable as offices, children at home can distract the most ardent worker, and some people don't like the isolation of home work.

Instead, a network of work centers located in suburban neighborhoods close to the homes of workers may be a better solution for many people. These work centers, which could include on-site day care, might be operated by one company or shared by a number of companies. Equipped with advanced communication technologies, such centers might make telecommuting possible for many millions of Americans in the years ahead.

As more people work from home or close to home, the distinction between work and home is blurring. In fact, this is the way it used to be, when work and family were one rather than two spheres. In the past, there was little separation between work and home for hunter-gatherer societies, nor was there much separation between work and home for farm families. In fact, the sharp division between work life and home life arose only about a hundred and twenty years ago in the industrial era, when factory work forced men to commute to massive complexes to take their place on the assembly line. But the modern economy allows people to work apart from office buildings and coworkers, integrating family and work once again.

Already, there is evidence that the gap between home life and work life is closing. Americans spend increasing amounts of time at work doing household errands and increasing amounts of time at home doing office work. This may be one reason people feel as if they're working more than they once did, when in fact they're working less.

A variety of surveys show that American workers spend less time working today than they did two decades ago. This fact flies in the face of the popular notion that people are working more, not less. The mistaken belief that people spend more time at work today arose in part from a series of Louis Harris surveys that are of questionable validity. A 1973 Harris survey asked Americans how many hours their job took each week—the answer was 41 hours. A 1980 Harris survey asked Americans how many hours they spent working, including keeping house or going to school—the answer was 47 hours. From these results, survey researchers announced that Americans were working more than they once did. But clearly, by including the time people spend doing housework or taking night classes, the question was far different in 1980 than in 1973.

A better measure of work time comes from time-use studies. In time-use studies, researchers ask people to keep a detailed diary of their activities throughout the day. The diaries show that people's work hours have actually fallen in recent decades—even when commuting time is included. People may believe they spend more hours at work than they once did, but they're spending a significant portion of their work hours not doing their jobs. Instead, they're running out to the drugstore to fill a prescription, picking up dry cleaning, making personal phone calls, shopping for groceries, paying bills, and doing other household errands. Time-use studies show that the number of hours a week people work for pay has fallen since the mid-1960s as they try to manage their home life from the office.

The same blurring of activities is happening at home. The amount of time people spend doing office work at home is rising, according to time-use studies. People spend more of their weekends doing job-related work than they once did. Employed men work an average of five hours on the weekend, while employed women put in three hours. Today's workers work twice as many hours on Sundays as they did in 1965.

Increasingly, employers look the other way while employees manage their lives from the office. In part, this is because the boss has the same work–family conflicts as employees. Many businesses allow employees to set their own schedules, and more employers are freeing their workers to do some of their office work at home. This change in work place and hours is occurring out of necessity. With most workers living in diverse and changeable families, flexibility is the key to recruiting and retaining workers. The labor force of the 1950s could accept rigid work schedules because most workers lived in nuclear families with a wife at home to manage family life. Rigid work schedules are incompatible with the family life of free agents because they leave no one at home to manage family life. Like so much else in the personalized economy, work schedules are coming under individual control.

Nearly half of American companies with ten or more workers now have flextime policies, where workers set their own hours or choose from several possible work schedules. Work at home is slower to catch on than flextime. Fewer than one in ten businesses allow employees to work at home during normal work hours, but this proportion is certain to grow as free agents demand it and as companies struggle to cut overhead costs, such as the expense of office space.

Whether companies offer flextime or allow employees to work at home is irrelevant to millions of Americans who work for themselves. As companies cut loose many of the business services they once performed in-house, such as market research and accounting, independent contractors are multiplying. A variety of tasks, from highly technical work to clerical and cleaning services, often can be handled more efficiently by independent contractors. These independent contractors are the nation's self-employed.

Today, about 10 million Americans are self-employed, or 8.3 percent of the work force. The Bureau of Labor Statistics projects that this percentage will fall to 7.9 percent by 2005. But its projection of decline may be wrong for several reasons. First, it includes only workers who earn most of their money from self-employment. Millions of Americans work more than one job. According to a Gallup survey, 16 percent of all full-time workers and 18 percent of baby boom workers moonlight. Many moonlight by running their own businesses on the side, working for themselves. These self-employed entrepreneurs do not show up in the Bureau of Labor statistics figures because their side business is not their main source of income.

The second reason the Bureau of Labor Statistics may be wrong about the decline in self-employment is that labor force projections based on current trends miss unforeseen structural changes in the economy. The employment structure of the personalized economy is quite different from that of the industrial economy, providing free agents with more incentives for self-employment. In the personalized economy, the bulk of employment will be in small, entrepreneurial businesses rather than in large, bureaucratic corporations. Businesses will interact in an entirely new way. Some call the newly emerging business structure the "virtual" corporation, meaning a corporation that is not a legal entity but a temporary network of companies that collaborate on a project to fulfill a marketplace demand quickly and efficiently. These networks of companies disband once projects are accomplished.

Many of the workers in the personalized economy will function like virtual corporations, plugging into companies to help create products or services, then moving on once the task is done. In this business environment, independent contracting will grow more rapidly than wage and salary jobs as increasing numbers of workers make a living outside of corporations. Universal health insurance coverage will spur the growth of this "virtual" work force. Cheap and portable information and communication devices also encourage the virtual work force, allowing people to carry entire filing cabinets of information around with them and to communicate with colleagues at will, whether they're at home or on a mountain top. In the future, free agents will seek income security rather than job security by developing a portfolio of skills in demand by a variety of businesses.

According to business consultant Charles Handy in his book, *The Age of Unreason*, the future structure of employment will look something like a shamrock. The first leaf of the shamrock will consist of highly paid core workers in corporations. These well-trained professionals will work long and hard for their companies, and they will be highly rewarded for their efforts. But they will account for a minority of workers in the future.

The second leaf of the shamrock will consist of independent contractors, the elite of the virtual work force. These are the workers who have the skills to plug into a variety of companies, perform a task, and move on. They are the management consultants, market researchers, accountants, cleaning services, trucking operations, and other businesses. The people who run these independent operations will be those who chose self-employment or were squeezed out of the first leaf of the shamrock. Some will make a lot of money, others only a moderate amount, depending on the value of their skills.

The third leaf of the shamrock will be the hired help. These are the underlings who work for the corporations and independent contractors, the laborers of the virtual work force. They are the uneducated or the uncommitted. They are the assembly-line workers, the secretaries, the temporary workers with little loyalty to the companies they happen to be working for at the moment. These workers are young people just getting a start, moonlighters, and homemakers who want to make a little money on the side. Some will work in company offices or stores; others will work from home. The economy's dependence on these contingent workers is already growing as businesses replace permanent employees with temporary help. The revenue growth of companies such as Manpower, Inc., even in the midst of the recession of the early 1990s, shows that the shift toward a "virtual" work force is already in progress. By hiring temporary workers, companies avoid the cost of benefits such as health insurance, unemployment insurance, vacation time, and so on. By not paying benefits, which now amount to about one-fourth of a worker's salary, companies can save money and improve their chances of surviving in the competitive personalized economy.

This is the future of the work force in the era of free agency. It is a world in which most workers will have to forge their own way in the economy, without the certainty of a career track, the comfort of a corporation, or the luxury of a paid vacation. This future workplace may frighten people accustomed to the security of an employer. But with increasing numbers of employers slashing their work force to boost profits, self-employment may seem more secure than depending on the goodwill of an employer.

To prepare for this kind of future, workers must begin to develop a portfolio of skills rather than a resume of jobs. They need to build their skills by collecting different experiences with a salable theme. The key to success is marketability. People with few skills, such as dishwashers, waitresses, or assembly-line workers, will be paid little. Those with specialized skills, such as software designers, will be paid a lot. This is the fast-changing, competitive, and technologically sophisticated economy with which free agents must cope. No wonder so many Americans feel insecure about the future. It will be unlike anything they've ever known, and the way it unfolds—whether in the direction of affluence or poverty—is almost entirely up to them.

✤ **IV** ✤

FREE AGENTS AND THE
MATRIARCHAL FAMILY

❖ 15 ❖

The Fight against Obligations

In 1966, researchers at UCLA fielded the first of what was to become an annual survey that continues to this day. The survey probed the backgrounds and attitudes of the nation's college freshmen. It was a lucky coincidence that this survey captured the attitudes of the first wave of baby boomers as they reached maturity. The battery of questions posed to 18 year olds, born in the first few years of the baby boom, revealed as much about the changing spirit of the times as their answers revealed about the college students themselves.

One of the most telling sections of the 1966 survey asked students to measure the significance of certain life goals. "Please indicate the importance to you of the following objectives," read the survey. The objectives included to "be very well off financially," and to "help others in difficulty." One objective in particular revealed the growing gulf between youthful free agents and older generations of Americans. "How important is it that you are never obligated to people?" read the question. The fact that researchers included this question on the survey at all was an early warning of the coming upheaval in family life.

The principles of maturity, which guided the parents of the baby boom during the 1950s, spelled out the myriad obligations people had toward one another: parents to children, husbands to wives, workers to employers, and citizens to communities. Baby boomers spurned these obligations. In 1966, more than one in four college freshmen agreed that being free of obligations to others was an essential life goal.

Those who wanted freedom in 1966 probably don't feel that way today. Now in their late forties, most are married and have children. Only 7 percent of all Americans regard freedom from obligations as one of their most important values. For baby boomers in middle age, who represent a large portion of the other 93 percent, the belief that someone can remain free of obligations must seem naive, if not undesirable. Such freedom may be essential to 18-year-olds hungry for experience, with the world's panoply of opportunities spread like a smorgasbord in front of them. But to a 40-year-old, obligations seem not only tolerable, but desirable. After a bruising day at the office, it's comforting to come home to people who care.

Baby boomers ate themselves sick at the smorgasbord of experience. Then they hunted for a safe place to sleep it off. That's when they discovered—or rediscovered—the comfortable haven of family life. But family life for baby boomers is neither as comfortable nor as safe as it was for older generations of Americans. Instead, the boomers have patched together an approximation of family togetherness founded on their own contradictory values.

Most Americans, including baby boomers, rank a happy marriage and children as essential ingredients of the good life, according to a poll by the Roper Organization. But neither marriage nor children tops the list of what it takes to live well. The number one ingredient of the good life is owning a home, followed by a happy marriage. Number three is owning a car, which is tied with having children. Fifth is having a lot of money. For free agents, materialistic values are just as important as family values because money buys independence.

A Roper poll documents the ongoing battle between the contradictory ideals of people today. Americans hold both family life and independence in high esteem. This is an unstable state of affairs that leaves most baby boomers at a loss for ways to resolve the deadlock between personal and family needs. When asked to identify the top elements of the American Dream, seven out of ten Americans say "freedom of choice in how to live one's life." Seven out of ten also say the American Dream means having "both a rewarding career and family life." Baby boomers want it all—

family commitment and freedom. Unfortunately, they can't pursue both with equal vigor. The parents of the baby boom split the duties, with men pursuing their careers while women managed the family. But baby boom women are as single-minded as baby boom men. More often than not, both men and women pursue their own interests at the expense of marriages and children.

Free agents live with paradox. On the one hand, they say family life is vitally important to them. Yet they let their families break apart as husbands and wives jockey for advantage. The numbers reveal just how radically and rapidly the failed marriages of free agents have changed the way Americans live. Among the 94 million households in the United States today, barely half are headed by married couples, down from a 74 percent majority in 1960. Just one in four households contains a married couple with children, down from more than four in ten in 1960. Another one in four households today consist of people who live alone, up from one in eight in 1960. Even more telling, people who live alone will begin to outnumber nuclear families during the early decades of the next century.

Free agency changed the nuclear family more than it changed any other social institution. As young adults, free agents attacked the nuclear family on all fronts. Baby boom women married late: the proportion of unmarried women in the 20 to 24 age group grew from 28 to 50 percent between 1960 and 1980 and stands at 63 percent today. Baby boomers remained childless far into their childbearing years: among women in the prime child-bearing age group, 25 to 29, the childless proportion rose from 31 to 42 percent between 1976 and 1990. Baby boomers divorced readily: the divorce rate began its steady rise in the mid-1960s, doubling by the mid-1970s.

The growing acceptance of singleness, childlessness, and divorce took their toll on the nuclear family. In 1960, Americans could expect to spend 62 percent of their adult lives in a nuclear family—the highest proportion in history, according to Rutgers University professor David Popenoe. Today, they can expect to spend only 43 percent of their adult lives with a spouse and children, the lowest proportion in history.

❖ 16 ❖

The Marriage Market

Nuclear families are breaking apart because free agents can't live together, yet men and women can't live apart. Despite thirty years of upheaval in family life, marriage remains a priority for Americans. It may not be the number one ingredient in living the good life, but it is number two.

Marriage is meaningful to baby boomers, but not for the same reasons it was important to earlier generations of Americans. According to a survey by Massachusetts Mutual Life Insurance Company, Americans rank "being happily married" far higher than "being married to the same person for life." A happy marriage comes in fifth among important values, while a lifetime marriage comes in a lowly fifteenth, less significant than individualistic values such as "living up to my full potential," or "being physically fit." To sociologists, these rankings show that the meaning of marriage has been transformed by individualism. Free agents value marriage as their personal ticket to happiness— a way to achieve companionship and a higher standard of living. In contrast, older generations of Americans value the communal nature of marriage—the lifetime commitment between two people and the stability this offers children and communities.

But even as middle-aging free agents pursue marriage as the route to the good life, happiness eludes them. A shrinking share of Americans reports being happily married. The percentage of Americans who say their marriage is "very happy" fell from 60 percent in the mid-1970s to 53 percent by the late 1980s. The decline in "very happy" marriages occurred for all durations of marriage, from marriages of less than three years to those of more than 30 years.

This trend goes against common sense. As unhappy couples divorce, happy couples should remain. With divorce more common, the proportion of couples "very happily" married should rise. Unfortunately, it doesn't work that way. Social scientists say today's marriages suffer from the "grass is greener" syndrome. With divorce the norm, people who marry today know it's not necessarily for life. The words "until death do us part" may still be heard in most marriage ceremonies, but they are spoken more in hope than in fact. Couples are free to divorce when the going gets tough. Because divorce is an ever present option, marriage no longer removes men and women from what sociologists call the "marriage market." Free agents marry for better, but not for worse. They're always open to a better deal, a way out if their relationship sours. Burdened by this attitude, marriages between free agents often do sour. The constant comparison of an all-too-familiar spouse with the allure of unfamiliar partners erodes marital happiness.

Americans have lost the "ideal of marital permanence," say sociologists. When people believed marriage was a lifetime commitment, they knew they had no choice but to learn to live together. Because of this belief, most viewed their relationship more positively, making it work. Until the mid-1970s, six out of ten couples described their marriages as "very happy." Now, faced with countless alternatives to their current relationship—not only other sex partners, but also the lure of a fast-track career, or even a single life-style—barely half are "very happy."

Nevertheless, Americans continue to believe in marriage. Nine out of ten baby boomers will marry at some point during their lives, but with the knowledge that they can always divorce. It wasn't always this way: divorce was uncommon before the free agents of the baby boom generation grew up. Until then, it was limited to Hollywood starlets and tabloid headlines. The baby boomers changed the rules. They still want to marry, but if things don't work out, they want a way out. Consequently, divorce is now almost as common as a lifetime marriage for people under the age of 50.

Marriage was once a moral commitment between men and women, regulated by law and controlled by social norms. Marriage bonds extended beyond husband and wife into the community. Religious and secular law either forbade divorces or allowed them only in a few circumstances. Falling out of love was not grounds for divorce. As people changed through the long years of marriage, community bonds—religious, legal, and judgmental— held couples together for better or worse.

The rise of individualism transformed marriage into a fragile emotional bond regulated by little more than hormones. The social norms against divorce have disappeared. Few religions still forbid divorce—even the Catholic Church regularly grants annulments. No-fault divorce allows couples to part simply because they feel like it. Friends and neighbors no longer care if someone divorces because many are in the middle of a divorce themselves. As husbands and wives change over the years, relationships based on nothing more than youthful emotional bonds are unlikely to last.

The fact is, men and women no longer need each other. Women today can earn a living. Men can buy the services of wives from dry cleaners, house cleaners, and day-care centers. Marriage has lost its meaning. It remains emotionally gratifying more out of tradition than logic. Yet because men and women still crave each other and always will, they team up for a while. Nonetheless, when their goals diverge, they go their separate ways.

Proof of the new, more casual relationship between men and women is revealed in three trends: the postponement of marriage, the rise in cohabitation, and the pervasiveness of divorce. The median age at which women first marry increased from its historic low of 20.2 years in 1955 to 24.1 years in 1991. For men, the median age at first marriage rose from a low of 22.6 years in 1955 to 26.3 years in 1991. It is no accident that today's men and women marry about four years later than their parents did. This is about how long it takes to graduate from college. Free agents invest in themselves and their own future before making a commitment to someone else.

Despite the older ages of first-time brides and grooms, men and women set up house together at about the same age as they did in the past. With divorce so easy and common, cohabitation— living together outside of marriage—has become essentially equivalent to marriage, even preferable because there are fewer legal problems when couples break up. The proportion of Americans who marry by the age of 25 fell from 72 percent in 1970 to 55 percent by the mid-1980s, a decline of 24 percent. But the proportion who live with someone of the opposite sex before age 25— with or without a marriage license—fell by only 8 percent, from 75 to 69 percent.

Today, it's almost the norm for couples to live together before marriage. The proportion grew from 11 percent in 1970 to nearly half by the mid-1980s. People live together before marriage because they want to make sure they're compatible before tying the knot, according to surveys of cohabiting couples. Forty-seven percent of currently cohabiting couples have definite plans to marry, while another 27 percent think they eventually will marry.

Though cohabitation is increasingly common in the United States, it is still far less common than in some other countries. In Sweden, for example, the great majority of young adults live together before marriage. Many never marry at all, making a significant dent in Swedish social statistics. One-fifth of all Swedish couples are not legally married. In the United States, only 5 percent of all couples are not legally married. As laws and regulations change to recognize the rights of cohabiting partners, unmarried couples are likely to become more common in the United States.

Still, marriage has meaning for free agents. Though most cohabitors think marrying would make little difference in their relationship, a significant minority cite advantages to being married: One-fourth of cohabiting men and one-third of cohabiting women say their economic security would improve; 28 percent of men and 38 percent of women say they would feel more emotionally secure; 30 percent of men and 36 percent of women think they would be happier.

But would they? Free agents long for the emotional security of marriage, but because they're wary of committing themselves to anyone else, they're unlikely to find security. Their spouse will be just as wary of commitment as they are, leaving their marriage vows open to renegotiation.

Over 1 million Americans divorce each year. For the past decade or so, the divorce rate has stabilized at more than double what it was in the 1950s. Because of so much divorce, only 55 percent of marriages today are between a bride and groom who have never been married before. About one in five marriages are between previously divorced men and women, while another 22 percent are between a never-married man or woman and a divorced man or woman.

While many consider the American divorce rate to be alarmingly high, it may in fact be settling at a natural level. Until recently, divorce was suppressed by the economic and social dependency between husbands and wives. This economic dependency was codified in the law, making divorce difficult. When the economics changed, the laws against divorce relaxed. Consequently, the likelihood of divorce grew rapidly at first, then stabilized at a high rate. The odds of divorce for couples marrying today are nearly fifty-fifty.

This may be a natural level of divorce for a society where men and women function as individuals in the economy, rather than as part of a family unit. During the industrial era, when women were economically dependent on men, individualism was submerged in the nuclear family. During the agricultural era, property rights made families the economic unit and individualism was submerged in the extended family and community. But before these economic systems evolved, when people survived by hunting and gathering, men and women functioned as individuals as they do today. In many ways, the hunter-gatherer life-style is more similar to current life-styles than the way Americans lived just a few decades ago.

The !Kung Bushmen of Africa's Kalahari Desert have been studied extensively by anthropologists and demographers. The !Kung are hunter-gathers, they have no permanent homes, no money, no property, and no hierarchy beyond kinship. The economic contribution of !Kung men and women is about equal. Both bring home the bacon or, in their neighborhood, antelope and vegetable roots. Among the !Kung, as is increasingly true among Americans, the individual skills of each man and woman form the basis of the economy.

The similarities between the relationships of !Kung men and women to contemporary American relationships are striking. These were exhaustively documented a few years ago by demographer Nancy Howell of the University of Toronto. According to her descriptions, relationships between !Kung men and women are similar to those between baby boomers today, starting with premarital sex.

Teenage sex is common among the !Kung, as it is among Americans. While many Americans are alarmed by teen sex, particularly premarital sex, it is only natural in a culture where there is a full ten-year span between the average age of sexual maturity and the average age at marriage. Premarital sex was less common among the parents of baby boomers because nearly half married in their teens. For them, the span between sexual maturity and marriage was only four or five years. As the number of years between sexual maturity and marriage expanded, premarital sex among teenagers became the norm. The proportion of Americans who believe premarital sex is wrong fell from 68 percent in 1969 to 40 percent in 1991, according to a Gallup survey. Among baby boomers, two out of three think premarital sex is okay.

For the !Kung, there are no formal rituals of marriage. Men and women simply start living together, which means they have a sexual relationship, and they share food, water, and shelter. The

casualness of marriage between the !Kung is similar to relationships between cohabiting men and women in the United States.

While !Kung men and women live together, they remain in
the "marriage market." The same is true for Americans now that
the "ideal of marital permanence" has given way to serial marriage. About half of !Kung marriages end in "divorce." For Americans under the age of 50, the proportion is about the same. In both
societies, long-term marriages are celebrated, and rare.

The lack of formal rituals in the relationships between !Kung
men and women is due to the fact that the sexes are not economically dependent on one another. !Kung society does not need to
regulate economic relationships between the sexes. The same is
also increasingly true in the United States as women gain economic power. The latest projections show that between 40 and 46
percent of the first marriages of baby boomers will end in divorce.
By 1990, more than one-third had already ended in divorce.

When free agents remarry, their chances of success are no
better. Demographers project that about 40 percent of the second
marriages of baby boomers will end in divorce.

With these odds, remarriage is losing its popularity. Among
women divorced in the late 1960s, 73 percent remarried within five
years of their divorce. But among women divorcing in the early
1980s, only 45 percent remarried within five years of their divorce.
These statistics are deceiving, however, because cohabitation is
even more common among the divorced than among single people. In fact, the entire decline in remarriage can be accounted for
by cohabitation. The divorced are more likely to live with a partner
today than they were several decades ago. In 1970, 58 percent of
divorced Americans had formed some kind of union—marriage
or cohabitation—within five years of their divorce. That proportion rose to 62 percent by the mid-1980s.

Clearly, sexual attraction still draws men and women together, but the friction between the divergent goals of free agents
pulls men and women apart. This friction intensified during the
past two decades and is documented in the Virginia Slims Opinion Poll.

When asked their opinion of men, 42 percent of all women say men are "basically selfish and self-centered." This proportion, nearly a majority, is up considerably from the 32 percent of women who thought so poorly of men in 1970. Fifty-three percent of women say men are more interested in their work than in their families, up from 39 percent who held this opinion in 1970. Fifty-five percent of women think most men want to keep them down, up from 49 percent who thought so in 1970. The proportion of women who think men are basically kind, gentle, and thoughtful fell from 67 percent in 1970 to just 51 percent in 1990. Yet two-thirds of men describe themselves as kind; over half say they are broad-minded. Fewer than 10 percent describe themselves as self-absorbed or egocentric.

The perspectives of men and women are polar opposites because their expectations of one another have changed radically in just one generation. With the coming of age of the baby boom generation, women abandoned their communal role. They demanded equal time for themselves and equal pay and equal opportunity in their careers. But men have been slow to respond, both at home and in the workplace. Among women who feel resentful about something in their lives (about half do), 49 percent resent the way their job or career has gone. Fifty-two percent resent how little their mate does around the house. In contrast, only 27 percent of men feel resentful about the amount of housework they do. Someone has to do the laundry, buy the food, and change the baby's diapers. All too often, women find that men still expect them to do these things, and so the battle commences.

Today, there are no rules to guide men and women on how to manage a life together. Whose job is more important? Who takes time off when children are sick? Who sacrifices to make the family work? Neither men nor women have been willing to sacrifice, and so houses are dirtier, meals are solitary affairs, and children spend their days with baby-sitters.

Housework is the hot core of resentment between men and women. Cooking, cleaning, and caring for one another is the communal work that nurtures the family. It is the glue that holds marriages together. One of the best predictors of marital happiness, in fact, is how satisfied husbands and wives are with the division of labor in their homes. This one factor does a better job of explaining marital happiness than nearly any other. Women are much more likely to say their marriages are troubled if they think they do too much at home. In contrast, men seem to be unaware of their wives' resentment and are surprised at the consequences. Women initiate fully two out of three divorces. A major factor behind many of these divorces is the unfair division of housework.

The housework problem is only going to get worse during the 1990s as baby boomers continue to raise children. Women's resentment toward men is rising because so many baby boomers are new parents, struggling with an unwieldy and often unworkable work load. Those most unhappy with the division of labor in their homes are wives with preschoolers, according to social science studies. Only 49 percent of wives with preschoolers are satisfied with how the work is divided up. In contrast, 76 percent of the fathers of preschoolers report being satisfied with the division of labor at home—a level of satisfaction that remains virtually unchanged throughout men's lives. In contrast, women's happiness at home is like a rollercoaster, with steep hills and valleys. Sixty-one percent of childless wives are satisfied with the division of household labor. This proportion falls below 50 percent among wives with preschoolers, then rises to 54 percent for those with school-aged children, to 57 percent for those with teenagers, and to a high of 68 percent for those whose children are grown. Even this highest level of satisfaction among women is less than the satisfaction level consistently reported by men throughout their lives.

During the past few decades, women have been doing less housework, and men have been doing more. But there's still a wide gap where resentment builds. In the mid-1960s, women spent twenty-seven hours a week doing the cooking, cleaning, and other household chores, according to time-use studies. Today, women spend twenty hours a week at these tasks. Men spend ten hours a week doing housework today, double the five hours they spent on housework in the mid-1960s. Husbands now do about one-third of the family housework, up from 15 percent in the mid-1960s.

In another study of who does what at home, sociologist Myra Marx Ferree reports that 29 percent of working women are "drudges"; that is, they work full time and also do at least 60 percent of the housework. Drudges are outnumbered by the 38 percent of working couples who are "egalitarian," meaning husband and wife share housework about equally. Ferree finds some improvement in these statistics: in the mid-1970s, "drudge" housewives outnumbered egalitarian couples.

Men are taking on more of the communal responsibilities of family life, but not fast enough to hold marriages together. Unfortunately, those most victimized by divorce are children.

❖ 17 ❖

The Baby Boom's Children

For decades, baby boomers ignored family life. They postponed marriage and delayed having children. They mocked the sense of duty felt by older generations toward the sanctity of marriage and the responsibilities of having children. Now these same baby boomers are in middle age. The importance of family life looms in their minds as the biological clock ticks on. But even in middle age, baby boomers remain free agents. Behind the facade of family togetherness, they are wary of commitment. The consequences can be read in government statistics documenting the breakdown of the nuclear family and the rise of a new kind of family to nurture the next generation of children.

Nothing symbolizes the conflict between the individualism of the baby boom generation and the communal instincts of the middle aged as much as children. Millions of baby boomers delayed having children well into their thirties. Many believed they never wanted children. Then the longings of midlife changed their perspectives.

In 1975, fully 25 percent of wives among the oldest baby boomers said they would never have children. Today, only 11 percent remain childless. Demographers once projected that one-fifth of baby boom women would be childless. Today, it looks like 15 percent may be closer to the truth. And that percentage will not set any records. It is higher than the level of childlessness experienced by the generation of women born in the 1930s (many of them the mothers of baby boomers), only 8 percent of whom were childless. But it is significantly lower than that experienced by the generation of women born in the first decade of the twentieth century (the grandmothers of the baby boom). Twenty-two percent of women born in 1910 never had any children. But the reason baby boomers will remain childless is far different from the reason for childlessness in their grandparents' generation. Women born in 1910 endured the Depression and World War II during their prime childbearing years. Those events made it hard to raise a family. Baby boom women put off having children not because of external events, but because of their outlook on life—they invested in their individual skills by going to college and starting careers.

Today, three out of four baby boom women have had children, ranging from more than 80 percent of the oldest boomers to about 60 percent of the youngest. Most baby boom families already include more than one child. Even among free agents, having at least two children is far more popular than having no children or only one. Most Americans believe it's better for children to have siblings. Overall, 57 percent of Americans say two children is ideal. Another 29 percent think three or more is ideal. Only 6 percent think one child or no children is best.

The desire for children is rooted in biology. It is no surprise, then, that the free agents of the baby boom generation are having children for the same reasons their parents and grandparents had them: they want the love and affection children bring, the pleasure of watching them grow, the sense of family they create, and the fulfillment and satisfaction they offer, according to a Gallup survey. In midlife, free agents want to belong to a warm and loving family, and children are the key to belonging.

Yet once they bring baby home from the hospital, free agents face the most trying experience of their lives: the sacrifice of their time, money, and personal goals for the well-being of their children. Even healthy children require parental sacrifice, but free agents find sacrifice to be a most uncomfortable role.

Today's parents recognize this failing. Eighty-eight percent of adults think it is harder to raise children today than it was for their parents. Eighty-six percent say they are often uncertain about the right thing to do. As parents, free agents are pulled in two directions. Their instincts tell them to take time for themselves, but the communal feelings of middle age admonish them to make time for their children. It is no wonder that parents are confused about their priorities.

When asked to list their priorities for the 1990s, 84 percent of mothers and 78 percent of fathers say a top priority is to spend more time with their family. But this is not their only top priority. A majority of mothers and fathers say advancing their careers is a top priority. Half of mothers and 61 percent of fathers say pursuing personal interests is a top priority.

One way to sort through these contradictory priorities is to examine how parents spend their time and how they would like to spend their time. This is what Hilton Hotels Corporation did in a 1991 time-use survey, asking parents to describe their weekends—both the reality and the ideal. The results show that for most parents the ideal weekend would be one in which they spend a lot more time pursuing personal interests and less time attending to household duties.

Mothers say they would like to spend twice as much time pursuing personal interests and dining out. In reality, they spend just six weekend hours on these activities, and they would like to double that to over twelve. Mothers want to spend less time doing chores like cleaning and running errands. They spend ten weekend hours on these duties, and they would like to cut that to three. Mothers spend eleven weekend hours caring for their children, an amount of time they think is about right.

Fathers also want to spend more time pursuing personal interests and dining out. In reality, they spend eight weekend hours doing these activities; they would like to increase the time to over fourteen hours. Like mothers, they want to spend less time doing chores. They spend six hours cleaning and running errands now, and they want to cut that to just two hours. In contrast to mothers, however, they would like to spend eleven hours caring for their children, up from the 7.5 hours they spend with their children now.

Though parents feel pulled in two directions, most also think they're doing a good job. Baby boomers give themselves a grade of A (31 percent) or B (52 percent) as parents. Only 16 percent give themselves a C, 1 percent a D, and no one flunks, according to a Gallup survey. In another survey probing parents' relationships with their children, 65 percent of all parents with children under age 18 (most of them baby boomers) say their relationship with their children is excellent, while another 32 percent rate it as good. Few regard their relationship with their children as poor.

But many social scientists would disagree, arguing that the family has been hurt by dual careers and divorce, both of which are outgrowths of individualism. With an average monthly mortgage payment of over $1000 for people buying homes today, with car prices equivalent to what homes cost only two decades ago, and with college costs rising much faster than wages, the only way baby boomers can afford the American Dream of a house, a car, and a college education for their children is to have both parents in the work force. Baby boom women work to support their families as do baby boom men. Three out of four baby boom women are in the labor force. A majority of new mothers are back at work before their babies celebrate their first birthday.

For two decades, mothers have been scolded for working outside the home. But working mothers may not be as big a problem for their families as working fathers. Most children, whether their mothers work or not, say they spend enough time with their mothers. Most say their mothers "almost never" miss events and activities important to them. In contrast, most children say their fathers "frequently" or "sometimes" miss important events. Many children say they would like to spend more time with their fathers.

Working fathers hurt family life more than working mothers, says Urie Bronfenbrenner, a Cornell University specialist in child development. Mothers adjust their work schedules to spend time with their children, he says. They're more likely than fathers to work part-time or part-year. They're more likely than fathers to take time off when their children are sick. Fathers have a harder time integrating work and family, partly because of tradition. Men are expected to put their nose to the grindstone. Those who ask for flexibility often lose status on the job, sidelined to the Daddy track. Those who choose to work part-time or who want flexible schedules while raising children may find their careers stalled. Because of this, many men don't ask for flexibility. That's why it still falls on women to shoulder family responsibilities, their own jobs, and the fallout from their husband's inflexible schedules as well. To do it all, mothers become schedulers, family life becomes rigid, and the pressure builds.

With working parents pursuing careers and with children attending day care or signing up for sports and after-school activities, each family member follows a different daily schedule. Integrating all these activities makes each family's schedule as unique as a fingerprint, says social historian Barbara Dafoe White-head. It is little wonder that families rarely get together for meals or that neighbors hardly know one another. One family's schedule rarely meshes with that of other families. These different schedules split communities apart. When family schedules were more uniform in the past, neighborhood parents did the same things at the same time, supporting one another in their proximity. Children played together, men carpooled to work together, women got together for coffee. Today, it's as though every family, and every person within the family, operates in a separate time zone, just as the many small towns of the United States did until Congress created standardized time zones at the end of the nineteenth century. Unfortunately, no Congressional Act can do a similar favor for American families.

Many millions of Americans are exhausted by the pace of modern life. Thirty-eight percent report constantly feeling under the gun. Seven out of ten say they want to slow down and live a more relaxed life, according to polls. This enormous desire to slow down is a consequence of the chaos of family life. Juggling work and family schedules is the principle source of stress in American families today, says Bronfenbrenner. Often, this kind of stress can lead to divorce, and divorce can devastate children.

Divorce has changed the nature of childhood. Most of the children born today will live in a single-parent family sometime before the age of 18. Currently, only six out of ten children live with both biological parents. This proportion ranges from 71 percent among children under the age of 4 to just 51 percent among children aged 15 to 17. The other 40 percent of children are scattered among a variety of family types, the largest portion of them single-parent families headed by women. Eleven percent live with their biological mother who is divorced from their biological father. Eight percent live with their biological mother who never married their biological father. Nine percent live with their biological mother and a stepfather. The remaining 11 percent live with their fathers, with adoptive parents, with grandparents, or in other types of families.

Many Americans see the rise of single-parent families as a social problem. Single-parent families are more likely to be poor than two-parent families, and their growth has led to a rise in poverty among children. But the problem may not be single-parent families, but society's lack of support for them. Studies of children's physical and emotional health reveal that children raised in single-parent families do almost as well as those raised in two-parent families. The children who fare the worst, both physically and emotionally, are those who experience the trauma of their parents' divorce and their mothers' remarriage.

The physical, mental, and emotional health of children is greatly affected by their living arrangement. The proportion of parents who report having an "excellent" relationship with their children is highest among happily married intact (two biological or adoptive parents) families. Fully 78 percent of happy couples say their relationship with their children is excellent. But the proportion is almost as high among single-parent families, 64 percent of whom report that their relationship with their children is excellent.

Among two-parent families with unhappy marriages, the proportion of parents who report an excellent relationship with their children drops to 54 percent. Among happy stepfamilies, the proportion reporting an excellent relationship is an identical 54 percent. In unhappy stepfamilies, the proportion who have an excellent relationship with their children falls to just 33 percent.

Other studies show that the children who fare the worst are those who experience divorce and remarriage. Children born into single-parent families do better than children whose families become single-parent through divorce. Among children ages 5 to 17, fully 76 percent of those living with their mother and a stepfather have behavioral problems, according to studies by the National Center for Health Statistics. Among children living alone with their divorced mother, 69 percent have behavioral problems. Among children in intact families, the figure is just 52 percent, and among those living with mothers who never married, the proportion is an even lower 49 percent.

A minority of children in two-parent or single-parent families are depressed or anxious (39 percent). In contrast, a majority of children in stepfamilies (59 percent) or who live alone with their divorced mothers (55 percent) are anxious or depressed. These patterns do not stem from poverty, because they hold regardless of income. Instead, they are rooted in family disruption.

With childhood becoming increasingly troubled by the disruptive life-styles of free agents, it was only a matter of time before children began to rebel. In keeping with the litigious nature of individualistic free agents, this rebellion is taking place in the nation's courts. Children are slowly gaining their own legal rights, separate from those of their parents. One of these rights is the ability to terminate parental ties in cases of neglect and abuse.

In Florida, for example, a state circuit court judge allowed a 12-year-old boy to terminate the parental rights of his natural mother so that his foster parents could adopt him. His father had already approved of the adoption, but his mother was unwilling to let him go. The judge allowed the boy to hire a lawyer. The lawyer argued in court that the boy's mother had abused and neglected him for years, and that the boy wanted the chance to find happiness with a family who cared about him. The judge ruled in the boy's favor, setting an important precedent by allowing a child to function as an individual under the law rather than as the property of his parents.

The law is slowly beginning to recognize children's rights separately from their parents' rights, according to legal scholars. Behind this trend is the growing recognition of individual rights within the family. Increasingly, the law is allowing contractual relationships to replace family relationships as friction between free agents builds. In a contractual relationship, both parties enter into a contract to protect their self-interest. In family relationships, in contrast, parties enter into a relationship because of shared commitments. With free agents wary of commitment, contractual relationships are by necessity taking the place of family relationships, even between parents and children. The examples range from no-fault divorce, which makes it legal for couples to divorce simply because they are no longer in love, to prenuptial agreements which maintain the individual ownership of property after marriage. They range from custody laws, which specify who gets the children, to the free-speech rights of ex-spouses. In another Florida case, the state's supreme court upheld a ruling that prevented a woman from saying bad things about her ex-husband to their children. "People used to settle affairs like this on their own," said the woman's attorney. "Now they go through the legal system."

As American institutions adapt to free agency, the social norms that once supported families are being replaced by legal norms. In response, the number of lawyers and judges grew by 132 percent between 1970 and 1990, from 273,000 to 633,000. During those years, the labor force as a whole grew by just 45 percent. Between 1990 and 2005, the number of lawyers and judges is projected to rise by another 34 percent, much faster than the 20 percent gain projected for jobs overall. Lawyers are in demand because free agents continually renegotiate their commitments, even within the family.

✤ 18 ✤

The Rise of the Matriarchal Family

Americans are of two minds when it comes to family life. Most believe the generic "American family" is in trouble. They can recite the facts: husbands and wives are divorcing; millions of children are being raised by their mothers alone; traditional values that once bound people together are disintegrating. Americans give the "American family" a failing grade. But paradoxically, most also believe their own family is doing fine. On a scale of 1 to 4, Americans rate their families at 3.5 or higher on attributes such as caring, loving, can always be counted on to help when needed, fun to be with, provides emotional support, and close. Seven out of ten Americans say their families are their greatest satisfaction.

This paradox occurs as baby boom free agents straddle two worlds. They remember the nuclear family of midcentury, but most of them live in a different kind of family today. As nuclear families break apart, they shudder at the consequences. Yet most free agents, even those who have been through a divorce, still find family life highly rewarding.

Families may have changed dramatically in the past two decades, but the importance of family life has not. Sixty-four percent of all Americans say their family is their greatest pleasure, and most would like to spend more time with their family. Americans rank spending time with their family a lofty third among thirteen favorite evening activities. Only watching television and reading rank higher than spending time at home with the family.

In 1939, when family togetherness was more duty than choice, spending time with the family ranked dead last among seven favorite activities. Americans even preferred an evening of card-playing to staying at home with the family.

Ironically, spending time with the family may be popular among free agents because of the many changes in family life, including working mothers, day care, and divorce. Free agents' opinion of family life might be entirely different if they were expected to sacrifice their own interests for their family's needs. But sacrifice is rarely demanded of family members today. Day care gives working mothers and fathers time away from their children. Books and magazines encourage parents to spend time alone, or alone together. Businesses market get-away vacations, candle-lit dinners, aerobics classes, and even gourmet chocolates with the message that mothers and fathers need to think of themselves. Mothers who martyred themselves for their children in the 1950s are now pitied rather than admired. The heroine of today's family is the mother who can say "me first."

With baby boomers now in their thirties and forties, the first generation of free agents is now in the most family-oriented stage of life. These are the years when people are most likely to be married and have children. Consequently, the 1990s is supposed to be a decade in which traditional nuclear families stage a comeback. Marriage is in vogue once again. American women are producing more than 4 million babies a year. Divorce rates are stable. But the long-awaited resurgence of nuclear families is temporary, a consequence of the baby boom's passage through midlife. Nuclear families are the dominant household type among people in their thirties and forties. Even so, baby boomers are much less likely to live in a nuclear family than previous generations of middle-aged Americans. Married couples with children are a majority of households only among boomers aged 35 to 39. Among both older and younger baby boomers, most households are not nuclear families. Instead, they contain married couples without children, unmarried parents with children, or people who live alone.

At current rates of divorce, most of the baby boom's children are expected to live in a single-parent family sometime before the age of 18. Mothers head nearly nine out of ten single-parent families, while divorced fathers see their children rarely if at all. Consequently, relations between children and their fathers are fragile at best.

The majority of children whose parents are divorced see their fathers infrequently, and most divorced fathers say they have no authority in child-rearing decisions. It is little wonder that one-fourth of adults say their relationship with their father is distant. Another one-fifth say it is "tense" or "cold and restrained." About half of those who feel distant from their fathers are the children of divorce, according to a Gallup survey. Among adult children whose parents are divorced, only one-third feel close to their fathers. Among those whose parents are still together, three-fourths feel close to their fathers.

Fathers complain that they are the disposable parent. They may be right. Since children cannot be split down the middle, and since free agents are not about to settle down and live a *Leave it to Beaver* life-style, fathers are fading into the background of their children's lives as divorce transforms a nation of nuclear families into a matriarchal society.

The emergence of the matriarchal family is not rooted in feminism. It is rooted in the fact that women today are the dominant parent in a majority of American families. Fifty-one percent of families with children are dual-earner couples. Among these couples, women as a rule do most of the housework and child-rearing. They also earn money to support the family. Though most wives earn less than their husbands, their incomes keep the family afloat. Another 23 percent of families with children are single-parent families headed by women.

With women playing all the parts, men are moving off stage. No longer the sole breadwinner, their role in family life is unclear. Many men are confused about what their role should be, and increasingly, it's no role at all.

Overall, women are the dominant parent in fully three out of four American families with children. This figure includes all of the nation's dual-earner couples as well as the vast majority of single-parent families. Men head just one-fourth of families with children today—the minority of couples in which the wife does not work, and the handful of single-parent families headed by men.

The matriarchal family is a consequence of the growing individualism of both men and women. It is a healthy grass-roots response to the dramatic change in the economic realities of life for younger generations of Americans. Rather than turn their children over to grandparents or institutions, baby boom women are building a life around them. Unfortunately, the social institutions that supported the nuclear family norm of midcentury have been slow to adapt to the needs of today's matriarchal families. But no matter how individualistic society becomes, it will not abandon its children to the fragile ties between men and women. New institutions are emerging to support matriarchal families and stabilize the lives of children.

Single-parent families are often blamed for many of the nation's worst problems—poverty, crime, and drug abuse. The fictional television character Murphy Brown became just such a scapegoat during the 1992 Presidential campaign when she had a child out of wedlock. Former Vice President Dan Quayle criticized the character as a poor role model because she failed to adhere to traditional family values. But in fact, the problems faced by single parents today are caused more by the failure of social institutions to adapt to the needs of matriarchal families than by any moral shortcomings within those families. Single parents must cope with the harsh personalized economy. But the social institutions they depend on are still designed for traditional nuclear families. They're caught between a slow-moving bureaucracy and a rapidly changing economy.

The rising number of children living in poverty, the growing inequality in the incomes of American families, pervasive drug abuse, rising crime rates, the spread of AIDS and other sexually transmitted diseases—these and many other problems are often blamed on the rise of individualism. The anything goes attitude of free agents is fertile ground for social disease, but these problems have grown over the past thirty years in part because society has been slow to adapt to the new realities of family life. The solution is not a return to the traditional family, an impossibility as free agents become an ever larger majority of Americans. The solution to these problems begins with building a support network for the matriarchal family.

One well-publicized area that desperately needs to change, for example, is the health insurance system. The current system arose to support families of the 1950s. At that time, nearly all families were married couples, nearly all husbands worked full time, and most wives stayed home. In this scenario, employer-based health insurance for full-time workers and their families provided Americans with adequate coverage. But this type of insurance is inefficient in providing coverage for matriarchal families. For dual-career couples, health insurance coverage is often duplicated. Each spouse's employer pays insurance to cover the same family, a wasted expense for business.

For families headed by women, the current health insurance system no longer does the job because many women work part-time or part-year. By law, businesses are not required to extend benefits to part-time workers, and consequently there are gaps in coverage. In a longitudinal study of health insurance coverage, the Census Bureau found that only 14 percent of people who worked full time were without health insurance for at least one month in a two-year period. The situation was far worse for part-time workers. Twenty-seven percent of part-timers lacked health insurance for at least one month in a two-year period. Among workers with job interruptions, fully 43 percent went without health insurance for at least one month. The health insurance system would provide better coverage of American families if businesses were required to cover all workers, both full time and part time, or pay into a government health care system that would fill in the gaps. This type of system would also give single parents dependent on welfare more incentive to go to work. No longer would they have to give up their family's health insurance coverage upon taking a job because they lost Medicaid benefits.

Matriarchal families have other needs as well. One is the absolute control over fertility. With their multiple roles as nurturers and breadwinners, women are too important to be at the mercy of unwanted pregnancies.

The rise of individualism was bound to free women of their biological destiny, long regulated by social norms, law, and science itself. First to disappear were the social norms against having children outside of marriage. In the early 1960s, before the baby boom generation was old enough to have children, only 13 percent of births were out of wedlock. Today, now that free agents dominate the childbearing age groups, unmarried mothers account for over one-fourth of all births.

An even larger proportion of babies are conceived out of wedlock—39 percent in the late 1980s, according to the Census Bureau. In the early 1960s, the proportion was 27 percent. The rise in premarital births is far greater than the increase in premarital conceptions because single women who find themselves pregnant are far less likely to marry now than in the past. Over half (52 percent) of women who became pregnant before marriage in the 1960s married before the birth of their child. In contrast, only 27 percent of pregnant single women today marry before their baby's birth.

Women are choosing to have children without a husband because they no longer depend on men's incomes to support them. Women earn their own money—perhaps not enough to live in luxury, but at least enough to get by. Single parenthood is a better choice than an unstable marriage for many women and children, particularly since children appear to do better when raised by a single mother than a divorced mother.

Abortion is at the center of the battle between traditional Americans and free agents. No issue is as symbolic of the tension between individualism and communalism as the decision on whether or not to carry a baby to term. On the side of individualism are the prochoice factions, arguing that the decision is up to a

pregnant woman alone. Those who oppose abortion are traditional, communally oriented Americans who argue that the un-
born child's life takes precedence over the personal agenda of a
pregnant woman.

Younger Americans are more likely than older people to
believe abortion should remain legal. Among people aged 18 to 29,
68 percent believe abortion should be legal under most circumstances, with 41 percent supporting it in all cases. Among baby
boomers, 66 percent believe it should be legal in most circumstances, with 34 percent supporting it in all cases. Among Americans aged 60 or older, only 57 percent favor abortion in most
circumstances, with 30 percent supporting it in all cases. With
over 1 million women having abortions each year in the United
States, and with a majority of the population in support of *Roe* v.
Wade, it is clear that the prochoice side is winning this battle. Even
if the Supreme Court returns the abortion decision to the states,
once the dust settles, the growing political majority of free agents
in every state will ensure that abortion remains a woman's decision, and her decision alone. Even a conservative Supreme Court
ruled that women do not have to consult their husbands before
having an abortion.

Childbearing is no longer linked to marriage or pregnancy. It
is also becoming separate from sex. In the era of free agents,
reproduction is moving into the realm of science fiction. Sperm
banks father thousands of children each year, fetuses begin their
lives in test tubes, grandmothers can give birth to their own
grandchildren. Women can bear children not genetically related to
them. Menopause no longer means the end of a woman's childbearing potential.

With individualism the most powerful social force in society
today, science is working to free women of their reproductive link
with men. In a market economy, where there is demand, there will
be supply. If there are customers, there will be products and
salespeople and money changing hands. Women of the baby
boom generation are the customers of the new fertility services.
While infertility itself is not increasing, baby boom women are

reaching the ages at which infertility is increasingly likely. Only one in twenty women under the age of 24 has fertility problems, compared with one in ten women aged 25 to 44.

The rapid expansion in infertility services strengthens the matriarchal family because it frees women of even their most basic reproductive link with men. Sperm banks father 65,000 babies a year in the United States. For over half a million Americans, their genetic father is a sperm-bank deposit. For other Americans— currently only a handful, though their ranks are growing rapidly—their genetic mother is a deposit at an egg bank. Egg donation, which started in the late 1980s, is now available from dozens of fertility clinics nationwide. This procedure is likely to become much more common in the years to come, allowing women for the first time in human history to give birth to children who are not genetically related to them.

The new fertility techniques are changing motherhood much more than fatherhood. They create children who can have up to three different kinds of mothers, according to John N. Edwards of Virginia Polytechnic Institute and State University: "Genetic" mothers donate the egg, "carrying" mothers donate their wombs, and what Edwards calls "nurturing" mothers donate their time to raising a child.

In contrast to motherhood, fatherhood is pretty much what it's always been. There are still only two types of fathers: genetic and nurturing. These two types of fathers have been present throughout history, but in the past, men who limited their contribution to genes alone were considered deadbeats. Today, they are the benefactors of the infertile.

❖ 19 ❖

Women as Kin Connectors

As divorce separates men from their children, the matrilineal line is growing in importance. Already, many more Americans feel closer to their mothers than their fathers. Nine out of ten say they have a close relationship with their mother, according to a Gallup poll. Seven out of ten describe their relationship with their father as close.

The growing strength of matrilineal ties is also evident in the desire for daughters. Americans now want to have daughters almost as much as they want to have sons. It wasn't always so: the strong patriarchal nuclear family of midcentury spawned lopsided preferences in favor of boys. In 1947, when Gallup asked Americans whether they would prefer a boy or girl if they had another child, 40 percent said a boy and only 25 percent said a girl. Today, 34 percent want a girl and 38 percent a boy. While men continue to prefer sons to daughters, 43 to 27 percent, women now prefer daughters to sons, 40 to 33 percent.

Women are the "kin connectors" of extended families, say researchers, which is one reason why daughters are increasingly valued. With divorce the norm, and with women almost always gaining custody of children following a divorce, having a daughter ensures that a mother will remain tied to an extended family throughout her life. Those who have sons and no daughters risk being cut off from their grandchildren if their sons divorce.

Free agents may bristle at family ties that threaten their freedom, but they welcome ties that help them keep their heads above water. Today, the extended family is growing in importance as baby boomers enlist the support of their parents, brothers and sisters, grandparents, and other family members in their effort to succeed in the complex and competitive world. Though most marriages between free agents fall apart, the bonds between mothers and children, grandparents and grandchildren, are stronger than ever. Social scientists have found, for example, that children who live with a single parent (almost always their mother) have more contact with that parent's relatives than children living with both parents have with their close relatives.

There are two reasons for the new vitality of the extended family: one reason is medical, the other social. Thanks to advances in the medical treatment of a variety of diseases, many more people live to old age than ever before. The odds that people will survive from the age of 20 to the age of 60, or approximately from the time they have children until the time they have grandchildren, have jumped from just over 50 percent a century ago to better than 90 percent today. Consequently, the children of baby boomers are much more likely to know their grandparents than any previous generation in history. Many extended families now include four generations.

The other reason for the vigor of extended families is social—free agents need them to stay afloat. Adult children depend on the financial and emotional support of their parents as they try to achieve balance in their lives. Four out of ten parents offer their adult children advice and emotional support at least once a month, according to surveys. One in four parents helps an adult child with household chores, including baby-sitting, on a monthly basis. One-third of parents occasionally give their adult children financial help.

Baby boomers, particularly baby boom women, keep the communication lines open so they can tap into this support. A quarter of baby boom women talk to their parents every day. Among men, just 9 percent have daily contact with their parents. Half of baby boom men and women talk to their parents at least once a week, and half visit their parents at least once a week.

Extended families can flourish today because relatives still live close to one another. Americans may be mobile, but most people don't move far. Seventeen percent of Americans move each year, but only 3 percent move to a different state. This fact makes the much talked about mobility of American society more myth than reality. According to this myth, children grow up and move away from home, beckoned by a distant ocean, or city lights, or fast-track careers. The myth says it's no longer over the river and through the woods to grandmother's house. Instead, it's over the freeway and through the airport terminal, a trip so expensive adults rarely see their parents or grandparents. In fact, the reality is otherwise: Most adult children live near their parents. Two out of three live in the same town or less than an hour's drive away. Likewise, two out of three parents live within a thirty-minute drive of at least one of their adult children—a proportion which, surprisingly, hasn't changed in the past three decades of social upheaval. Researchers have found that adult children live farther from their parents when they're single, then move closer to home after they marry and have children.

Extended families rarely live together under one roof as they did in the past, but this does not mean extended families are less important in modern society than in traditional societies. Most parents live apart from their grown children out of choice. Ninety-six percent of Americans aged 60 or older say the best relationship between parents and grown children is one in which they get together regularly to eat and talk. Only 3 percent say the best relationship is to live together. In communally oriented cultures, extended families are more likely to live under one roof. Over half of the Japanese, for example, say living together is the best relationship between grown children and their parents.

But living under one roof does not make extended family relationships any better. The Japanese are renowned for the high esteem in which they hold their older family members, but this esteem may be more ritual than reality. Older Americans are more confident about their relationships with their children than are older Japanese. Eighty-four percent of older Americans say their children are very interested in their well-being. Among older

Japanese, only 67 percent feel that their children are very interested in their well-being.

By the year 2000, one-third of Americans with grandchildren under the age of 18 will be baby boomers. As baby boom women assume leadership of their extended families, they can look forward to spending time with their children and grandchildren. But baby boom men may find themselves isolated and lonely. Even now, family life is less important to men than it is to women. Among men aged 30 or older, a 45 percent minority say that their family is one of the most important parts of their lives. Among women, a 60 percent majority say that their family is of paramount importance to them.

Matriarchal families are diverse. As the nuclear family disappears, a variety of matriarchal families are taking its place, including never-married mothers, divorced mothers, and stepfamilies. One-third of Americans now live in a stepfamily—either as a stepparent, a stepchild, or a stepsibling. By the year 2000, fully half of Americans will be members of stepfamilies.

Because of the diversity of matriarchal families, society is redefining the very concept of "family." Free agents are questioning whether the legal privileges and protections offered to traditional families—married couples—are a denial of individual rights. They're asking businesses to reconsider the meaning of "family" coverage in health and other benefits. They're asking government to broaden the legal definition of "family."

Business and government are listening. In New York, the courts ruled that a homosexual couple can be considered a family under New York City's rent-stabilization laws. In cities from West (Seattle, Washington) to East (Tacoma Park, Maryland), the same benefits granted to married couples are extended to domestic partners. Private companies such as Levi Strauss, Lotus Development, and MCA, Inc. are broadening the definition of family to include unmarried couples.

Virtually all Americans regard married couples as families. Eight out of ten also regard mothers and children as families, whether or not the mother was ever married. Three out of four regard cohabiting couples with children as families. In keeping with their individualistic perspective, younger Americans are more accepting of new kinds of families than older people. Among adults under age 30, 87 percent regard unwed mothers and their children as families. Among people aged 60 or older, a smaller 73 percent consider an unwed mother and her children to be a family. Just 64 percent of people aged 60 or older consider cohabiting couples with children to be a family, versus 84 percent of adults under age 30. As younger Americans replace older generations, family diversity will be accepted by ever-larger majorities of the population. In turn, the legal definition of "family" will expand, further weakening the traditional nuclear family.

Free agents have changed family life more than most people even suspect. In middle age, baby boomers are firmly committed to family life, but only because they've recreated it in their own image. Many Americans hope the past few decades of family change is only a temporary breakdown of traditions, something that can be fixed. Politicians and special-interest groups tell people to clean up their act and return to the nuclear family. But the on-going family change is not a temporary breakdown; it is an evolution. People cannot return to midcentury life-styles. The realities of the personalized economy and their own survival instincts tell them to move on. In this transitional period, children suffer most because the social institutions are not yet designed to support the growing majority of matriarchal families. But as free agents gain political power over the next few decades, social institutions will begin to adapt. Then Americans can stop admonishing one another for their failings and start to cope with the new way of life.

❖ V ❖
FREE AGENTS AND THE ETHICS OF INDIVIDUALISM

The Ten Commandments

Yoko Ono first attracted John Lennon's attention at a show of her art. One of her pieces consisted of a ladder standing under a canvas attached to the ceiling of the gallery. A magnifying glass hung from the canvas, allowing the viewer to read a tiny word printed on the canvas. Upon climbing the ladder and peering through the magnifying glass, John Lennon saw the word "yes."

Legend has it that this moment changed John Lennon's life. Yoko Ono's avant garde art certainly intrigued Lennon. They fell in love, and the two free spirits became role models for millions of free agents worldwide who were ready to "just say yes" to experiences frowned upon by the baby boom's parents, including sex, drugs, and rock-and-roll. This anecdote captures the mood of the first free agents in their youth, when they were willing to accept, ignore, or excuse virtually any behavior. In middle age, this attitude has changed. Right and wrong now have meaning as free agents embrace values and accept limits. But they have not adopted many of the traditional moral values of their parents and grandparents. As is true in so many other facets of life, the perspectives of free agents are unique.

There is no more important set of traditional moral values for Americans than the Ten Commandments. These rules, thousands of years old, are moral basics: no killing, no stealing, no adultery. Since the first generation of free agents came of age, however, the Ten Commandments began to lose their grip on the American psyche. Baby boomers and younger generations are much more likely to question these values than older Americans, according to sociologist Margaret Mooney Marini of the University of Minnesota. Americans born since World War II are less likely than older people to believe that the Ten Commandments apply to them.

Researchers have studied this shift by asking a representative sample of Americans how seriously they take the Ten Commandments. Respondents to the survey rate how well each commandment applies to themselves today. If a commandment applies fully, respondents give it a rating of 1. If it does not apply at all, they give it a rating of 0. Researchers sum the ratings to arrive at a total score. Overall, Americans give the Ten Commandments a score of 8.51. Not surprisingly, "Thou shalt not kill" receives the highest rating, an 0.95. Also not surprising, given Americans' insistence on twenty-four-hour shopping, "thou shalt keep the Sabbath holy" receives the lowest rating, an 0.6.

But when researchers compare the answers of older generations to those of younger ones, they find statistically significant differences between the answers of Americans born after 1945 and those born before that date. Those born from 1946 to 1955, the oldest baby boomers, give the Ten Commandments an overall score of 8.38. Those born between 1956 and 1963, the youngest baby boomers, given them an overall score of 7.96. These scores, say researchers, are significantly lower than those of older generations, and they appear to be related to the rapid social change beginning after World War II.

Americans born between 1926 and 1935 (the parents of the baby boom) give the Ten Commandments a score of 8.95. Those born between 1906 and 1915 (the grandparents of the baby boom) give them a score of 9.2. The significantly higher scores given the Ten Commandments by Americans born before World War II are the result of different attitudes, says Marini, rather than a consequence of the chronological maturity of these generations.

Free agents may not have abandoned traditional moral prescripts, but they are less likely than their parents or grandparents to follow them personally. This doesn't mean free agents are devoid of moral beliefs. Indeed, now that most baby boomers are raising children, this life-transforming experience is causing them to embrace moral values with a passion not seen since the 1950s.

People who have a stake in society care deeply about right and wrong. For free agents, that stake is their children. But the rules important to free agents are not the same ones that governed their parents. The moral issues have shifted away from those spelled out by the Ten Commandments, which banned work on the Sabbath, taking the name of the Lord in vain, adultery, and the longing for material goods. Instead, the new moral guidelines seek to control behavior that has the potential of harming individual free agents and their families.

In communal societies of the past, strict moral guidelines were important for keeping order. Having such rules helped to suppress behavior that could disrupt the all-important social networks upon which agricultural economies are built. As the need for these social networks diminished with the rise of the industrial and then the personalized economy, the importance of the Ten Commandments eroded. Materialistic longings and working on Sundays might have damaged the communal spirit of old, but they benefit free agents in the economic competition of the personalized economy. The commandments against murder and stealing, in contrast, are still highly regarded by all generations of Americans. These commandments regulate acts that have the potential to harm the majority of free agents, though they may benefit the criminal minority.

If free agents were to draw up a revised list of Ten Commandments, they certainly would keep those honoring mothers and fathers, since so many are now parents themselves. They would also keep those against adultery and lying, although they probably would allow exceptions. But they would drop the Commandments banning work on the Sabbath, materialistic desires, and taking the name of the Lord in vain. They would replace these commandments with some of their own making: no smoking, no drinking and driving, no drug use, and no sexual experimentation—particularly by their children.

It is no surprise, given their self-centeredness, that the moral wrath of free agents falls on the few rather than the many. A minority of Americans smoke, so smoking is declared taboo. A minority of Americans are pregnant at any one time, so it's safe to criticize drinking during pregnancy. The new morals, unlike the Ten Commandments of old, do not infringe on the activities of majorities. Free agents are willing to restrict individual freedom as long as their freedom is not at stake.

Smokers are easy targets for the moral wrath of free agents. Smoking is something that nearly everyone agrees is unhealthy. The attempt to convince smokers to give up their bad habit has been fairly successful. The proportion of Americans who smoke fell from 42 percent in 1965 to 28 percent in 1991. Now free agents are taking it a step further. They want to keep smokers from exposing others, including their children, to second-hand smoke. Though a minority of Americans smoke, a majority are exposed to second-hand smoke. Seventeen percent of Americans currently live with smokers, and 58 percent once lived with a smoker. Overall, 45 percent of these Americans are at least somewhat worried about the harmful effects of second-hand smoke on their personal health. This proportion ranges from a low of 34 percent among Americans aged 50 or older to over half of Americans under the age of 50.

Free agents value their own health so highly that they are unwilling to let smokers endanger it, even at the expense of liberty. Nearly half (44 percent) of Americans favor a complete ban on smoking in public places. An even larger proportion, more than two-thirds, want to restrict smokers to certain areas of hotels, restaurants, and workplaces. At home, nonsmokers are equally aggressive: most would ask a guest not to smoke in their homes; most would object if a person wanted to smoke at their dinner table. A majority of Americans do not want to make discrimination against smokers illegal.

A near majority of the population, 47 percent, want to ban all cigarette advertising, though few think cigarette companies are at fault for smoking-related illness. Instead, most Americans think the labels on cigarette packages provide plenty of warning about the dangers of smoking, and blame individual smokers for their illnesses. This fact may explain why Americans are increasingly judgmental toward smokers. When asked whether they harbor negative feelings about any particular group, including blacks, Jews, business, labor, and so on, Americans are most likely to have bad feelings about smokers: one in three admits to being biased against smokers. This is the only group that a growing proportion of Americans feels hostile toward and is not embarrassed to say so.

The attitude of Americans toward drinkers is more tolerant, and for good reason. Two-thirds of Americans drink on occasion. While the moral guidelines of free agents allow social drinking, the combination of drinking and driving is considered a major transgression. This issue has taken on increasing importance since free agents felt their children were endangered by other people's drinking habits. Thus, free agents have become increasingly intolerant of drinking and driving, and the proportion of baby boomers who drive after drinking has fallen substantially. Among those aged 25 to 34, the share who say they drive after drinking fell from over half to just one-third between 1985 and 1990. Among those aged 35 to 44, the share fell from 33 to 28 percent. Americans today go so far as to support the invasion of privacy to curtail drinking and driving. Three out of four favor random police checks at toll booths to test drivers for signs of drinking or drugs.

As free agents matured beyond the ages when people are most likely to drink excessively (the young adult years), they have carried their crusade against inappropriate drinking into other areas as well. Once scientific evidence showed that drinking during pregnancy could harm a fetus, drinking during pregnancy became a moral transgression equivalent to drinking and driving. Today, many Americans believe waiters and waitresses should refuse to serve alcohol to pregnant women in restaurants. When the readers of *Child* magazine were asked whether the staff at restaurants should refuse to serve alcohol to pregnant women, a full 58 percent said yes.

As fewer baby boomers indulged in recreational drugs over the past few decades, free agents turned against drugs with the passion of the newly converted. According to a 1990 survey, only 10 percent of Americans reported using illegal drugs in the past 12 months. With such a tiny minority at risk of going to jail, free agents are willing and even eager to punish offenders. Do as we say, not as we did, is the message millions of baby boomers send their children, particularly as the association between crime and drugs grows stronger. More than half of baby boomers smoked marijuana at least once, according to a Gallup survey. One of them is the President of the United States, though he claims (with some embarrassment) that he didn't inhale. One in five baby boomers regularly smoked marijuana, and an equally large proportion say they experimented with LSD or other psychedelic drugs. Despite, or perhaps because of this experience, the baby boom's attitudes toward drug use have shifted a full 180 degrees. Though most baby boomers were not irreparably harmed by their experimentation with drugs, many have friends who were. They don't want drugs hurting their children.

By the late 1980s, Americans rated drugs as one of the biggest problems facing the nation. Eight out of ten baby boomers believe the liberal attitudes toward drugs in the 1960s were bad for society. Eight out of ten Americans think it is reasonable for employers to require job applicants to take drug tests. By 1990, just one in three Americans thought smoking marijuana in a private residence should be left up to the individual, down from a 55 percent majority who felt that way in 1978. In that year, fully 11 percent of the nation's high school seniors reported using marijuana daily. It was then that the baby boom generation discovered the dangers of drugs and began to campaign against them. The proportion of high school seniors who believe that regular use of marijuana could cause them "great harm" rose from 35 percent in 1978 to 79 percent in 1991. By 1991, only 2 percent of high school seniors regularly smoked marijuana. Free agents also turned their fury on drug dealers, now that the dealers were no longer their friends and roommates. Over half of Americans think police should be allowed to search the houses of drug dealers without a court order. Most Americans support a mandatory death penalty for known drug dealers.

Sexual promiscuity is another moral battleground for free agents. Baby boomers changed their minds about the wonders of the sexual revolution for several reasons, including AIDS, which is a leading killer of baby boomers. Parenthood is another reason. When the baby boom generation began to have children, teenage abstinence started to look like a good idea.

The oldest baby boomers are the most sexually experienced generation of Americans now living. They started the sexual revolution, paving the way for younger boomers to demand and get greater sexual freedom. Among older baby boomers, 72 percent say their parents did not allow them much sexual freedom. Among younger boomers, this proportion drops to 59 percent. Free agents in their forties have had an average of nearly ten sexual partners since the age of 18, according to a study by the National Opinion Research Center. Those in their thirties have had an average of eight sex partners. In contrast, their parents (Americans in their sixties) have had fewer than five sex partners, on average. Despite their sexual experience, only 46 percent of Americans aged 30 to 49 think the liberal attitudes of the 1960s toward premarital sex were good for society. Among baby boom parents with children under the age of 18, 60 percent want their children to have less sexual freedom than they had.

These attitudes toward sexual promiscuity are partly a consequence of the AIDS epidemic. More than one in four baby boomers is "very" concerned that he or she will get AIDS. With AIDS now the third leading cause of death among people aged 25 to 44, one in five baby boomers knows an AIDS victim. When Magic Johnson announced that he carried the HIV virus, the public became even more concerned about the disease. Seventy percent of Americans said they were more likely to practice safe sex after the announcement. Eighty-eight percent of parents said they were more likely to talk to their children about AIDS. Because Americans think AIDS is a greater threat to public health than to civil liberties, they're willing to consider putting aside civil rights to protect public health. Between 40 and 50 percent of the public says it would be appropriate to test all employees for the HIV virus, for example.

But on sexual issues that do not directly affect free agents and their families, there is much greater tolerance than in the past.

Homosexuality is one of these issues, despite the fact that the AIDS epidemic in the United States began in the homosexual community. The well-publicized horror stories of homosexual AIDS sufferers may have increased the nation's tolerance for homosexuality by showing homosexuals as the victims that they are of a dread disease. Overall, Americans are now more likely to favor than oppose legalizing homosexual relations between consenting adults. Forty-eight percent favor it today, while 44 percent oppose it. Among Americans under the age of 50, well over half favor legalizing homosexual relations versus just 30 percent of Americans aged 65 or older. While the public splits about fifty-fifty for and against homosexuals in the military, Americans under the age of 50 are far more accepting of it. Six out of ten Americans under the age of 50 favor allowing gays in the military.

In the revised list of Commandments, free agents would endorse heartily those tenets against stealing and murder. Among the oldest free agents, attitudes toward crime have shifted from a gleeful chuckle over Abby Hoffman's *Steal This Book*, published over two decades ago, to overwhelming support for law and order. With children to protect, homes stocked with possessions, and cars as extensions of their living rooms, free agents are now more likely to identify with crime's victims rather than those who, because of possible social injustices, commit crimes.

Free agents are eager to crack down on criminals, and they strongly support the death penalty. The proportion of all Americans who favor the death penalty for convicted murderers has grown from a minority of 42 percent in 1966 to a majority of 76 percent in 1991 as Americans changed their minds about this issue. Today, there is virtually no difference in attitudes toward the death penalty by generation. Significantly, fully half of Americans who support the death penalty favor it not for its deterrent effect, but as revenge for victims, proving that the moral wrath of free agents knows no boundary. Only 13 percent favor the death penalty to deter crime.

Most Americans think convicted murders should have fewer avenues to appeal their sentences. Though most Americans support the right to bear arms, they want tougher laws restricting the sale of firearms, including the registration of all handguns. They think the Supreme Court went too far in protecting the rights of defendants in criminal cases during the past few decades. The more conservative Supreme Court now in place is right in line with the thinking of most Americans on the crime issue. Criminal cases now make up a larger proportion of the cases the Court accepts, partly because the conservatives on the Court are eager to overturn previous rulings that expanded the rights of criminals, according to *The New York Times*. In the 1990–1991 term, the Court overturned five of its own precedents, all on the issue of crime. While many free agents quake at the thought of the Court overturning the *Roe v. Wade* abortion ruling, most applaud its get-tough attitude toward criminals.

At the core of the moral values of free agents is self-interest. The issues that galvanize them are those that threaten them personally: smokers beside them in a restaurant; drunk drivers on the road; carjackers in a parking lot; drug dealers outside their children's school; boys with unknown HIV status dating their daughters; gun-toting criminals on the streets. Free agents are trying to build a fortress around themselves and their families. As they do, they pick and choose their issues with care. If the majority indulges, free agents look the other way. If the minority indulges, it's fair game for regulation.

There is no denying that American society has been in dire need of some controls after decades of an anything goes attitude. In their youth, baby boomers bent over backwards to avoid passing judgment. But now the pendulum is swinging strongly in the other direction. Middle-aged free agents are eager to protect their stake in society. Behind these protective instincts are the self-interests of individuals rather than the shared interests of communities.

❖ 21 ❖

The Rise of Crime

On the highway, in restaurants, in supermarkets, at work and at home, Americans are becoming increasingly indifferent to what others think of them. Raised to be independent rather than obedient, free agents place less value on the basic social graces than do older generations of Americans. With self-interest rather than shared interests dominating social interactions in the personalized economy, it is no surprise that people are less polite than they used to be. Good manners and proper attire were critical to maintaining social and economic ties in communal societies. Over the past few decades, however, they have lost much of their importance as the personalized economy allows free agents to navigate their own course. Proper attire has given way to casual dress, even on the most formal of occasions. Politeness is no longer essential to getting ahead, kindness is seen as a weakness rather than a strength.

The Roper Organization has documented a sharp decline in what it calls the "standard social graces" in the past decade. Americans place less importance on appearance and manners as they become more tolerant of diversity, reports Roper. The proportion of Americans who say "politeness" is very important to making a "good impression" fell by 14 percentage points between 1985 and 1992, to 72 percent. The proportion who regard table manners as very important to making a good impression fell by 13 percentage points to 56 percent. The share who regard neatness of appearance as very important fell by 15 percentage points to 54 percent. These traits are waning in importance because today's parents are more concerned, by a margin of 61 to 49 percent, with instilling a sense of responsibility in their children rather than teaching them good manners.

A sense of responsibility helps children succeed in the personalized economy. It means people think independently, judging situations based on their own sense of right and wrong rather than letting others make the decisions. By contrast, politeness or kindness can hamper success. Politeness depends entirely on the judgment of others. When people act politely or kindly, they want others to think well of them. Politeness can dull the competitive edge of free agents. Kindness can leave them vulnerable to the self-interest of others. Those too polite or too kind to seize upon opportunities as they fly by in the fast-paced personalized economy will lose to free agents less concerned with what others think of them.

Kindness and politeness are important in communally oriented societies, where people must get along with one another for economic success. But for free agents, success is earned independently and often anonymously. This anonymity erodes ethical as well as social standards. Consequently, dishonesty is on the rise among Americans. The attitudes of Americans born after World War II are significantly different from those born before the War.

In a survey measuring Americans' ethical standards, researchers asked respondents to rate how justifiable nine dishonest acts were on a scale of 1 (never) to 10 (always). The nine acts are: failing to report damage to a parked car, accepting a bribe, lying, keeping money a person finds, taking a car for a joy-ride, buying something that was stolen, cheating on taxes, not paying a transit fare, and claiming government benefits to which a person is not entitled. Overall, Americans give these dishonest acts a score of 2.13—very close to never justifying them. But the generations born after World War II give these acts a significantly higher score than older generations—in other words, they are more willing to justify dishonesty. Most telling of all, educated respondents are more likely to justify unethical acts than those with less education. In their search for a competitive edge, the independent, well-educated generations of free agents are willing to bend the rules, shaking the ethical foundations of society as they do.

The indifference of free agents toward public judgment has disturbing consequences that ripple through society. One of the consequences can be found in the margins of the personalized economy, among poverty-stricken young adults. There, violent crime is a chronic problem.

The indulged children of the postwar middle class were not the only ones to become free agents. The children of the poor also grew up to be free agents. Among the middle class, the maturing of free agents eroded ethics and broke down the sense of community. Among the poor, the anything goes attitude of free agents and the harsh economic realities of the personalized economy have been much more devastating, resulting in pervasive drug abuse and a rise in violent crime.

The violent crime index, which measures the combined level of murder, forcible rape, robbery, and aggravated assault, rose from 160.9 crimes per 100,000 population in 1960 to a record level of 663.7 in 1989, a more than 300 percent increase in the past three decades. The violent crime index rose steadily until the early 1980s, in sync with the changing demographics of the population. With the huge baby boom generation in its teens and twenties—the most crime-prone ages—crime was predicted to rise through the 1960s and 1970s, and it did. But as the baby boom moved out of these age groups in the 1980s, crime was predicted to decline, and it did for a while. Between 1981 and 1984, the violent crime index fell from 594 to 539 crimes per 100,000 people. Then, to the surprise of many, it took a U-turn in 1985 and began to rise again, reaching record levels by the end of the decade. In 1991, 24,000 Americans were murdered, a record number. Americans' concern about crime is rising along with the violence.

Young adults are often the perpetrators of this violence. In any society, young people are more likely than older generations to rebel against the prevailing social norms. Poverty-stricken young adults, indifferent to community standards, and with few economic alternatives, feel that they have nothing to lose by

choosing a life of crime. This pathological individualism is resulting in a near-total breakdown of the social fabric in many of the
nation's central cities. In the ghetto version of the personalized
economy, crime is one of the few remaining routes to economic
success. Drug dealing, robbery, and murder have become commonplace in blighted neighborhoods.

Ironically, the victims of this trend are teenagers and young
adults. The increase in violent crime since the mid-1980s has
disproportionately affected the young and minorities. The percentage of older Americans who fall victim to crime is dropping,
while the rate among young Americans is rising, according to the
Bureau of Justice Statistics. In 1964, 31 percent of murder victims
were aged 15 to 29. By 1989, 45 percent of victims were in this age
group, including those involved in drug wars and innocent by-
standers caught in drive-by shootings. Most of those who commit
murder are also under the age of 30.

The fast-paced and competitive personalized economy, together with the loss of social norms and the erosion of ethical
standards, hits society's economically vulnerable populations the
hardest. In the United States, 22 percent of children under the age
of 18 were poor in 1991, up from 14 percent in 1973. For blacks, the
statistics are even worse. Forty-six percent of black children under
the age of 18 live in poverty. Unemployment rates for black teenaged males hover around one-third. Even those with jobs aren't
faring well: the median income of black men fell by 5 percent
between 1985 and 1991, to just $12,962, after adjusting for infla-
tion. In contrast, the median income of white men fell by just 1
percent during those years, to $21,400.

The consequences of this economic erosion are gruesome.
Life expectancy among black men has been falling since the
mid-1980s. Homicide is the fourth leading cause of death among
all black men, and it is the leading cause of death among black
men aged 15 to 19. Firearm mortality for black men aged 15 to 19
has doubled just since 1984, from 35.8 to 79.5 deaths per 100,000
population. While firearm mortality has increased among white
men aged 15 to 19 as well, the rise is far smaller than that among

blacks, growing from 17.8 to 21.7 deaths per 100,000. Black teen-aged males are now nearly four times more likely to be killed by gunfire than white males in this age group. These are the conse-quences of a one-two punch: the loss of moral and ethical stan-dards throughout society coupled with the loss of economic hope in the margins of society.

With rates of violent crime taking a U-turn, Americans report crime growing in their local areas. A majority of Americans think violent crime is more of a problem in their community than it was ten years ago. Yet paradoxically, fully 90 percent of Americans feel safe and secure at home at night—perhaps because their homes are rigged with dead-bolt locks and security systems. Only 38 percent of Americans feel more uneasy on the streets than they did a year ago, while most feel just as safe as ever. The proportion of Americans who are afraid to walk alone at night within a mile of their home is virtually unchanged from the 43 percent level of the 1970s. This feeling of security in the face of rising rates of violent crime can be accounted for by the fact that the proportion of Americans victimized by crime is shrinking—despite the increase in violence. In 1975, 32 percent of households included people who had been victimized by crime. By 1989, the proportion had fallen to 25 percent, a 22 percent drop.

Rather than affecting everyone, the rise in crime is increas-ingly concentrated in pockets of pathology, particularly the central cities of the nation's largest metropolitan areas. The central city horror stories make the headlines nationally, spreading alarm across the country. Free agents have responded personally to this: having children to protect, they turn with a vengeance on crimi-nals, calling for more police, more jails, and harsher sentences. But until the root causes of central city crime are dealt with by offering the poorest free agents a legitimate way to succeed in the person-alized economy, violent crime will continue to plague the nation's central cities.

❖ 22 ❖

The Rise of Tolerance

Individualism may have eroded moral and ethical standards, but it has had positive consequences for society as well. Free agents are more accepting of diversity than are older generations of Americans. According to University of Texas sociologist Norval D. Glenn, individualism leads to greater tolerance for diversity. As people withdraw from social groups, they are less likely to see the world in terms of "us" and "them." Consequently, younger generations of white Americans are far less prejudiced toward blacks and other minorities than older generations.

Recent events seem to challenge this assertion. The not-guilty verdict in the first Rodney King assault trial, the Los Angeles riots, and a barrage of headlines reporting racial bias in cities across the country appear to contradict the long-term trend toward greater acceptance of minorities. But the dismay with which Americans of all backgrounds greeted the not-guilty verdict in 1992 and the horror with which most people regard incidents of racial bias are in fact symptoms of a growing tolerance for racial diversity—and a growing intolerance of racial prejudice. Americans have become so intolerant of prejudice that bias crimes once buried inside the nation's newspapers are now front-page headlines.

As younger generations of free agents replace older, less tolerant generations, Americans' attitudes toward a variety of racial issues are changing. The proportion of Americans who believe there should be laws against interracial marriage fell from a majority of 59 percent in the early 1960s to a minority of 25 percent in the late 1980s.

More Americans now approve than disapprove of marriage between blacks and whites, according to a Gallup survey. Forty-eight percent of Americans approve of interracial marriage, versus 42 percent who disapprove. In 1968, just 20 percent of Americans approved. Behind the rise in approval for interracial marriage is the tolerant attitudes of free agents. Sixty-four percent of Americans aged 18 to 29 approve of interracial marriage, as do 56 percent of those aged 30 to 49. But among Americans aged 50 or older, just 27 percent approve of interracial marriage. As those who approve of interracial marriage become a larger share of the population, approval becomes the majority opinion.

The percentage of white Americans who think whites have a right to keep blacks out of their neighborhood fell from a majority of 54 percent in the early 1960s to a minority of 24 percent by the late 1980s. As younger generations replace older ones, the percentage of white Americans who would vote for a black for President has grown from about one-third of the population in 1958 to three-fourths today. The percentage of Americans favoring integrated schools has grown from only 30 percent in the 1940s to over 90 percent today.

The tolerance of free agents is also a pragmatic approach to an increasingly diverse population. Minorities are a rapidly rising percentage of Americans. The growing racial and ethnic diversity of Americans is particularly striking among the young. In the forty-seven states that report on the racial and ethnic origin of mothers, only 65 percent of newborns today are non-Hispanic whites, according to the National Center for Health Statistics; the rest are minorities. By 2000, over one-third of the nation's children under the age of 18 will be black, Hispanic, Asian, or some other minority.

As the nation's children become more diverse, the adult population also becomes more diverse. Overall, the number of white Americans grew by just 6 percent between 1980 and 1990, while the black population grew twice as fast, by 13 percent. The Hispanic population grew by 53 percent, while the Asian population more than doubled. The number of whites fell in both the

Northeast and Midwest during the past decade. The number of Asians nearly doubled or more than doubled in every region.

The nation's largest metropolitan areas are home to most minorities. While only about half of all Americans live in the nation's fifty largest metropolitan areas, these areas are home to two-thirds of blacks, 70 percent of Hispanics, and three-quarters of Asians. It is in these crowded and rapidly changing areas where racial tensions are at a peak, particularly because the recession of the early 1990s robbed minorities as well as the white majority of economic opportunity.

Los Angeles is the largest, most diverse, most rapidly growing and most rapidly changing metropolitan area in the nation. The metropolitan area grew by fully 26 percent between 1980 and 1990, gaining more than 3 million people. Today, more than half its residents are Hispanic, black, or Asian. The number of Hispanics in Los Angeles grew by 73 percent during the 1980s; the number of Asians grew by 138 percent. Many of Los Angeles' new residents are immigrants, barely speaking English and competing with blacks and other minority citizens for jobs. Take a diverse, rapidly growing, and changing mixture of people, add in a recession, and the ingredients for racial tension and violence are all in place. The not-guilty verdict in the 1992 Rodney King assault trial was the catalyst, not the cause, of the Los Angeles riots.

Outside the nation's metropolitan multiracial neighborhoods, racial tension is unavoidable for yet another reason. While the white majority is more accepting of blacks and other minorities than it once was, there is a new chasm opening between the attitudes of blacks and whites. Whites are less willing than they once were to see blacks as a disadvantaged group that needs society's help, and more likely to insist that black problems be solved through individual effort. While a majority of whites say they want to see blacks get a better break, only 35 percent favor increased federal spending to attack urban problems. In contrast, 61 percent of blacks want increased federal spending. A majority of whites think blacks are to blame for black problems, versus 32 percent of blacks who feel this way. Only 12 percent of whites versus 51 percent of blacks think blacks and other minorities should receive hiring preferences to make up for past inequities. Most whites, but a minority of blacks, think there are enough laws and regulations aimed at reducing racial discrimination.

Even within the black population, the attitudes of younger generations of free agents are diverging from those of older generations. The percentage of blacks who "completely" agree that blacks and other minorities should get preferential treatment to improve their position differs sharply by age. Among those aged 65 or older, a majority of 56 percent agree "completely" that preferential treatment is necessary. Among those under the age of 30, fewer than one-third "completely" agree that preferential treatment is needed.

The percentage of blacks who agree "completely" that "there hasn't been much improvement in the position of black people in this country" ranges from a majority of 62 percent among blacks aged 65 or older to 44 percent among blacks aged 18 to 24 and 35 percent among those aged 25 to 29. Twice as many young blacks as elderly blacks disagree with the statement that "there hasn't been much improvement." Among blacks under the age of 30, 24 percent disagree with this statement; among those aged 65 or older, only 13 percent disagree.

As individualistic free agents gain power, the feeling among most whites and a growing share of blacks is that each individual must forge his or her way in the personalized economy regardless of sex or race. Free agents believe success depends on individual effort. In contrast, the traditional civil rights approach favors rules and regulations to smooth the way for disadvantaged groups. The tension between these two philosophies is one of the factors behind current racial conflicts. The argument is not about the merits of racial equality; it is about the way to achieve equality.

The reemergence of racial issues in the nation's collective consciousness has more to do with the rise of individualism than with a rise in intolerance. As more Americans identify themselves as free agents and regard individual effort as the key to getting ahead, they take offense at affirmative action programs designed to aid groups rather than individuals. In the next few decades, the battle over civil rights will be transformed by the rising importance of individual rights. Free agents—black and white, male and female, able-bodied and disabled—will demand both individual rights and equal opportunity. Finding the right balance between protecting individual rights and ensuring equal opportunity is the challenge facing free agents as they lead an increasingly diverse country.

❖ 23 ❖

The Rise of Self-Interest

French statesman and writer Alexis de Tocqueville writing about Americans more than 150 years ago, said "Individualism disposes each citizen to isolate himself from the mass of his fellows and withdraw into the circle of family and friends; he gladly leaves the greater society to look after itself."

In 1831, when de Tocqueville wrote those words, he could not foresee how accurate his critique of individualism would be more than a century later. In the early nineteenth century, the individualism of Americans was insignificant compared to what it is today, when free agents leave society to itself, with serious consequences for the future of the nation.

More interested in personal pursuits than in public duties, free agents promote their own agendas at the expense of local and national needs. They withdraw into special-interest groups rather than work for the shared interests of the community at large. The consequence of this withdrawal is a loss of trust in others. Americans are far less trustful of one another than they once were. The proportion who think most people can be trusted has fallen from a majority of 54 percent in the mid-1960s to a minority of 38 percent in 1991. Americans are also less trusting of society's institutions. Between 1973 and 1991, the percentage of Americans with a great deal of trust in organized religion fell from 66 to 56 percent. The share who trust the public schools fell from 58 to 35 percent. Trust in the Supreme Court fell from 44 to 39 percent, while trust in Congress fell from 48 to 18 percent. Trust in the presidency hovered at just 50 percent in 1991.

Surveys taken in 1992 reveal a startling degree of political alienation among Americans. Over half of all Americans agreed that "people like me" don't have any say about what the government does, according to a poll by the Times Mirror Center for the People and the Press. Only 43 percent of Americans thought elected officials cared about what they thought. Fewer than half believed the government was run for the benefit of all the people.

Then something happened. The Presidential election of 1992 lit a fire under millions of previously disinterested free agents. The baby boom ticket energized the Democratic campaign, while Ross Perot's run for the Presidency excited free agents fed up with the political establishment. Seizing upon the opportunity to elect two of their own, free agents rallied for Clinton and Gore. Voter turnout among Americans under age 60 was 20 percent greater than in 1988. The election became a battle between two generations and two ways of life. Record numbers of Americans registered to vote in the weeks before the election. Millions tuned in to the Presidential and Vice Presidential debates. Books by Ross Perot and Bill Clinton, mapping out plans for the future of America, became best sellers. The percentage of Americans casting a vote in the November 1992 election rose to 55 percent, the highest level since the Presidential election of 1972. Interestingly, as if they sensed defeat, voter turnout among people aged 60 or older was 21 percent lower than in the 1988 Presidential election.

In retrospect, 1992 will be seen as a watershed year in American political history, the year free agents finally came to power. All eight Presidents in office before Clinton, from Eisenhower through Bush, were World War II veterans. All were born in the first quarter of the twentieth century, with the exception of Eisenhower who was born in 1890. All reached maturity before television, before mothers worked, or before divorce was commonplace. The string of World War II veterans who exited the White House in January 1993 dominated the nation's politics for forty years. The long tenure of that world view partly explains the political alienation of Americans in recent years. Americans felt politicians were out of touch because so many in fact were out of touch with the growing majority of free agents in the electorate. Free agents wanted a leader who could help them cope with life in the personalized economy.

The passing of the torch to baby boom free agents was inevitable during the 1990s based on the demographics. Finally, the baby boom's huge numbers were working in its favor. Because the middle aged are much more likely to vote than young adults, middle-aged baby boomers were a power in the voting booth in 1992, for the first time equal in strength to their elders.

The victory of free agents was also predictable based on the new style of campaigning that emerged in 1992. This should have tipped everyone off well before election day that free agents were the key to winning the race. With candidate Clinton playing the sax on Arsenio Hall and appearing on Phil Donahue, MTV, Larry King Live, and the morning news shows, he reached free agents live, unedited by political handlers. George Bush at first resisted this "unmediated" approach to the public, preferring traditional methods. But as Bush's approval ratings declined, he finally felt compelled to make a few talk show appearances. The change in political communication mirrors the life-style differences between older generations and free agents. Americans aged 50 and older are still loyal to the traditional media—the television networks and the newspapers. Free agents, in contrast, are media browsers as they wield their remote controls. Clinton played this to his advantage, popping up on a variety of television programs and channels from early morning to late at night, reaching free agents on their turf whenever they happened to tune in.

This "guerrilla" style of campaigning will characterize Presidential campaigns from now on. Clinton ambushed voters with his message. In contrast, the more traditional campaign style of older generations of politicians depended on staged political events designed for the network news. Free agents pay far less attention to staged news events than older generations of Americans. This fact has fundamentally changed the news itself.

During the 1950s and 1960s, television offered Americans a common fare of news. Each day people waited patiently until 6:30

P.M. when the network anchorman would tell them what was happening in the world. The three network news organizations decided what was newsworthy and informed the public of their decision. With no alternatives, the nation's attention focused on the same stories at the same time, from the intrigues of the Cold War to the much-celebrated arrival of the Beatles to the United States.

Television, once the agent of mass culture, now breaks it apart. With well over thirty television channels reaching most households, and with VCRs allowing people to see the movie of their choice, television no longer creates a common culture. The networks once commanded over 90 percent of television households during prime time. Now they must scramble for the attention of only about 60 percent of television households. Dozens of other channels capture the other 40 percent. People still watch network news, but they can also watch Headline news, CNN's twenty-four-hour news, local news, prime-time news shows, business news, or even live satellite feeds from news reporters around the world. Consequently, what's "news" to one person may not be "news" to another. The question, "did you see the news?" is now likely to be greeted by a blank stare rather than an affirmative nod.

Overall, 70 percent of Americans get most of their news from television, up from just over half in the late 1950s. The share of Americans who get most of their news from newspapers fell from 57 percent in 1959 to 43 percent today. At least 60 percent of those aged 50 or older read a newspaper every day. A much smaller share of Americans under age 50 read daily newspapers, ranging from just 23 percent of those aged 18 to 24 to 49 percent of those aged 35 to 49.

In a study by the Times Mirror Center for the People and the Press, researchers discovered that different generations of Americans are interested in different news events. Political summits between world leaders, the fall of Communism in Eastern Europe, and the opening of the Berlin Wall did not capture the attention of younger Americans as much as they did that of older Americans. *The Washington Post* claimed that the young must be "doofuses" for not paying attention to these stories. But there are good reasons for the greater interest of older Americans in these events. The events touched them personally—older Americans fought a war in Europe, they remember the building of the Berlin Wall, they lived through the Cold War, and they have ancestral roots in Europe. In contrast, a large proportion of younger Americans have no common heritage with the European past.

When researchers asked younger Americans how closely they followed events that had more relevance to them, their interest level was just as high as that of older generations. The freeing of Nelson Mandela, the invasion of Panama, political upheaval in China, abortion—these issues were as likely to capture the attention of the young as of the old. These events interested younger Americans partly because so many are black, Hispanic, or Asian.

The roving attention spans of free agents allow few events to unify the country. In fact, the only remaining unifying events are natural or man-made disasters. These are a hit in the television ratings for good reason. According to psychological studies, people pay more attention, unconsciously, to negative than to positive words. This fact may explain why people are drawn more to bad news than to good news, says Stanford University psychologist Felicia Pratto. It also explains why negative campaigning often works. This unconscious focus on the negative may be an evolutionary adaptation that helps protect people from harm, Pratto suggests, forcing people to pay attention to potentially dangerous situations.

When disaster strikes, the nation is once again united. Though most disasters present no danger to the majority of Americans, they remain psychologically compelling. For this reason, disasters are the most watched news stories, according to surveys that track Americans' responsiveness to the news. The explosion of the Challenger space shuttle continues to be the single most closely followed news story since the Times Mirror began to track public attentiveness to the news in 1986. Eighty percent of the public followed the Challenger story "very closely."

Also ranking among the top ten most closely followed news stories are the 1989 San Francisco earthquake, the Los Angeles riots, the 1987 rescue of the toddler from a well in Texas, the end of the Gulf War in March 1991, Hurricane Andrew, and the buildup of the Gulf War in the fall of 1990. With the nation's attention pulled in many directions at once, disasters are likely to be the only news that majorities of the public follow.

Understanding the new role of the media and particularly the power of television, candidate Clinton played his cards right. The White House was a big win for free agents, but it's only the first of many. Another victory lies ahead as free agents take over the nation's corporations. Americans born in 1946 or later accounted for fewer than 10 percent of the nation's corporate elite in 1992, defined by *Business Week* as the CEOs of the thousand most valuable publicly traded U.S. companies. The average age of this "elite" is 56, but with the oldest baby boomers about to enter their fifties, a majority of corporate leaders will be free agents within a decade.

Free agents in the Oval Office and the corner office will bring much needed change to a dispirited public. For one, it should help end the political gridlock in Washington. This gridlock, long blamed on a Republican President and a Democratic Congress, is caused less by political labels and more by the opposing views of older and younger generations of Americans. The political battle over parental leave, for example, was not between Republicans and Democrats so much as it was between generations. As the political might of free agents begins to overpower that of older generations, things will start to move again.

The Republicans tried to paint candidate Clinton as another in a long line of "tax and spend liberals," but the public may be pleasantly surprised to discover that he is not. Unlike previous Democratic Presidential candidates, free agent Clinton may create a new mix of economic and social policies that defy the labels devised by the generations born before World War II. If he does not do this, free agents are likely to vote him out of office in 1996 and elect someone who better meets their needs.

The needs of free agents are many, beginning with government policy that will support them rather than the traditional lifestyles of the industrial economy at midcentury. Just as they are more concerned with themselves than with society at large, free agents are also more interested in domestic issues than in foreign policy. Under the leadership of free agents, domestic issues will be at the top of the political agenda. Obsessed with their own health and physical fitness, free agents will support spending public funds to improve the nation's fitness. Given the right leadership, they will rebuild the nation's infrastructure, reform the educational and health care systems, and develop a high-tech economy. The baby boom generation, in its formative years during the race to the moon, still believes in technological miracles.

Unlike communally oriented older Americans, free agents are not anxious to meddle in other countries' affairs. Over half of Americans aged 50 or older agree "completely" that "it is best for our country to be involved in foreign affairs," according to a Times Mirror poll. In contrast, a minority of Americans under age 50 "completely" agree with this statement. Most Americans under age 35 "completely" agree that "we should pay less attention to problems overseas and concentrate on problems at home." Among Americans aged 50 or older, a minority "completely" agree with this statement. In keeping with their "live and let live" philosophy, free agents are also less likely to favor military intervention than are older Americans. A minority of free agents believe that "the best way to ensure peace is through military strength," versus a majority of Americans aged 50 or older.

With a free agent in the White House, the transformation of American society will quicken. For local communities across the nation, the consequence of this transformation could be disastrous as Americans turn away from public life. De Tocqueville foresaw this consequence in the early nineteenth century. "Individualism," he wrote, "dams the spring of public virtues." Communities across the nation are already suffering from Americans' withdrawal from public life as maturing free agents abandon local organizations. While local groups dwindle, national lobbies that promise to promote the personal interests of their constituents grow in power and influence. The National Rifle Association gets bigger while volunteer fire companies beg for help. The American Association of Retired Persons whips its millions of members into a frenzy of self-interest, while community service groups dwindle from lack of local attention. The proliferation of special-interest media, including direct-mail, cable channels and programs, and specialty magazines and newsletters, link Americans more closely to like-minded people in far-flung locations than to the diversity of voices in their own communities.

The community groups that maintained the all-important social networks of communal societies are dying because they offer few benefits to free agents in the personalized economy. Overall, Americans are less likely to belong to groups or organizations than they were several decades ago. When the oldest baby boomers were in their twenties in 1974, only 25 percent of Americans did not belong to some kind of club or group. Today the figure stands at 35 percent.

Some social observers argue that Americans' community spirit is reviving, citing a rise in volunteers as evidence. Fifty-four percent of households reported volunteering in 1990, up from 45 percent in 1988, according to Independent Sector, a nonprofit organization which encourages giving and volunteering. But even behind the rise in volunteering are the self-interests of free agents. Most volunteers have ulterior motives: Fully 60 percent of volunteers contributed their time to an organization or activity from which they derived personal benefit.

The unwillingness of free agents to join local groups is decimating the nation's volunteer fire companies. These organizations, responsible for protecting lives in communities across the country, are suffering from a sharp loss of volunteers. The number of volunteer firefighters fell from 884,600 in 1983 to 772,650 in 1990, a 13 percent drop in just seven years, according to the National Fire Protection Association (NFPA). The NFPA does not know why fewer people are volunteering, but the individualistic life-styles and attitudes of free agents are a major factor. In 1983, volunteers represented four out of five municipal firefighters across the nation. By 1990, they were just three out of four as communities were forced to pay firefighters as their volunteers disappeared.

The percentage of Americans who belong to fraternal service groups (such as the Moose or Masons), fell from 15 percent in the late 1960s to 9 percent by 1991. The percentage belonging to a church social group fell from 42 percent in 1974 to 33 percent in 1991. The trend away from groups is even invading college campuses, where the percentage of freshmen who plan to join a fraternity or sorority fell from 31 percent in 1967 to just 17 percent in 1990.

Free agents, spurning organized political parties, are more likely to identify themselves as independents than either Democrats or Republicans. Among all Americans of voting age, 38 percent identified themselves as independents, 32 percent as Democrats, and 28 percent as Republicans, according to a Times Mirror poll taken in the summer of 1992. Independents form the plurality of Americans under the age of 50, while Democrats are the largest block of voters among Americans aged 50 or older. The youngest free agents are the most independent, which may be why Americans under the age of 30 were most likely to vote for Ross Perot in the 1992 election. Fully 48 percent of people aged 18 to 24 say they are independents, as are 43 percent of those aged 30 to 34, and 39 percent of those aged 35 to 49. The independent share drops to 32 percent among Americans aged 50 to 64, and to just 28 percent among those aged 65 or older.

The organizations gaining ground in the personalized economy are those that promote the personal and professional interests of free agents. The percentage of Americans belonging to sports clubs, for example, grew from 12 percent in 1967 to 18 percent in 1991. Obsessed with their own bodies, millions of free agents belong to local health clubs where they lift weights and do aerobics. Likewise, the share of Americans belonging to academic or professional associations grew from 7 percent in 1967 to 16 percent in 1991 as college-educated free agents sought to strengthen their specialties.

With millions of Americans indifferent to local organizations and even tuning out national affairs, the consequences are felt in odd and unexpected places. One such place is in government statistics: A rising proportion of Americans refuses to take part in government surveys and censuses. The consequence of this refusal is a growing gap between how we live, and what we know about how we live.

The two most meaningful ways in which the government probes the life-styles and living conditions of Americans are the census and the Current Population Survey. The findings from the census and the survey are the principle means by which government officials determine the direction of public policy. They also form the backbone of data about consumers used by businesses.

In taking the census every ten years, the federal government sends a questionnaire to every household in the country. While the primary purpose of the census is for reapportioning seats in the Congress, the census also collects information about life-styles, incomes, educational levels, occupations, commuting patterns, and housing quality block by block. When the 1990 census knocked on people's doors a few years ago, 4 million people refused to respond, up from 2.8 million who refused to do so in 1980. An estimated 1.6 to 1.8 percent of Americans did not answer the census, the first increase in the census net undercount rate in modern history.

When the Census Bureau takes the Current Population Survey, which it does every month by interviewing a representative sample of about 60,000 households across the country, its primary task is to determine the monthly unemployment rate. The Census Bureau also asks its sample of households a variety of other questions about their jobs, incomes, and families. Today, however, an increasing proportion of Americans are refusing to tell Census Bureau interviewers about themselves. More than one-quarter of respondents to the Census Bureau's Current Population Survey now refuse to divulge their incomes. Just a few decades ago, the refusal rate was below one in ten.

Even when Americans agree to report their income to the

federal government, they're increasingly likely to report the wrong number. When the Census Bureau compares the income statistics it collects to other, independent sources, it finds that Americans underreport their income by 11 percent. They underreport self-employment income by 30 percent, interest and dividend income by a full 40 percent. While some people underreport their income simply because they have a faulty memory, others do so because they're hiding "under-the-table" money from the tax collector. The competitiveness of the personalized economy, coupled with free agents' indifference to rules and regulations, results in a growing underground economy.

Income underreporting is a problem for other government surveys as well, such as the Consumer Expenditure Survey. This quarterly survey collects information on household spending which is used to determine the inflation rate. But Americans who answer it are less and less likely to tell the whole story. The clue is that many households, especially the poorest, spend much more money than they say they make. Most of the gap, according to government specialists, is due to the underreporting of income, and this is a growing problem. In the 1960s, the poorest households reported spending one-third more money than they made, according to a study by Susan E. Mayer of the University of Chicago and Christopher Jencks of Northwestern University. By the mid-1980s, the poorest households reported spending five times as much money as they made.

The reluctance of free agents to take part in public life, from joining local fire companies to answering the census, is a consequence of their desire for anonymity. Privacy is important to free agents. It is the guard at the gate of individualism, keeping society's social and legal norms from intruding on their personal needs and goals.

While the Supreme Court may argue about whether the Constitution guarantees the right to privacy, most Americans think it does. Seventy-nine percent of the public thinks privacy is a fundamental right, along with the rights to life, liberty, and the pursuit of happiness. Concerns over the invasion of privacy have soared with the maturing of free agents and the widespread use of computers in the personalized economy. Eight out of ten Americans are concerned about threats to their privacy, up from 64 percent in 1978. The proportion of Americans who are not at all concerned about threats to their privacy fell from 19 percent in the late 1970s to just 6 percent in 1990.

Those most concerned about privacy are Americans under the age of 50. The fear of "Big Brother" lurks in the minds of most free agents, who worry that the more others know about them, the less freedom they enjoy. Over 80 percent of Americans younger than 50 are at least somewhat concerned that their privacy is threatened by the increasing flow of computerized information. A 75 percent majority of those aged 50 or older are at least somewhat concerned about the invasion of privacy. One-third of Americans under the age of 50 have decided at some point not to apply for a job, a credit card, or insurance because they did not want to provide certain types of information about themselves. In contrast, only 25 percent of Americans aged 50 or older have not applied for something to protect their privacy.

Typically, free agents want it both ways. They want easy access to the personalized economy which credit cards and other computerized information allow them. Yet they worry about the unrestricted use of that personal information. Most Americans under the age of 50 say they would be unhappy if the credit, catalogs, insurance, and other products that result from the use of personal information were no longer available to them. Most also say they would be upset if they could no longer use credit cards. Among Americans aged 50 or older, only 35 percent would be upset about this. Consequently, over 70 percent of Americans under the age of 50 think its all right for companies to sell mailing lists with their names and addresses. Only 54 percent of Americans aged 50 or older think this practice is permissible.

Privacy issues will continue to be important in the personalized society because they involve the freedom of free agents to do as they please. But the right to privacy will have to be encoded in law. Free agents are too competitive and too willing to bend the

rules to entrust privacy protection to the good will of the institutions (banks, insurance companies, medical offices, credit card
companies, all levels of governments) that collect such information. With the public pressing for privacy protection, it is likely
that the information people reveal about themselves when they
apply for loans, credit cards, or insurance will become jointly
owned by the individual and the business collecting the information. Businesses will be allowed to repackage and sell this information to others only with the consent of those who supply it.
Free agents will feel far less concerned about their privacy when
they have the ability to deny others access to their personal
information. Today, people have to make an effort to keep their
names off mailing lists. In the future, the system is likely to work
in reverse. People would have to check a "yes" box on a mail-order
form or answer in the affirmative on the phone before their names,
addresses, or other personal information could be used. Once they
have control over it, however, few free agents will deny companies
access to their personal information. They may want privacy, but
their economic survival depends on being well connected to the
personalized economy.

Free agents must connect with the personalized economy for
economic security, but their social ties to society are tenuous. As
De Tocqueville once warned, individualists gladly leave society to
look after itself. Free agents are indifferent to local needs. Multiply
those local needs by thousands of communities nationwide, and
growing social problems result, such as poverty, homelessness,
failing schools, and an eroding infrastructure. As free agents
begin to lead the country, they must find a way to solve these
problems or risk the collapse of society at its core. They must find a
way to take care of one another once again. This cannot be done
through preaching morals or teaching values. The solution lies in
the one mechanism that motivates free agents to get out of bed
each morning: self-interest. Free agents must see how their self-
interest and the needs of the community converge. Then they
must put their self-interest to work for the community.

❖ VI ❖

FREE AGENTS AND
THE 21ST CENTURY

❖ 24 ❖

Growing Old, but Not Gracefully

Free agents will not grow old gracefully. The battle is about to be waged. Aging threatens the most cherished possessions of individualistic Americans—their financial, emotional, and physical independence. Free agents risk financial ruin in old age because of the extraordinary expenses of raising and educating children as well as saving for a lengthy retirement. They risk emotional isolation because of their propensity to divorce. They risk physical dependence as their odds of illness rise with age.

As the baby boom generation enters its fifties beginning in 1996, the first battle will be against the labels of old age. Free agents will revolt against any attempt by society to designate them old at the age of 50, 55, 60, and even beyond. Marketing campaigns that now place people 50 and older into a separate category of "mature" consumers will be ignored by free agents who rebelled against maturity in their youth and still bristle, even in middle age, at the "mature" label. Special privileges and discounts offered to "senior citizens" from organizations ranging from the American Association of Retired People (AARP) to hotels and restaurants will be spurned by free agents unwilling to think of themselves as "seniors." Free agents will turn off patronizing sales pitches targeting the older market, including any use of the terms *golden* or *silver* as euphemisms for old. Free agents will not even begin to consider themselves "older" until well beyond the age of 60. Until then they will be working, supporting children, and balancing the demands of work and family. They will be living a middle-aged life-style well into what is considered old age today.

The second battle will be against the aging process itself. Free agents by the millions will turn to antiaging remedies. They will form enormous markets for products and services that promise to stop or slow aging, from skin creams to face lifts, from special diets to exercise regimens. Free agents are already obsessed with their own physical well-being. When the effects of aging begin to make themselves felt, free agents will be consumed with avoiding them.

The third battle in the war against old age will be psychological. Beginning in their seventh decade of life, between the ages of 60 and 70, free agents may begin to accept and even enjoy the fact that they are the older generation. But this will happen only after the life-style transition from middle to old age. The transition will be psychologically tumultuous, making their teenage years look placid by comparison. Free agents will need to regroup their families when their parents die and they assume leadership of the extended family. They will need to rethink their finances when their children graduate from college. They will need to rearrange their time upon retirement, and they will need to reorganize their activities as their bodies age. The many profound changes marking the transition between middle and old age will give free agents a different perspective on the world, just as middle age itself has altered their opinions and priorities. These new perspectives will drive many free agents on a spiritual quest, a renewed search for the meaning of life.

With the many changes of old age looming ahead, it is a wonder free agents don't dread growing old. According to a Gallup survey, however, two out of three baby boomers say the thought of growing old does not bother them. Eighty-one percent say they have a positive attitude toward retirement, according to a Merrill Lynch survey. Indeed, free agents look forward to having more free time after their children are grown and their careers are ended. In the final decades of life, free agents could concentrate on their own needs once again, rather than the demands of children and jobs. They could spend their time traveling, developing hobbies, pursuing intellectual interests, and exploring their spiritual natures. But will the old age awaiting free agents allow them these pleasures, or will they find leisure elusive? The answer to both questions is yes. The baby boom is such a large and diverse generation that its old age also will be diverse. Many boomers will enjoy an affluent and leisurely old age, while others will escape poverty only by working well into their seventies. Millions of other baby boomers will be poor in old age, dependent on government handouts and the charity of their families to make ends meet. Baby boomers are deciding now, in middle age, which of these old ages is in their future. The danger is that free agents will make the wrong decision, opting for pleasure today rather than security tomorrow.

✤ 25 ✤

The End of Early Retirement

The baby boom generation is the largest in American history. This fact alone ensures that the baby boom's retirement will be very different from that of its parents.

Upon retirement, free agents will resolve one of the greatest conflicts in their lives today: balancing the competing demands of career and family. The end of this conflict means the beginning of much more free time, something free agents value more highly than work. But this is where their numbers get in the way. Because of the size of the baby boom generation, the first generation of free agents will not be able to retire any time soon, certainly not at the early age typical of their parents. For many baby boomers, retirement is likely to remain out of reach until they are well into their sixties or even seventies.

Few baby boomers have accepted this fact yet. Over 70 percent want to retire before the age of 60, according to a Gallup survey. Fewer than 30 percent of baby boomers expect to work after their sixtieth birthdays, but the great majority will have to work far longer than that.

Many free agents are already fantasizing about leaving the work world behind, though they face at least two more decades in the labor force. More than a third of baby boom men and women say they plan to "reduce their job commitment to allow more time for other things" in the next five years, according to a Gallup survey. Eleven percent of men and 23 percent of women say they plan to quit work entirely in the near future.

These plans are likely to remain on the drawing boards. Most baby boomers will have to put off their retirement for years. Those who delayed having children until they were well into their thirties will face the expenses of parenthood for decades to come. Consequently, the baby boom's life story will have an entirely different ending from that of today's elderly.

Most of the baby boom's parents had their children when they were young. When the boomers left home at the age of 18 or 20, their parents were still in their early forties. Consequently, their parents could retire in their fifties or early sixties, their financial commitments over. In contrast, the many baby boomers who started families in their late thirties will still have children in college when they're approaching 60. Few will be able to afford to pay for college tuitions in retirement. Instead, they will have to work into their sixties to pay college bills. Though younger generations may be eager to push boomers into retirement, the political might of the baby boom generation in old age ensures that as long as boomers need jobs, companies will have to keep them on the payroll. Laws against age discrimination will proliferate. No legislator will dare cross swords with the politically powerful baby boom generation.

There are other reasons to suggest that the free time enjoyed by the baby boom's parents may be unique to that generation. Today's older Americans have more free time than any previous generation of older Americans. This fact does not bode well for the leisure future of the baby boom. Today's older Americans have more than fifty hours of free time each week, according to time-use studies, more free time than any other age group. In addition, older Americans are least likely among all age groups to feel pressed for time. Only 25 percent of people aged 55 to 64 say they always feel rushed, for example. Among people aged 25 to 54, over 40 percent always feel rushed.

Today's older men have more free time than their fathers did because they retired at a younger age. In 1960, 92 percent of men aged 55 to 59 were in the labor force. By 1990, that figure had fallen to 80 percent. During those years, labor force participation rates among men aged 60 to 64 fell from 81 to 56 percent. In the 1950s, a majority of men aged 65 to 69 were still working. Today, only one-fourth are still in the labor force, with the great majority retiring by choice because they could afford not to work. Today the average age at which older Americans receive their first Social Security check is 64. Previous generations of Americans did not begin to collect Social Security retirement benefits until an average age of 68.

In contrast to the decline in labor force participation rates of men, those for older women have increased over the past several decades as working women became more common, replacing older generations of housewives. Though today's older women are more likely to work than their mothers were, their free time has also increased over the past few decades because they're doing less housework than previous generations of women. Today's older women spend one-third less time cleaning than older women did two decades ago. Many also spend less time cooking because today's elderly are much more likely to go out to eat than were older people in the past.

As the baby boom generation approaches retirement age, the early retirement trend of the past few decades will come to a halt. Labor force participation rates among older men and women will rise. Baby boomers will work longer because their generation will stretch the Social Security system to its limit. The age at which baby boomers can begin to receive full Social Security benefits is already moving up by law. Those born in 1960 or later will not receive their full Social Security benefits until the age of 67, rather than 65. At the same time, businesses will end their early retirement plans when the baby boom approaches retirement age because of the expense of funding the early retirement of such a huge generation. In addition, employers may not want boomers to retire early because there are too few people to replace them, since the generations that follow the baby boom are much smaller.

❖ 26 ❖

The Money Supply

People can afford to retire when they have enough money set aside (savings) or promised them (Social Security, pensions) to support them for the rest of their lives. For the parents of the baby boom, the financial trends worked in their favor, allowing them to accumulate enough money to retire at a relatively young age—younger than any previous generation of older Americans. In contrast, it will be a struggle for the baby boom generation to do as well as their parents. The same financial trends are working against the boomers.

In the past twenty years, the incomes of older Americans have grown more than those of any other age group. Consequently, elderly Americans are more likely to be comfortably middle class today than they were several decades ago. In contrast, middle-aged Americans are less likely to be middle class than they were a few decades ago. The diversity of free agents and the changing structure of the economy has made some people richer and some poorer, shrinking the middle class among the middle aged. This income polarization also will occur among older Americans once free agents enter old age.

The proportion of Americans aged 65 or older with incomes clustered around the middle of the income distribution grew from 51 to 59 percent between 1964 and 1989, according to an analysis of the Census Bureau. Most of the growth in the elderly middle class occurred as older Americans escaped the poverty of old age through the expansion of the Social Security system. The share of elderly Americans with incomes less than half the median fell from 39 percent in 1964 to 32 percent in 1989. At the same time, the share with incomes more than twice the median climbed only slightly, from 9.2 to 9.4 percent.

In contrast to the growing middle class among the elderly, the middle class shrank among the middle aged as free agents entered their thirties and forties. Among 25- to 44-year-olds, the proportion with incomes less than half the median grew from 13 percent in 1964 to 17 percent in 1989. The share with incomes more than twice the median also grew, from 13 to 16 percent. Consequently, the proportion of people aged 25 to 44 with incomes clustered around the middle of the income distribution fell from 74 percent in 1964 to 67 percent in 1989.

Behind this income polarization is the life-style diversity of free agents. Free agents will bring this diversity with them as they age. Those who are economically successful in middle age, and who plan ahead for old age, will rank among the affluent elderly. Those who do not plan ahead will be the elderly poor.

Today's elderly benefited economically from a unique convergence of events that make them the most affluent elderly generation in history. During their careers, wages rose rapidly, even after adjusting for inflation. Also during their careers, a growing proportion of workers were covered by pensions. Then, just as they began to retire, the Social Security system was indexed for inflation, allowing Social Security benefits to keep pace with the cost of living even as wages began to stagnate. And when they began to trade in their large homes for smaller ones, housing values skyrocketed.

The consequences of these trends are evident in the income statistics. Between 1967 and 1991, the median income of households headed by people aged 65 or older increased by 64 percent after adjusting for inflation. In contrast, the household incomes of younger Americans grew much more slowly if at all. The median income of households headed by people aged 35 to 44 increased by 17 percent between 1967 and 1991, after adjusting for inflation. Among households headed by 25- to 34-year-olds, median income during those years grew by just 3 percent. For households headed by people under age 25, it fell by 13 percent.

The incomes of older Americans grew faster than the incomes of any other age group during the past two decades. So did their net worth, boosted by the rising value of their homes. Retired Americans aged 55 or older had a median net worth of $94,000 in 1989, twice the median net worth of the average household and 47 percent greater than their net worth in 1983, after adjusting for inflation. In contrast, the net worth of the average household rose by just 11 percent during those years.

The size of the baby boom generation worked in favor of today's older generations. Many of the elderly received relatively generous pension and medical benefits because employers were encouraging them to retire early to make room for midlife baby boomers rising through the ranks. Social Security checks are largely untaxed and indexed to inflation because millions of baby boom workers can afford to maintain a smaller older population in relative comfort. Housing values rose rapidly because millions of baby boomers were competing with one another for homes. While it has been said that the elderly live on "fixed" incomes, their household incomes rise every year as the government adjusts Social Security benefits for the cost of living. If anyone lives on "fixed" incomes, it is workers in the competitive personalized economy. Younger generations of workers have no guarantees, and the incomes of the youngest workers have fallen sharply over the past few decades. The future for today's younger workers does not look promising either, since it will be up to them to pay off the growing federal deficit.

The rising fortunes of the nation's older generations are behind the well-publicized decline in the nation's savings rate over the past few decades. Many blamed free-spending baby boomers for the decline, but the boomers were not wholly at fault. As their homes increased in value, older Americans felt less need to save money the old fashioned way—in savings accounts. The savings of Americans aged 45 or older fell by 7 percent between 1963 and the mid-1980s as older people spent a larger proportion of their incomes, according to an analysis of the Survey of Consumer Finances by the Brookings Institution. Older Americans could afford to spend more and save less because their home equity was rising rapidly. During those same years, in contrast, the savings of households headed by people aged 25 to 44 fell by only 1 percent. Traditionally, the 25 to 44 age group does not save much money because it has the expenses of raising children.

The parents of baby boomers were recipients of good fortune when they reached old age. Free agents cannot expect to be so lucky. Financial planning will be essential for comfortable retirement for baby boomers. Yet most still are not serious about saving money for retirement. Over half of baby boomers say they do not feel financially prepared for it, according to a survey by Merrill Lynch. Most do not have a separate pool of retirement savings apart from an employer-sponsored account. This is an especially serious problem for baby boomers because they need to amass a huge pool of savings to finance not only their own retirement, but also their children's college educations. Among baby boom savers, college and retirement needs compete for savings dollars.

Many free agents are deluding themselves about retirement. Three out of four baby boomers expect their standard of living in retirement to be better than it is today, or at least no worse. Only 24 percent expect their standard of living to fall. But given the meager savings that baby boomers have accumulated so far, most will find it difficult to match the incomes of today's elderly. This means that baby boomers will have to make do with very little money in old age.

Despite the fact that today's older Americans are the most affluent elderly generation in the nation's history, their incomes are not that impressive. Most free agents would find it difficult to live on the household incomes of Americans aged 65 or older, a median of $17,000 in 1991. At the low end, the median income of women aged 65 or older who live alone was just $9,700. At the high end, the median income of elderly married couples was $25,500. Free agents accustomed to incomes far above this level may be surprised at how little they have in retirement.

Granted, those who are retired from the work force don't need as much money as the middle aged. Most no longer have mortgages, owning their homes free and clear. They no longer have career expenses—professional wardrobes, commuting costs, lunch tabs, and so on. Nor do they have the expenses of child rearing—clothes, shoes, food, allowances, or college bills. But baby boomers will need even more money in retirement than their parents do today because boomers will live longer. In addition, free agents are far more materialistic than today's older generations. While old age is likely to mute these desires, materialism will continue to remain an overriding desire for free agents throughout their lives.

Social Security is the most important source of income for half of retired Americans today. Yet the average Social Security recipient receives just $6500 a year in benefits. Baby boomers are likely to receive even smaller Social Security checks in old age as their numbers drain the system of funds. On top of that, they're likely to pay more taxes on their Social Security checks than do today's elderly.

Only 15 percent of baby boomers expect Social Security to be the main source of their income in retirement. Many of them lack confidence in the system and don't believe they will ever receive Social Security benefits. Three out of four Americans under the age of 45 do not believe the Social Security system will pay them benefits of equal value to those received by current retirees, according to a survey of retirement confidence by the National Taxpayers Union. Even worse, a majority of working Americans don't believe they will receive Social Security benefits at all. Only 43 percent of 18- to 34-year-olds and 49 percent of 35- to 54-year-olds expect to receive any Social Security benefits. In reality, however, baby boomers are likely to find themselves desperately dependent on a bare-bones Social Security system because of meager pensions and inadequate savings.

Thirty percent of baby boomers believe a pension will be their biggest source of income in retirement. This figure is nearly the same as the 33 percent of currently retired Americans who say their employment pension plan is their most important source of income. But if boomers plan to depend on their pension to support them in retirement, they should prepare to live on very little. The average elderly private pension recipient receives just $5800 a year in pension benefits. Yet this figure is generous compared to what baby boomers can expect as companies scale back their pension plans to cut costs. Already, employer-provided pension coverage is slipping among full-time employees, from 48 percent in 1972 to 46 percent in 1988, according to the Social Security Administration. One reason for the slippage is the decline of unionization. Typically, unions negotiate generous pension coverage for their workers. Seventy-seven percent of men who belong to unions have pension coverage, versus only 44 percent of men who are not in unions. But union membership among the employed fell from 36 percent in 1945 to just 16 percent today. With fewer workers backed by unions, pension coverage is falling most dramatically among younger men. Between 1972 and 1988, pension coverage fell by 14 percentage points among men aged 16 to 24, by 11 percentage points among men aged 25 to 29, and by 8 percentage points among men aged 30 to 34.

Forty-two percent of baby boomers expect their savings to account for the largest share of their income in retirement. Among the current generation of retirees, just 9 percent say savings is their most important source of income—and this is a generation known for its propensity to save. It will be even harder for baby boomers to save enough to retire in middle-class style. The Survey of Consumer Finances shows that as of 1989, only 44 percent of households headed by people aged 35 to 44 had a retirement account, and it had an average of $8000 in it. Among households headed by people under age 35, 23 percent had a retirement account containing an average of $4000.

Some baby boomers may expect to finance their retirement with money they inherit from their parents. But only a tiny proportion of boomers can look forward to this windfall. Just 5 percent of all workers expect an inheritance to be a major source of income in retirement. Ten percent say it will be a minor source of income, and fully 85 percent say it will not be a source of income at all. Though the baby boom's parents are the most affluent elderly generation in history, they are not wealthy enough to allow their many children to retire in comfort. According to the Urban Institute, the average net wealth of Americans born between 1929 and 1938 amounts to $293,000. When that figure is divided by four, the average number of children in baby boom families of the 1950s, each boomer ends up with less than $75,000. While this might finance a few European vacations or a year or two of college, it's not enough to support someone through two or even three decades of retirement. On top of that, many baby boomers will watch their parents' estates be eaten up by rising medical bills and nursing home costs.

Unlike their parents, baby boomers will not be able to count on rapidly rising home values to finance their retirement. Smaller generations of Americans follow the baby boom into the housing market. Consequently, housing values in general are not likely to outpace inflation over the next few decades. But the value of the baby boom's homes depends on where boomers live. Housing values will continue to outpace inflation in rapidly growing areas, while they will increase little or even fall in areas where the population is growing slowly or declining. Unless baby boomers have enough savings to "buy low" and enough foresight to "sell high," it is unlikely that they will be able to take advantage of these trends.

If free agents want to be as affluent in old age as today's elderly, they will need to sacrifice their current standard of living for their future well-being. Sacrifice is not something that comes easily to free agents. In 2011, when baby boomers start to retire, they will need an annual income of $46,000 just to match the modest $17,000 median household income of today's elderly, assuming a 5 percent inflation rate. After 20 years of retirement, in 2031, they will need fully $125,000 a year to match the median household income of the elderly today. It will take a large savings account, coupled with Social Security benefits and pensions, to generate that much income each year.

The financial outlook for the first generation of free agents is grim unless boomers start planning realistically for their future. Most baby boomers will not match the modest affluence of today's elderly. After several decades of improvement in the living standards of older Americans, there will be a decline in standards when baby boomers begin to retire. Everything that worked in their parents' favor is working against them. Social Security will be scaled back; employers will be stingier with pensions and early retirement plans; housing values are likely to rise no faster than inflation; day-care costs are crimping the boomers' savings when their children are young; college costs will crimp their savings when their children are older. There is nothing in any of the trends to suggest that the baby boom generation as a whole will be able to retire in the style to which they have become accustomed in middle age.

Though many free agents will enjoy affluence during this decade and in the first decade of the twenty-first century, for most this affluence will end with their careers. Baby boomers will have to work far longer than they expect before they can retire. When they do retire, they will have to adapt to a lower standard of living. They will leave less to their children than their parents left to them. This paring of life-style will create a culture of simplicity beginning in the second decade of the twenty-first century. By necessity, many free agents will curtail their accumulation of material goods and pursue spiritual experiences. And since the end of every millennium is accompanied by spiritual anxiety about the future, a spiritual awakening in the first half of the next century is virtually assured.

❖ 27 ❖

The Fortunate Few

Though most baby boomers will have little money to spare in their old age, some will be affluent. And because the generation is so big, the affluent are certain to number in the millions. They will be the envy of the rest of the generation, moving to resort and retirement communities, pursuing personal interests, and traveling around the world.

Upon retirement, most older people stay put, but a significant number move to another community. Surveys of pension recipients (a relatively affluent group of elderly) suggest that the proportion who move after retirement is about 44 percent, with about half of the movers going to a different state. In the past few decades, the movers among today's elderly have turned some parts of the country, such as Florida and Arizona, into rapidly growing retirement areas. During the next two decades, retirees will continue flocking to these established retirement communities. The Census Bureau projects that over half of elderly Americans will live in just ten states in 2010, including the retirement meccas of California and Florida. The elderly population will grow 26 percent overall, but by more than 50 percent in both Florida and Arizona, and also by more than 50 percent in less well-known retirement states such as New Hampshire, North Carolina, and Georgia.

When affluent baby boomers retire after 2020, it is unlikely they will settle in the crowded and overdeveloped retirement areas of today. Instead, they will create new retirement communities in areas surrounding the old ones. When baby boomers bought their

first homes, they created the exurbs—new suburban developments that spread outward from the old suburbs built by their
parents. They will do the same when they retire, turning forests
and farms into boomer resorts and retirement communities. These
areas are likely to be in regions adjacent to current retirement
hotspots as retirement zones spread outward from their crowded
cores. The states that will boom when baby boomers retire are
Vermont, Virginia, South Carolina, New Mexico, Nevada, Ore-
gon, and Washington. In addition, affluent boomers are likely to
retire to the islands of the Caribbean, to Canada, and to Mexico—
places the boomers are growing familiar with as they travel the
globe. Once Fidel Castro is consigned to the history books and
Cuba regains economic and political stability, the island nation is
certain to become a retirement mecca for affluent boomers.

A tiny proportion of today's elderly live in formal retirement
communities—developments established solely for retirees, providing them with a variety of services such as restaurants, laun-
dries, golf courses, and swimming pools. It is unlikely that fiercely
independent free agents will favor this type of living arrangement
in old age. It may suit the communally oriented older generations
of today, but there are too many rules in such places to suit free
agents. It is more likely that free agents who move to retirement
areas will buy homes or apartments in independent suburban
developments. One feature that will be common to these developments, however, is walls. In old age, free agents who can afford it
will escape the all-pervasive crime by choosing homes or apartments in walled suburbs. There, gates and security guards will
protect them from the chaotic world they helped to create.

Inside those gates, affluent free agents will enjoy personal
interests, making up for lost time. The career and family pressures
on middle-aged Americans today prevent many of them from
pursuing hobbies. Consequently, Americans have fewer hobbies
than they once did. In 1982, Americans claimed to have six
different hobbies, on average. By the end of the 1980s, they had
only four. When the Roper Organization quizzed Americans
about 22 different hobbies, it discovered declines in all of them,

from reading to music, from bowling to fishing. In retirement, Americans are likely to pick up where they left off in middle age. They will pursue hobbies once again. The hobbies likely to be most popular among retired free agents are familiar pastimes like reading, cooking, fishing, and gardening. Other hobbies that will be popular among free agents are music (such as developing an archival knowledge of rock-and-roll), collecting things (such as "antiques" from the 1950s and 1960s), using computers to experience "virtual reality," and travel.

Many baby boomers will spend a good portion of their free time traveling. As young adults, free agents made globe trotting common. Those who went to college often studied in foreign countries. Consequently, baby boomers are almost as well traveled as the oldest Americans, though they have had much less time in which to see the world. Among the oldest baby boomers, for example, about two-thirds have been to a foreign country. Among Americans aged 60 or older, 78 percent have traveled outside the United States.

Just as free agents will not choose to retire in crowded retirement areas, they also will not choose to travel the beaten path. While Europe will continue to draw millions of U.S. tourists, baby boomers will escape the crowds by traveling to more exotic locales. Instead of going to Europe, they will travel to China or Kenya. Instead of visiting Mexico, they will fly farther south, to Brazil. Instead of the Caribbean, they will explore the islands of the South Pacific.

While affluent free agents will travel in style, many baby boomers will not have the money to afford luxurious accommodations. They will need simple accommodations wherever they choose to travel, creating a global network of Motel 6s. These motels will not be quite as primitive as youth hostels, however. They will offer separate sleeping quarters and private bathrooms for privacy-conscious free agents.

Vacations that combine travel, meals, and lodging with educational experiences will be immensely popular when the baby boom generation retires. College-educated Americans are more likely to have traveled outside the United States than those with less education. Eighty-six percent of Americans with a college degree have been to a foreign country, for example, versus 62 percent of those with a high-school diploma or less. Travel packages of the future typically will include educational experiences in order to appeal to well-educated free agents. Some of these packages will be traditional, such as learning to paint or play chess. Others will be offbeat, such as learning how movies are made or learning how to be an astronaut. Free agents will satisfy their craving for experiences from the safety of packaged tours.

✤ 28 ✤
Old and Alone

Free agents who enter old age with their marriages intact will be the lucky ones. They will account for most of the affluent elderly, with two Social Security checks and possibly two pensions in retirement. Couples will travel together and explore new interests. They may find their marriages improving after years of struggle. Studies show that midlife is hard on marriage. Marital satisfaction hits a low as parents raise preschoolers, the demands of children leaving little emotional energy for a spouse. But in later life, when children are grown and retirement allows husbands and wives to spend more time together, couples often experience a "second honeymoon."

Many free agents won't be so lucky, risking emotional isolation in old age because of their propensity to divorce. As free agents grow older, divorce will become a game of musical chairs. When the music stops, someone will be left standing alone—this time permanently. Baby boomers may do well to take Margaret Mead's advice about relationships. The first one is for sex, the second for children, but the third should be for companionship.

Free agents also risk losing the emotional gratification of grandchildren in old age because they postponed childbearing. Many free agents will not become grandparents until they are far too old to take an active role in the relationship. Divorce is likely to intrude as well, since the children of free agents will be as likely to divorce as their parents. Consequently, many baby boomers will have complex relationships with their grandchildren. In the era of the matriarchal family, where women rather than men head the majority of families, maternal grandmothers will be most fortunate. Social science studies show that maternal grandparents are closer to their grandchildren after a divorce than are paternal grandparents, since it is mothers who most often get custody of children.

About 15 percent of baby boomers will never have children, according to Census Bureau estimates. Studies show, however, that childless older Americans are just as happy in later life as those with children. Their lives are just as satisfying, and they are no more likely to be lonely than older parents. Parents develop interests and activities that revolve around their children. The childless develop other interests and activities that give them just as much pleasure. The only circumstance in which the childless are at a disadvantage is when they get sick. Adult children are the most likely caretakers of the frail elderly, and the childless lack this support network. Consequently, they are much more likely than elderly parents to be institutionalized. The unmarried, childless old are almost three times more likely to end up in a nursing home than the old who are married and have children. For childless baby boomers, the death of a spouse threatens emotional isolation. But even for those with children, widowhood is likely to mean living alone.

As the incomes of the elderly rose over the past few decades, living alone became the dominant life-style among the widowed elderly. The more affluent a society, the more likely older people are to live alone rather than share a household with relatives after the death of a spouse. As the number of elderly Americans grew during the past few decades, the number of single-person households became a larger share of all households, growing from 13 percent in 1960 to 25 percent in 1990, becoming one of the most common household types. When the huge baby boom generation reaches old age, the number of single-person households may surpass the number of nuclear families or empty nesters (married couples with no children living at home) to become the most common household type in the United States. This will be a milestone in American history. Never before has solo living been the dominant living arrangement.

Because of their fierce independence, most free agents will insist on living alone following the death of a spouse, if they can afford it. But because they will not be as affluent as today's older Americans, many will not be able to afford independent living. They will have to move in with their children. Since poverty is likely to grow among the elderly as baby boomers age, households containing three or more generations will become more common in the next century as economically strapped free agents try to find a way to live more cheaply. But because the baby boom generation is so big, there still will be many millions of free agents who can afford to live alone.

Most of the elderly who live alone are women. From the age of 55 on, in fact, women are much more likely than men to live alone. The proportion of women who live alone rises from about one in five among those aged 55 to 64, to one in three among those aged 65 to 74, to a majority among women aged 75 or older. In contrast, the proportion of men who live alone peaks among men aged 85 or older at just 28 percent.

Only half of women aged 65 to 74 live with their husband. Among those aged 75 to 84, the proportion drops to less than one-third. By ages 85 or older, only one woman in ten still lives with her husband. Among men aged 85 or older, in contrast, nearly half still live with their wives.

Women are more likely than men to live alone because they are far more likely to be widowed and less likely to remarry after widowhood. The chances are seven out of ten that a wife will outlive her husband. But if the decline in mortality rates at older ages continues, widowhood will be slightly less common among baby boomers than among today's elderly. Women will continue to live longer than men, but not quite as long as they do today. According to projections by the Social Security Administration, 37 percent of women aged 65 or older will be widows in the year 2040, down from half of women aged 65 plus today. Among women aged 75 or older, half will be widows in 2040, down from two-thirds today.

Widowhood is already uncommon for men because women live longer than men and because widowed men are more likely than widowed women to remarry. Widowhood will be even less common among men when baby boomers are aged. Among men aged 65 or older in 2040, only 13 percent are projected to be widowers, down from 14 percent today. Among men aged 75 or older in 2040, only 20 percent will be widowed, down from 24 percent today.

The number of widows in the United States increased rapidly during this century as the gap in life expectancy between men and women grew. In 1920, women outlived men by only two years on average. Today, newborn girls can expect to outlive newborn boys by an average of seven years. In 1920, there were only 1.4 million elderly widows; today, there are 8.4 million. By the time the entire baby boom generation is aged 65 or older in 2040, there will be 15 million widows aged 65 or older, according to projections by the Social Security Administration. The number of elderly widowers has grown much less, climbing from 669,000 in 1920 to 1.8 million today. In 2040, there are likely to be 4.5 million elderly widowers.

A 65-year-old woman today can expect to live four years longer than a 65-year-old man. But most women marry men who are a few years older. Among men and women marrying for the first time, grooms are, on average, two years older than brides. The gap is even larger for people who remarry. Among previously married men and women, grooms are four years older than brides, on average. The greater age difference between remarrying men and women is especially relevant to free agents, among whom remarriage is common.

The odds that a woman will outlive her husband have grown significantly in the past century. In the 1890s, a woman had only a 57 percent chance of outliving her husband, while today, the chance is 69 percent. Only 31 percent of men outlive their wives today, down from 43 percent in 1890. According to mortality projections, baby boom women will become widows at an average

age of 67. They can expect to be widows for an average of fifteen years. Fewer than one in ten will remarry.

Because of their diverging life-styles in old age, baby boom women must prepare for a different future than baby boom men. Though baby boom women face the likely trauma of widowhood, they can turn to the matriarchal families they head—their children and grandchildren—for support. Baby boom men are more likely to have wives to help them in old age. But if they are divorced, widowed, or remarried, their relationships with their children may be distant. They could find themselves estranged from their own families and stranded by illness in old age.

❖ 29 ❖

Improving Health

The baby boom generation may be young enough yet to benefit from current advances in medical science. These advances are every bit as important as the discovery of antiseptics in the nineteenth century and antibiotics in the twentieth century. The advances include better diagnostic equipment (such as magnetic resonance imaging); better surgical techniques (laser surgery); better corrective techniques (gene therapy); better prevention through diet and exercise; and the growing ability to prolong health (though not life) for an indefinite period.

These medical advances may help free agents live longer and healthier lives than any previous generation of Americans. They are occurring just in time, because in the 1990s free agents will begin to succumb to physical conditions that strike people as they age into their late forties and early fifties.

The fact that the baby boom generation is about to experience a myriad of health problems guarantees that the current system of health insurance will change. Health insurance has already become a major political issue, with voters electing leaders who promise universal insurance coverage. Some type of universal coverage is likely to be in place by the end of the 1990s. While this will lower the cost of health insurance for many Americans, it is likely to mean higher taxes if it is funded by taxpayers, or lower wages and more unemployment if businesses must fund it. But most Americans are willing to make these sacrifices for the security of universal coverage.

It is not as easy to predict the direction of health care as baby boomers age. While a good argument can be made for shifting resources into preventive medicine, for many baby boomers about to experience a variety of chronic conditions, it is too late for prevention. The boomers will form a huge voting block demanding funding for research and development into high-tech cures. The self-interest of free agents makes them more than willing to throw money at their health problems, demanding complex procedures, expensive equipment, and exotic drugs. With this demand driving health care over the next four decades, the cost of health care will continue to rise faster than the general cost of living. Cures that cannot be funded by society as a whole will be borne by private patients, and the current system of health care rationing— one based on income—will continue. Still, this will be an improvement over the current health care system, which currently fails to insure 14 percent of Americans.

Behind the growing demand for a better health care system will be the rise of chronic illness among baby boomers. Three chronic conditions are likely to strike a significant proportion of baby boomers during the 1990s: arthritis, high blood pressure, and hearing problems. The proportion of people who suffer from arthritis rises sharply in the 45-to-54 age group—the age group now filling with baby boomers. Only one in ten 35- to 44-year-olds has arthritis, versus one in five 45- to 54-year-olds. The proportion of people with high blood pressure increases from 11 percent among those aged 35 to 44 to 20 percent among 45- to 54-year-olds. Hearing problems also become much more common among 45- to 54-year-olds, with 12 percent of those in this age group reporting hearing problems. This proportion is likely to rise among baby boomers since many damaged their hearing by listening to too much ear-shattering rock music in their youth.

Menopause usually begins when women reach their late forties, which explains why books about menopause now appear on the best-seller lists. Though new fertility technologies suggest that even menopause need not end a woman's reproductive years, few free agents will choose to spend their time changing diapers in their fifties or sixties. Most older baby boom women have already decided not to have more children. Among married women born between 1946 and 1955, only 31 percent can still bear children. Fifty-eight percent have been surgically sterilized (or their husbands have had vasectomies), ensuring that there will be no accidental pregnancies. As the enormous baby boom generation says goodbye to childbearing, reproductive issues will begin to fade from the headlines of newspapers. Even the abortion debate will soften as the nation's attention shifts to the different priorities of a postfertile population.

One of these priorities will be staying alive. Some argue that ongoing medical advances could extend life expectancy beyond the age of 100. But during the baby boom's lifetime, life expectancy is more likely to rise slowly to around 85 years, up from 75 today.

This growing longevity is a cause for celebration. It is also a cause for concern because it will contribute to the problems that will confront the Social Security system. If Americans were to receive Social Security benefits for the same number of years as retiring workers received them in 1940, then baby boomers would not begin to receive Social Security benefits until they reached their midseventies, according to calculations by the Social Security Administration.

Length of life has increased enormously since the turn of the century. In 1990, a newborn boy could expect to live to age 48, while a newborn girl could expect to live to age 51. Today those figures are 72 and 79 years, respectively. Most of this dramatic increase in length of life is due to the sharp decline in infant deaths in the past 100 years. It is not that older people are living so much longer, but that more people are living to be old.

This fact is greatly misunderstood by most people. Take the life expectancy figure of 51 for newborn girls in 1900. Many people interpret this to mean that women died around the age of 51. But at the turn of the century there were many women far older than 51. Women's life expectancy was only 51 years not because women died at that age, but because so many girls died before reaching adulthood. If children survived the diseases of childhood, they stood a good chance of living well into old age.

Though most of the rise in life expectancy over this century can be traced to efforts at combatting infant mortality, in the past few decades there has been substantial progress in lengthening the life of adults. But the figures are not nearly as dramatic. At age 40, Americans can expect to live another 38 years. At the turn of the century, a 40-year-old could expect to live only 28 more years. Today, at age 65, Americans can expect to live another 17 years, up from 12 years in 1900. This gain of five years, while significant, pales in comparison to the more than twenty-five-year increase in life expectancy at birth.

As life expectancy increased, the gap between the life expectancy of men and women grew. Women, it appears, are biologically sturdier than men. Though some predicted that the life expectancy gap between men and women would shrink as women went to work and experienced the same stresses as men, health research suggests the opposite has occurred. The healthiest women are not housewives, but working women, according to sociologists Lois M. Verbrugge and Jennifer H. Madans. At all ages, working women spend fewer days sick in bed, and they suffer from fewer acute illnesses (such as colds or flu) or chronic conditions (such as heart problems or emphysema) than housewives. Working women are also more likely than housewives to report feeling healthy. In fact, the healthiest women of all are the busiest—those who work, are married, and have children. Credit female hormones or blame male hormones, but the fact is that women have a biological edge. The consequence, unfortunately, is a lengthy widowhood.

Though death rates are falling in old age, this does not mean older people today are any healthier than older people in the past. On the contrary, it often means the old must live with disability and illness. While life expectancy at age 65 has grown from 12 to 17 years during this century, "active life expectancy" (defined as the average number of years remaining before people lose their ability to perform the activities necessary for daily life, such as bathing, dressing, money management, and so on) at ages 65 to 70 is just ten years, according to social scientists. At age 85, life expectancy is five years for men and six for women, but "active life expectancy" is just three years.

Length of life may be increasing, but quality of life is not necessarily improving. In a study of elderly Canadians, researchers found that the elderly were disabled for 80 percent of the extra time they gained as life expectancy rose. People are living longer, but they are not living better. A majority of Americans rate their health as very good or excellent until they reach their midsixties. Among elderly Americans, only 36 percent rate their health this highly. Four out of five people aged 65 or older suffer from at least one chronic illness—a health condition that won't go away. The most common chronic condition is arthritis, affecting nearly half of people aged 65 or older, while high blood pressure affects one in three and hearing problems trouble nearly three out of ten. Cataracts or heart disease each affect more than one in ten of those 65 or older.

As free agents age, feeling good for as long as possible will be a top priority. Free agents are fortunate in that they are likely to be healthier in old age than are the old today because of the ongoing advances in health care.

Death rates for some of the leading causes of death have been falling for decades as medical science progresses and as Americans learn more about prevention. Heart disease causes one-third of all deaths in the United States, but death rates from heart disease have fallen dramatically, down by 22 percent between 1970 and 1991. Death rates for heart disease are likely to continue to fall in the future because of advances in the treatment of heart disease through drugs and corrective surgery. In addition, the baby boom knows more about how to prevent heart disease than did today's elderly in their middle age. Four out of ten boomers exercise strenuously at least several times a week, according to a survey by

Prevention magazine. A majority of Americans now avoid fatty and high-cholesterol foods. Health-conscious boomers should live longer and feel better in old age than many of today's elderly.

Even if heart disease were entirely eradicated, however, life expectancy would not increase dramatically. With heart disease eliminated, life expectancy at age 65 would increase by just five years, and at age 85 by just over three years. The increase is small because those who survive heart disease would then die of some other cause. The older people get, the more vulnerable their deteriorating body organs are to a variety of diseases. Today, fully 73 percent of people die of multiple causes, up from just 35 percent in 1917, because the average age of death is higher than it was in the early part of the century. The human body just seems to break down after 80 or 90 years of life.

The number two killer in the United States today is cancer, responsible for one-fourth of all deaths. Unlike heart disease, death rates from cancer have increased over the past few decades, rising by 25 percent between 1970 and 1991. While there is the possibility that a breakthrough cure for some cancers will be discovered in the next few decades, this too would have surprisingly little effect on life expectancy, according to demographers. If cancer were entirely eradicated, Americans' life expectancy would rise by about two years.

The third leading cause of death is cerebrovascular disease, such as stroke, accounting for 7 percent of all deaths. Death rates from cerebrovascular disease have fallen by 44 percent since 1970 and they are likely to continue to decline because of the same factors that are lowering death rates from heart disease. Better diets, more exercise, and less smoking are warding off these killer diseases.

Accidents are the fourth leading cause of death. Death rates due to accidents have dropped by fully 36 percent since 1970. Many fewer people are dying in car accidents partly because of the middle aging of the baby boom generation. Those most vulnerable to car accidents are teens and young adults. In addition, seat-belt laws and the speed limit of 55 miles per hour have succeeded in saving lives.

Lung disease, pneumonia, diabetes, suicide, AIDS, and homicide account for the remaining top ten causes of death. Only 1.4 percent of all deaths are caused by AIDS, which killed about 30,000 Americans in 1991. People aged 25 to 44—baby boomers—are most likely to die of AIDS. But even if a cure for AIDS is not discovered in the next few decades, this disease is likely to affect boomers much less in old age than it does today because, unfortunately, most of those with AIDS will already have died.

The key to aging gracefully is not avoiding death, but postponing illness for as long as possible. The growing concern of free agents with diet and fitness is an attempt to do just that. Today, these obsessions spring from the vanity of free agents. Their health consciousness will grow far beyond their waistlines, however, as the problems of aging begin to emerge. Free agents will pay sharp attention to health advice about diet and exercise in order to avoid disease and early death. The American diet has already begun to change as the public's knowledge of prevention grows, but eating habits will change more radically as aging free agents stop taking their health for granted. Low-fat foods will become the norm rather than the exception. Restaurants will routinely offer low-fat, low-cholesterol meals. Fruits, vegetables, and grains will become central to the American diet while meat moves off stage—a condiment rather than the centerpiece of a meal. These changes in eating habits and attitudes are likely to benefit free agents in old age.

Free agents will also benefit from technological devices that will enable them to remain independent far longer than the current generation of elderly. Today, 13 million Americans, more than half of them aged 65 or older, use what the National Center for Health Statistics calls "assistive technology devices." These devices range from simple things such as canes and braces to complex equipment such as wheelchairs, hearing aids, scooters, adapted automobiles, and handicapped-accessible computers.

The elderly now comprise the majority of the users of traditional devices, such as walkers. But free agents are already a major segment of the market for some of the newer devices such as scooters, TDD/TTY communications devices for the deaf, adapted automobiles, and handicapped-accessible computers. As technologically sophisticated free agents become increasingly disabled with age, and as the disabled become increasingly integrated into society, high-tech devices are likely to come into widespread use. This trend is already underway. The number of people using wheelchairs, for example, increased by 96 percent between 1980 and 1990.

America's housing is also likely to change as elderly free agents insist on independent living. Today, 7 million Americans have homes equipped with accessibility features, including ramps, elevators, hand rails, and extrawide doors. Not surprisingly, free agents are a large share of the population with specially adapted homes. Half of Americans who live in homes with ramps are under the age of 45. Nearly half of those living in homes with lowered counters or extrawide doors are also under the age of 45. Adapting homes to allow people to function independently will be a booming industry as free agents age. Because of these adaptations, most free agents will be able to remain independent well into advanced age.

But when failing health makes independent living impossible, free agents will depend on a multilevel support system to help them function. The first level of support will be family care. Today, 16 percent of people aged 65 or older who do not live in institutions need someone to help them with at least one of their daily activities, including help with bathing and dressing, getting around outside, preparing meals, doing housework, or keeping track of bills or money. The proportion rises with advancing age to 45 percent among people aged 85 or older.

The proportion of free agents who will depend on family care in old age is likely to be far smaller. Though families are the primary caretakers of the frail elderly today, baby boomers have relatively few children compared to their parents. In addition, daughters rather than sons are most likely to help out. Because many baby boomers have only one or two children, many have no daughters. And because the baby boom's daughters will be free agents pursuing their own careers, they may have little time to physically care for their elderly parents.

Free agents whose families cannot help out will have to depend on the second level of support: inhome care by paid caregivers. Inhome care is much less expensive than caring for someone in a nursing home. It is likely to become much more common as society struggles to bring health care costs under control and as more homes are equipped for the disabled.

The third level of support will be hotel-like communities where the ailing elderly can live in relative independence—in their own apartments, for example—but with necessary medical services nearby. Similar to nursing homes, these facilities will house people who can still get around and who are still alert, but who need more supervision than daily home visits can provide.

The fourth level of support for free agents will be nursing homes. These will be reserved for those truly in need of 24-hour medical supervision. Today, 22 percent of Americans aged 85 or older are in nursing homes. Among free agents, the proportion will be considerably smaller. Technological devices, family help, inhome caregivers, and health-care hotels will keep most free agents out of nursing homes. In addition, possible medical breakthroughs that could greatly reduce the incidence of dementia—the most common reason older people end up in nursing homes— may make institutional care less common.

As baby boomers become physically dependent with age, their life-style will depend on how much money they have. The affluent will equip their homes with assistive devices, hire inhome caregivers, or move to comfortable, hotel-like medical communities, perhaps joining their ailing friends there to reminisce about the good old days of the 1990s. The life-styles of the poor will be quite different. Many will already live with their children in three- or four-generation households, too poor to maintain their own homes or apartments. Family care will be much more common among the poor. But for those with no families or with families too busy to help out, nursing homes may be the only solution. Some of these sick and destitute free agents may opt for the fifth level of support: the right to die.

The right to die is at the heart of free agency itself—the power of each person to decide his or her own ultimate fate. The debate over the right to die may be raging in the medical establishment, but the issue has been settled in the minds of most Americans, particularly among the younger generations. Over half of Americans say people have a moral right to end their lives if they have an incurable disease or if they are in great pain. Americans under the age of 50 are much more likely than older Americans to believe suicide is acceptable under these circumstances. An even larger majority of Americans, 84 percent, want life support to be discontinued if there is no hope that they could recover from a serious illness. As free agents face the prospect of a lingering and painful death, the right to die will become encoded in the laws of the land. Those likely to be the sickest in old age and most likely to choose to die, will be the poorest free agents, those who by choice or circumstance lived for today during their middle years.

This grim finale will be the lot of a minority of baby boomers. For the majority, their obsession with health and fitness today will pay off in the decades to come. Most are likely to feel good in old age. Most will be able to live independently, without the help of others. Boomers may have to work much longer than their parents did, but at least they will be capable of working. And if the more roles people play the healthier they feel, then the boomers who must work well into their old age may end up being the healthiest of them all.

✤ 30 ✤

Spiritual Therapy

During the next two decades, the baby boom's parents will die and boomers will begin to head extended families. More of the boomers' friends will die, reminding them of their own mortality, their children will grow up and have children, and many boomers will succumb to chronic illness. These changes will challenge whatever peace of mind free agents achieved in middle age. It will create a psychological shock wave that will consume free agents and bring a new perspective to Americans. Free agents will begin an earnest search for the meaning of their life. The aging of free agents will bring a spiritual renewal to the United States in the twenty-first century.

Americans are one of the most religious people on earth, and free agents are no exception. The coming of age of the first generation of free agents has not changed Americans' basic religious beliefs. But it has changed the way people practice them.

As free agents have come of age, Americans have become much more cynical about religious institutions. The proportion of Americans who think religion can answer most of today's problems fell from 82 percent in 1957 to 63 percent in 1990. During those years, the share who thought the influence of religion on society was increasing fell from 69 to 39 percent.

But personal religious beliefs have barely budged. The proportion of Americans who believe in God is stable at more than 90 percent. The proportion who believe in an afterlife stood at 75 percent in 1957 and 71 percent in 1990. The proportion who have been to church in the past seven days has been steady at just over 40 percent for decades.

With the maturing of free agents, there has been a surprisingly small increase in the proportion of Americans who do not have a religious preference, from 5 percent in the early 1970s to 8 percent in 1990. A more significant shift has occurred in the proportion of people who say religion is "very important" in their own lives, falling from 75 percent in the 1950s to just over half in 1990. Free agents are less likely than older generations of Americans to say religion is very important in their lives today. Fifty-five percent of all Americans and 48 percent of baby boomers say religion is very important for them today. Among 18- to 29-year-olds, the figure is just 38 percent. But, interestingly, when baby boomers are asked to look into the future, 64 percent of them say religion will be more important in the coming years.

It is popular to claim that the baby boom generation has returned to its religious roots in middle age, now that it is raising children. But in fact, most of the boomers who abandoned their religious upbringing in their youth still have not returned to the church or temple. According to a survey by Wade Clark Roof, professor of religion and author of *A Generation of Seekers: The Spiritual Journeys of the Baby Boom Generation*, 96 percent of baby boomers were raised in a religious tradition. Of these, 58 percent abandoned that religion as young adults. Among these dropouts, only one-third (or 18 percent of all baby boomers) have returned to the fold. The remaining two-thirds of the dropouts (or 38 percent of all baby boomers) still are not involved in traditional religious activities.

But this does not mean they are not religious. In fact, many are, though both religious dropouts and returnees prefer the term *spiritual* to *religious*. Even among dropouts, 38 percent read the Bible and 30 percent practice daily prayer. Many baby boomers would describe their religion as a spiritual quest. In the future, a majority of baby boomers will embark on such a quest.

The profound changes baby boomers will experience in the coming decades, such as the death of their parents, the birth of their grandchildren, and the beginning of a new millennium, will drive them to search not for the meaning of life in general, but for the meaning of their own life in particular. While the coming exploration will take many shapes, in its most popular form it will blend the findings of psychology with the longings of religion, a unique mix of science and spirituality. We will see the emergence of a religion of individualism, or spiritual therapy. Self-obsessed free agents brought psychotherapy out of the closet and into dinner-table conversation. Now they are about to make it a religious experience. Like psychotherapy, spiritual therapy will be personal and private rather than institutional. Its answers will not be generic, but individual, explaining personal motivations and behavior. Its goal will not be the greater good, but to make free agents feel good about themselves, the lives they've led, and the legacy they leave behind.

This more personal approach to religious experience is already evident among younger Americans who are less tied to denomination, congregation, and traditional religious authority. Among members of mainline Protestant churches, for example, the proportion who say the institution of the church most helps them find meaning and purpose in life is above 70 percent among Americans aged 60 or older. But among people in their thirties, the proportion who find the institution most meaningful is just 53 percent, and among those in their twenties, it is just 44 percent. In contrast, private religious experience—rather than the institution of the church—is most helpful to 50 percent of those in their twenties and 40 percent of those in their thirties. Among those aged 50 and older, just one-quarter find the most meaning in private religious experience.

This private expression of faith will define the spiritual search in old age of the first generation of free agents. Denominational loyalties are weak among the majority of baby boomers, with a large proportion believing people should explore different religious traditions rather than stick to one faith. A minority of baby boomers say they are likely to spend more time in the years ahead attending religious services, reading the Bible, or being actively involved in their church. But half of baby boomers say they will spend more time exploring the basic meaning and value of their life.

This exploration will take them in diverse directions, reflecting the diversity of free agents themselves. A preview of what is in store can be found in bookstores today. *The Road Less Traveled*, a book mixing psychology, religion, and personal growth, has been on *The New York Times* best-seller list for over a decade, longer than any other book. Its critics claim that it is self-indulgence masquerading as a spiritual quest. But this is exactly the kind of spiritual search on which free agents will embark, one that allows them to focus on themselves.

Two other best-selling books, *The Tao of Pooh* and *The Te of Piglet*, by Benjamin Hoff, offer a combination of self-help and spiritual discovery, or "spiritual advice." This genre is a natural outgrowth of the 12-step recovery programs popularized by baby boomers in the past few decades. But as free agents age, the focus of their spiritual quest and of the books, magazines, multimedia computer disks, and support groups that follow, will be less about self-help and more about self-understanding. It will be less about changing themselves, their marriages, or their jobs, and more about accepting themselves, their children, and their circumstances as they are, with all their short-comings. There will be less advice and more affirmation of whatever decisions free agents made in their youth and middle age.

The mix of ideas in this spiritual quest will be eclectic. Some will be borrowed from eastern religions, which have already made significant inroads into the baby boom's religious perspectives. Reincarnation, for example, is believed in by 36 percent of religious dropouts, 23 percent of church returnees, and even by 19 percent of boomers who never rejected their religious traditions, according to Roof. Reincarnation is an ideal belief for highly individualistic free agents. It suggests that they will never die nor give up their place in the world, that they will continue to live on through one lifetime after another.

Grief therapy will also become widespread as free agents age, helping them accept the deaths of their parents, their spouses, their friends, and finally their own mortality. Old age consultants will be popular, too. They will help people determine the best life-style for their old age—recommending the best places to live, the type of community in which to live, the best approach to staying healthy, and how to manage their money through a lengthy retirement.

Baby boomers will also seize upon science as a quasireligious experience, particularly the small percentage of baby boomers who do not believe in some kind of God. During the next few decades, free agents raised during the race to the moon will be looking for life elsewhere in the universe. Their search will use instruments, such as radio signals, rather than manned vehicles. Books and other media that popularize the search, as well as the most recent scientific findings about the way the universe works, will satisfy many free agents' need for a deeper understanding of why things are the way they are. These preoccupations will keep some baby boomers from facing their own mortality and it will help others accept it.

Free agents will find the diverse spiritual quests of their old age immensely rewarding, helping to buoy their spirits when illness strikes or as death approaches. Though some free agents will despair at growing old, unable to cope with their aging bodies, most will find satisfaction in their final decades of life. They will enjoy looking back at how they reshaped America in their image. They will reflect on their power as a generation and try to help like-minded younger generations of free agents make their way into the future. Younger generations may not listen to their elders, but free agents have no one to blame but themselves. These are the children they taught to be independent.

Free agents were raised to think of themselves first and foremost. Old age will allow them to do so unencumbered by children, careers, or even spouses. They will have few obligations and more free time. But they will still be busy, this time with hobbies, travel, extended families, and spiritual pursuits. Even with their children grown and their careers ended, free agents will find plenty to do. The leisure opportunities of the personalized economy will grow far beyond what is available today when the giant baby boom generation has more leisure time. Even in retirement, free agents are likely to wonder how they will do everything they want to do each day. And they will wonder how they ever managed to go to work and raise children in the distant past— their middle age.

✤ VII ✤

FREE AGENTS, FOR BETTER OR WORSE?

❖ 31 ❖

The Final Judgment

There is little anyone can do to alter the ongoing evolution of society. The course society is on was established in countless ways over many decades. Just as the beating wings of a single butterfly can change weather patterns half a world away, so too the way people live today is the result of the combined actions taken by millions of people over hundreds of years. And just as it is impossible to change the weather, it is also impossible to stop or even significantly alter the direction of society's evolution.

Still, this has never prevented people from worrying about whether society is headed in the wrong direction. Is society changing for the better or for the worse? Are free agents and the personalized economy good or bad?

There are two ways of examining these questions: One is through the traditional perspective of equating the simple passage of time with human progress. This tradition assumes that human culture improves with age—new cultures are always superior to the ones preceding them. According to this viewpoint, agricultural economies improved on the hunter-gatherer economies they supplanted. In turn, the industrial economy was better than the agricultural system. The conclusion that must be drawn from this perspective is that free agents and the personalized economy are better for human society than the industrial economy they replace.

There is a contrarian view, however, and one that is increasingly popular today. In this view, human progress is not dependent on time. Some societies are better than others, and inferior cultures often replace superior ones. This perspective is at the core of the debate over the arrival of Columbus in the New World. Is this an event to be celebrated or mourned?

Of course, whether the evolution of human society is good or bad depends on how good and bad are defined. Is a "good" culture one that does the least environmental damage? Is a "bad" culture one that allows little personal freedom? Before a judgment can be made about free agents and the personalized economy, there must be a definition of what is good. A workable definition may be one devised by the nineteenth-century English philosopher John Stuart Mill. He defined a good society as one offering the "greatest happiness for the greatest number." With some editing of this definition to account for population growth (after all, one society should not be considered better than another simply because it has a larger population), the good society becomes one that offers "the greatest happiness for the greatest proportion of the population." By this definition, human society has not been on a steadily upward path, but has deviated from the ideal of "progress" a number of times in the past.

Perhaps the most significant deviation was the shift from a hunting and gathering to an agricultural economy. While the popular belief is that agriculture improved human life, in fact it made life much harder for many more people. The evidence lies in a comparison of the bones of ancient hunter-gatherers with those of ancient farmers. Anthropologists commonly find evidence of nutritional deficiencies in the bones of early agriculturists. In the bones of ancient hunters and gatherers, they rarely find evidence of nutritional problems. Farming populations are vulnerable to both nutritional deficiencies and famine because their diets are less varied than those of hunter-gatherers, often limited to a few food types. Hunter-gatherers, in contrast, are much less likely to experience famine or nutritional deficiencies because they eat a large variety of foods.

Agricultural societies are also vulnerable to infectious disease because their populations are larger than those of hunter-gatherers. Most infectious diseases require a large "host" population to survive. Hunter-gatherers are less vulnerable to infectious disease because they live in small, isolated bands where infectious disease cannot establish a foothold. The anthropological evidence suggests that life expectancy—which is one measure of the "greatest happiness for the greatest number"—actually declined as human societies shifted from hunting and gathering to farming.

Industrialization improved life for millions of people. It improved the production and distribution of food and it supported scientific advances that eradicated many infectious diseases. It allowed millions of people to escape poverty and join a burgeoning middle class, which eventually included the majority of the populations of the United States and many other Western countries. By Mill's definition, the "greatest happiness for the greatest number" may have reached its zenith in the United States during the three decades following World War II. Then, the middle class was growing rapidly, infectious diseases such as measles and tuberculosis were fast disappearing, poverty rates were falling, and life expectancy was climbing.

Some might disagree with this point, arguing that the decades following World War II were good for some people, but difficult for others. Life was good for white males who followed the rules. For blacks, women, singles, gays, the disabled, and anyone else who deviated from the rigid norms of the time, life was not so good. These critics believe society can do better. The emergence of free agents and the personalized economy may be a step in that direction.

Will the personalized economy offer greater happiness for a greater number? The case can be argued either way. Free agents are transforming society in both good and bad ways. Though the bad (i.e., high rates of divorce and violent crime) seems overwhelming today, some of the worst characteristics of the personalized economy are a consequence of the transition between two ways of life. Until the transition is complete, it is difficult to judge whether free agents will create a better society, whether the personalized economy will be a boon to the billions or a new dark age in human history.

One bit of evidence is reassuring. Despite all the changes of the past few decades, Americans are as happy now as they were nearly forty years ago when social scientists began to keep detailed records of their emotional well-being. In spite of social and economic turmoil, there has been virtually no change in the proportion of Americans who say they are happy. Consistently, about one-third of Americans say they are "very" happy; slightly more than half claim they are "pretty" happy; only about one in ten say they are unhappy. In 1957 these proportions were 35, 54, and 11 percent, respectively. In 1991, in the midst of recession and a serious bout of national pessimism, the proportions were nearly identical, at 31, 58, and 11 percent, respectively. Since these proportions have held steady through dramatic social, economic, and technological change, it may be fair to say that happiness has not yet suffered at the hands of free agents.

But this may not hold true in the future. The intrinsic nature of free agency creates social problems that must be resolved before the next stage of human history improves upon the past. Solving these problems will require a rethinking of the way in which society works. Before free agents can become eager participants in the nation's future, governments must harness their self-interest and put it to work collectively for the public interest.

THE TRAUMA OF DIVORCE

Divorce is the most obvious social problem resulting from the independent nature of free agents. Divorce is now commonplace among Americans under the age of 50. Consequently, free agents have replaced traditional nuclear families with a diversity of matriarchal families. Within their matriarchal families, women play all the roles—they are breadwinners, nurturers, and family heads. In contrast, men are shadowy figures with little permanence in many families.

Most Americans today would argue that matriarchal families are less desirable than nuclear families. Typically, they are much poorer than nuclear families, and the children of single-parent families are often traumatized by divorce. On the other hand, social science studies show that the emotional well-being of children raised by never-married mothers is nearly as good as that of children raised by happy couples, and certainly better than that of children raised by parents who are unhappily married. The evidence suggests that single-parent families do not hurt children. Rather, it is the conditions too often associated with single-parent families—poverty and divorce—that harm children.

While these are serious problems, their overwhelming nature today may stem in part from society's transition from divorce as the exception to divorce as the norm. Society has yet to find a role for divorced spouses, and so children often lose a parent when spouses divorce. Some baby boomers have managed to include divorced spouses in their complex extended families. Many free agents speak, sometimes fondly, of their in-laws and their ex-laws. Former spouses and their families can be integrated into modern family life. In some cases, this integration is occurring through the personal efforts of ex-spouses to remain friends despite differences or because of the children. In other cases, it is occurring by order of the court. Across the country, the courts are awarding grandparents visitation rights to their grandchildren. A handful of states now prevent spouses who have custody of the children from moving out of state. Better enforcement of child support awards will improve the financial situation of single parents, especially when child-support payments can be routinely and automatically withdrawn from the noncustodial spouse's paycheck. As society adapts to divorce socially, economically, and legally, the traumas are likely to ease.

THE THREAT OF LONELINESS

Another potential problem for free agents is the risk of emotional isolation as more people live alone. So far, however, loneliness does not seem to be growing. Matriarchal family ties appear to be just as strong if not stronger than those of nuclear families. Friendships also count just as much as they once did. The proportion of people who are very satisfied with their friendships has not changed appreciably in decades. And surveys reveal that Americans are getting more comfortable doing things by themselves.

Only 3 percent of Americans say they have no close friends, according to a Gallup poll. Three out of four are satisfied with the number of friends they have, and eight out of ten are satisfied with the closeness of their friendships.

Regardless of age, only about 10 percent of Americans say they frequently feel lonely. Television, telephones, and frequent get-togethers with family and friends appear to do an adequate job of linking free agents together. With the likely widespread adoption of personal communication devices, the threat of loneliness could diminish in the future. Lonely or not, however, at least no one will be alone, except those who voluntarily flip the switch for a little peace and quiet.

THE CONFLICT BETWEEN WORK AND FAMILY

The fast-paced, competitive, personalized economy demands more work for less pay. For this reason, virtually all adults between the ages of 20 and 60 must work. A larger proportion of Americans are in the work force than ever before, including a majority of women with infants. The demands of the personalized economy create enormous stresses on families raising children.

Some of these stresses are transitional, arising because the workplace has not yet adapted to the new families of free agents. These conflicts are likely to ease once the workplace offers employees greater flexibility in getting their jobs done. With health insurance coverage extended to all Americans, more may choose part-time employment while their children are young. Flextime and work-at-home options will also make the scheduling of daily life less complex.

Advances in telecommunications will allow many more people to work at home yet interact with coworkers as if they were in an office. Home offices of the future may include an entire wall covered with multiple flat-panel television screens. Each screen will display a coworker. Colleagues can see and communicate with one another instantaneously just as they do in the office. One of the video panels may be trained on a day-care center. Through the video link, parents can communicate with their children while they are at work. In this way, families will be able to spend their day emotionally close though physically remote. Coworkers will enjoy the camaraderie of the office from the comfort of home.

THE POLARIZATION OF INCOMES

The diversity of free agents has polarized incomes. The middle class has been shrinking, while more people join the ranks of the rich and others slip into poverty. Though there are indications that this polarization stabilized in the late 1980s, it is not likely to reverse because of the diversity of skills and life-styles among free agents.

The consequence of this polarization is chronic poverty. Poverty rates have been creeping upwards for over a decade. But it is difficult to ascertain whether chronic poverty is a transitional problem or an intractable part of the personalized economy. The current welfare system does not offer incentives to draw poverty-stricken free agents away from their dependence on welfare. In fact, Americans who choose to rely on welfare today are making a rational economic choice. Why give up government-paid health insurance for a low-paying job that offers no health insurance? Why drop off children at a day-care center when the cost of day care slices take-home pay below the level of a welfare check? Until incentives are put in place, chronic poverty will continue. With the right incentives, it is likely that welfare dependency will be far less common, and poverty will be a far more temporary condition than it is today.

THE LACK OF SKILLS

Most Americans believe the public schools are failing to prepare students for work in today's economy. This realization is a good sign, indicating that the educational system is about to change, ending this transitional problem.

The personalized economy demands a much more highly trained worker than did the industrial economy, which demanded little more of workers than their physical presence on an assembly line. Many of those assembly-line jobs are now done by machine. Today's factory work force must know how to design, operate, and maintain those machines. With fewer middle managers, blue- and white-collar workers must think for themselves rather than do what the boss tells them to do. With the economy changing rapidly, workers must be able to apply their knowledge in a variety of settings. They must be flexible enough to cope with several career changes throughout their lives. They must be familiar with the ever present and ever changing computer, and they must be able to manipulate the basic resource of the personalized economy—information.

The problem is that the public schools are still producing assembly-line workers for an industrial economy. Employers complain that high school graduates are not qualified to do the work that must be done. Their complaint is valid. While high school graduates are no less educated than they used to be, employers need workers with more skills than ever before.

In 1960, most Americans were high school dropouts. In that year, only 41 percent of adults even had a high school diploma. Today, 78 percent have a high school degree. In 1960, only 8 percent of Americans had been to college for at least four years. Today the proportion is 21 percent. More Americans are better educated than ever before. Not only do educational attainment statistics support this claim, but there are other indicators as well. The proportion of Americans currently reading a book or novel climbed from 21 percent of the public in 1949 to 37 percent in 1990. The proportion who have bookcases or bookshelves in their homes—one possible sign of a more educated public—climbed from just 58 percent in 1953 to 84 percent in 1990.

Even the well-publicized declines in average S.A.T. scores are largely an artifact of the growing diversity of students who take the test. In 1941, when the S.A.T. was first established, only 11,000 students took the test, most of them affluent white males. In 1990, over 1 million students took the test, a large share of them minorities and the poor. Between 1980 and 1990, S.A.T. scores rose within nearly every racial and ethnic group. But because more of the test takers were disadvantaged minorities, their lower (but rising) scores pulled down the overall averages.

The problem is not that Americans are less educated than they used to be, but that they need to be much better educated to do the work required of them. The public school system has not failed outright so much as it has failed to make the transition to training workers for a new economy.

The ten fastest-growing occupations between 1990 and 2005, according to projections by the Bureau of Labor Statistics, will be home health aides (trained workers who provide inhome health care services); paralegals; computer scientists; personal and home care aides (workers who provide a variety of light housekeeping tasks for those in need of home care); physical therapists; medical assistants; operations research analysts; human service workers; radiology technicians; and medical secretaries. All but one of these occupations (personal and home care aides) require highly specialized skills, including computer literacy and the ability to manipulate information.

The ten occupations that are projected to have the largest job growth between 1990 and 2005 are retail sales, registered nurses, cashiers, general office clerks, truckdrivers, general managers, janitors, nursing aides, food counter workers, and waiters and waitresses. While these ten jobs are likely to be plentiful, most are dead ends. The two that offer the most financial opportunity (nurses and managers) again require specialized skills.

The Bureau of Labor Statistics projections make two things clear. One, finding a job in the personalized economy won't be hard for those willing to work at McDonald's or drive a truck. Two, prospering in the personalized economy will be much more difficult, requiring specialized training, computer literacy, and the ability to extract and manipulate information. This is what the public schools must teach the nation's children if the country wants citizens who can cope with the new economy.

The public outcry about the educational system will bring about much-needed change. Public schools are likely to become more European in style, with specialized apprenticeship programs for high school students who might otherwise drop out and for those who do not want to go on to college. These programs will train people to do the work of the personalized economy (medical diagnostics, computer programming, and computer-aided design, for example). They will replace the industrial training programs of today (carpentry, auto repair, and typing). Worker retraining will become a much more significant part of the nation's overall economy, with free agents learning to cope with several career changes during their lifetimes.

THE DANGER OF CRIME

Crime is an intrinsic problem of a society run by free agents because there are fewer universally agreed upon social norms that keep people in line. With free agents following their own drummer, some of those drummers are likely to be dangerous.

There are two possible scenarios for the future of crime in the United States. The optimistic scenario is that crime, now common in the nation's inner cities, will be reduced when economic opportunities are brought to inner city residents. With few legitimate jobs available to today's urban poor, many opt for a life of crime, a rational economic decision. If those living in the inner cities can be included in the personalized economy, they will be able to earn a living legitimately and the crime wave may ebb.

But that's a big if: The personalized economy may be leaving whole segments of the population behind. If true, the worst-case scenario is that criminals will become domestic terrorists on a national scale. Daily life could become feudal in nature. Like barons of the Middle Ages, gangs will divide the country into territories. Citizens will have to buy protection by paying off the local gang. Life will become even more violent and dangerous than it is today. Only those rich enough to live in security compounds and drive bullet-proof cars will be free from the feudal power structure.

If the personalized economy cannot make room for the most disadvantaged Americans, free agents face a frightening future. Already, a whole generation of inner-city Americans has been left behind, unlikely ever to catch up. If the educational system can change fast enough, today's inner-city children may be saved, channeled into productive careers rather than abandoned to the streets.

THE POWER OF THE MEDIA

In the personalized economy, most interactions are between strangers rather than between friends, neighbors, or even acquaintances. To cope successfully with so many anonymous interactions, free agents must know something about the people with whom they interact. This explains why demographic information, opinion polls, and attitude surveys have such a hold on society, and it explains why the media have become so powerful.

The anonymity of the personalized economy makes people dependent on the media to explain the increasingly complex world. This wasn't always the role of the media, according to historical studies. The media now place news stories in a broader context than they once did, presenting them as social problems or trends rather than as individual events. This point is borne out in a comparison of the front pages of newspapers a century ago with those of today, according to an analysis by K. G. Barnhurst and J. C. Nerone. A century ago, the front page of a newspaper was densely packed with diverse stories that left readers to draw their own conclusions. In newspapers today, the front page is much simpler in design, offering readers a few major stories. Rather than simply reporting events, the stories attempt to give readers the "big picture." If a house burns down, explains Barnhurst, it is no longer a singular event, but evidence of a chronic wiring problem in the nation's aging housing stock.

This power of the media to present the "big picture" creates a problem for free agents who are easily manipulated by well-crafted messages. Those who put together compelling stories can capture enormous audiences. This is the tactic used almost daily by sophisticated special interest groups as they try to promote the needs of their constituencies. From the National Organization for Women (NOW) to the National Rifle Association (NRA), special interest groups harvest demographic and economic statistics from the millions produced by the personalized economy. They process these statistics into studies and market them to the press in time for the morning headlines or the evening news. The hotly competitive media is eager to play along, exposing the public to a constant barrage of reports about how poorly women (NOW), or gun-owning Americans (NRA), or children (Children's Defense Fund), or the elderly (AARP) or some other constituency is faring in society.

For free agents, the consequence is emotional paralysis, the feeling that problems are enormous and hopelessly complex. Because problems seem insoluble, people give up, becoming apathetic and alienated. This inertia already plagues Americans, preventing them from applying proven solutions to costly problems. For example, the Head Start program is known to aid disadvantaged children, yet funding for Head Start was cut sharply in the 1980s with no public outcry. Childhood immunizations save lives and reduce health care costs, yet until recently, participation in immunization programs was shrinking with little protest.

Public inertia is one of the greatest problems politicians face today. If they want public support for their programs, they must break through the public's paralysis. This will require the utmost political skill. Politicians need to produce their own well-crafted messages of hope and progress. Most important, politicians will have to convince free agents that it is in their best interest to support initiatives. If those in power can do this, they may motivate free agents to do their part in solving society's problems.

THE OBSTACLE OF SELF-INTEREST

Free agents are motivated by self-interest. They are unwilling to sacrifice their own comfort for the common good or even for their own good in the future. An example is the failure of free agents to save for their own retirement. Baby boomers are loath to sacrifice any portion of their paycheck today for a more comfortable old age.

There is a way around this problem. The self-interest of free agents must be seen as a tool rather than an obstacle. This can be done through a system of rewards and punishments. If free agents are paid for being good and punished for being bad, they will pay attention. The solution to the savings problem is to reward free agents for saving money. The tax-deductible Individual Retirement Account (IRA) was just such a device, but its rewards were reduced in the mid-1980s to the point where most Americans no longer benefited from them. When an expanded IRA makes a comeback, free agents will again have an incentive to save for the future. That's when the saving rate will begin to rise again.

The self-interest of free agents also gets in the way of the common good. This can be seen in Americans' attitudes toward the environment. On the one hand, most Americans say they want a clean environment, on the other hand, they're unwilling to sacrifice for it. Free agents are armchair environmentalists— demanding that someone else do something about the problem while they sit in comfort. Most free agents aren't willing to change their life-style to save the earth.

Nearly eight out of ten Americans call themselves environmentalists, according to a Gallup poll, but few sacrifice for the cause. They want the government to force businesses to clean up their act, but they are unwilling to do anything about their own. Most Americans are not willing to carpool, for example. Only 5 percent take public transportation to work, according to the 1990 census, down from 6 percent in 1980. Most Americans are not willing to pay more for environmentally safe products. A minority return bottles or cans, recycle newspapers, sort trash, buy biodegradable products, or buy products in refillable packaging. Among the good Samaritans who do return bottles or recycle newspapers, most do so only because they get money in return or they are required to do so by law.

Free agents support the common good only if it does not adversely affect them, and if it adversely affects others, that is not their problem. From cutting the federal deficit to siting landfills, free agents demand action when they are immune from the consequences. They block action if they must make the sacrifice. Finding a way to make the self-interests of free agents work for the public good will require a realistic approach toward the attitudes of free agents. It is fruitless to pretend that free agents are altruistic when they are primarily concerned with their own well-being. It is also fruitless to exhort free agents to sacrifice for the good of society because that's a sacrifice they won't make. Instead, the nation's leaders must develop a workable system of rewards and punishments that will harness the self-interests of free agents and move society forward.

THE NEED FOR GOVERNMENT

With few social norms to guide them, free agents must put order back into society through law. This is paradoxical in a way because free agents have been rebelling against rules all their lives.

Now they desperately need them. Free agents don't need just any law, however, but rules and regulations that support their way of life.

Government, so far, has been slow to respond. Consequently, free agents often ignore government, refusing to answer censuses and surveys, cheating on taxes, and often making a living in defiance of government regulations. An increasing number of businesses operate illegally, finding fertile ground in today's competitive business environment. A part of the underground economy, these businesses typically sell legal products and services but in defiance of government regulations or tax collectors.

All types of businesses can be found in the underground economy. This economy includes gypsy cabs that operate without a license, nightclubs that operate without the proper permits, street vendors who sell handcrafted products and pocket their take without reporting it to the tax collector. It includes baby-sitters, car mechanics, house cleaners, and others who make money on the side and don't report the income. A small portion of the underground economy consists of illegal businesses—drug dealing, prostitution, bookmaking, car theft, and organized crime.

The underground economy is growing as companies shed workers, subcontracting many of the tasks once performed in-house. This restructuring gives Americans more reasons and opportunities to work off the books, maintaining their slim profit margins by avoiding taxes and regulatory costs.

The biggest problem created by the underground economy is the defiance of government regulations that ensure public safety. The consequences of ignoring safety rules can be disastrous, as was the case in the 1991 nightclub fire in New York City that killed over 80 people. The nightclub was illegal because it did not have a license. One of the reasons it did not have a license is that it had only one exit. People died because the sole exit was blocked by fire.

Government regulatory authorities enforce building and fire codes, the safety of the food supply, and the health and safety of workers and citizens alike. As more businesses try to duck the regulators, enforcement becomes harder and more costly, and public safety erodes.

Rather than treat free agents like criminals, governments must rethink their approach to regulation. They need to reexamine their rules and regulations, continually updating them to make them responsive to the new economic and social realities. Currently there are many regulations still on the books in communities across the country that were designed for the industrial economy, examples of which are laws prohibiting people from working in their homes. These regulations were established decades ago to prevent illegal manufacturing operations that could have weakened the power of unions, endangered workers, and turned residential areas into industrial zones. Today these regulations are in direct conflict with the realities of the personalized economy, where millions of people work quietly at home on their computers.

Once governments update their rules and regulations, they need to do something business has been doing for years: they need to market themselves to the public, explaining the rationale behind their rules and regulations. Governments must continually remind people of how the law—specific rules and regulations— benefits them.

Third, governments must offer rewards for compliance as well as punishment for defiance. Governments could offer tax credits or discounts on government services (such as garbage collection) for businesses with up-to-date permits or licenses. Reward structures such as these appeal to the self-interest of free agents and make them willing, if not eager, participants in enforcement. The federal government's child and dependent care tax credit is one such example. This credit encourages people to hire legal rather than illegal day-care providers. But this reward system is not yet fully operational. The burdensome paperwork required of parents who hire household help discourages millions of Americans from obeying the law.

The political alienation of many free agents today stems in part from the slow transition governments at all levels are making to the new economy. The bureaucratic structures of the industrial economy are getting in the way of the fast pace of the personalized economy, hindering people rather than helping them. Just as businesses have gotten leaner and meaner, governments too must act faster by putting more power into the hands of their front-line representatives. And government officials must change their attitudes, learning to please rather than obstruct the public, their customers. This is not just the latest rhetoric of management theory, but a real change in the role of government brought about by the personalized economy.

If government authorities see themselves as educators rather than regulators, the attitudes of citizens toward government will change. City building departments, for example, could vastly improve their image in the eyes of the public (and perhaps lower the costs of enforcement) through education. Building departments need to market themselves to the public by repeatedly explaining their benefits—in brochures distributed to the public, in newspaper columns, on local television stations, in community seminars, and so on. The public, developers and private citizens alike, must hear the message that the building department is there to help them build safely. The department is there to shield them from lawsuits in case of fire or some other problem. Inspection reports can show that they followed proper procedures, for example. This change in perspective, from enforcer to educator and benefactor, would not cost much. And it would lower enforcement costs by encouraging the public to participate in rather than hide from government regulation.

SAVED BY THE BYTE

The almost daily technological miracles spewed out by the rapidly changing personalized economy promise a better life for many people. New technologies give people more control over their lives, from the mother who can stay in constant contact with her children because she carries a cellular phone, to the disabled worker who can earn a living with the assistance of a computer.

The personalized economy is also less damaging to the environment than was the industrial economy—E-mail and word processing save a lot of paper. Computer-controlled thermostats programmed to regulate temperatures in different zones of a building save heating and cooling costs. Miniaturized products use less raw material. The more powerful the microchip, the fewer natural resources society consumes. The first computer filled an entire room. Now much more powerful computers are carried in briefcases.

If the social problems created by free agents can be tackled and solved, human society could be far better in the future than at any previous time in the past. Free agents are highly dependent on technology, to be sure, but technology itself is cheap, abundant, and readily available.

There is only one catch: people must be able to use the technology of the personalized economy. Those who cannot use computers, telephones, faxes, modems, and their successors will fall by the wayside. In a society of free agents, that wayside is likely to offer little comfort.

In any society, there is a body of knowledge and an array of technologies that must be mastered before people succeed. Hunter-gatherers must know about plants and roots and how to throw a spear. Farmers must know how to plant and plow. Factory workers must know how to assemble parts and work as a team. In each economy, those who cannot learn to do the work of the society become wards of that society. Many die young, while others are cared for by their families. Some become homeless, while others turn to crime.

In the personalized economy, people must know how to use computers even as the meaning of "computer" changes every few years, from mainframes to desktop machines to notebooks to the forthcoming generation of personal digital assistants. People must also know how to manipulate the flow of information, using it to their advantage, from helping them gain a competitive edge in the business world to marketing themselves to employers or clients.

The public schools should teach children how to use computers and manipulate information, along with reading, writing, and arithmetic. Once children learn the basics, vocational programs, colleges and universities, and job training programs can teach teenagers and young adults the specialized skills needed for prosperity. With the educational system preparing people for the personalized economy, this new era in human history has the potential to bring the greatest happiness to the greatest number of people.

To make this potential a reality requires three things: One, it requires acceptance—Americans must accept the fact that their society is in the process of evolving into a new economic order. This evolution cannot be reversed, and attempting to reverse it will be self-defeating since these changes are inevitable.

The second requirement is a willingness to rebuild the institutions of society to work with rather than against free agents. Americans must accept that free agents are motivated by self-interest. They must be willing to establish a system of rewards and punishments that appeal to those self-interests. Then free agents will work together for their own good and, while they're at it, do good for society as a whole.

The third requirement is time. A transition from one economic order to another does not happen overnight. It requires at least two generations. The still powerful communally oriented older generations of Americans will slowly be replaced by free agents. This replacement is occurring now. As more baby boomers gain political and corporate power over the next decade, the rebuilding of society can begin in earnest, a process that is likely to take an additional generation to complete. In approximately thirty years, the first generation of free agents, the baby boomers, will be the nation's elders. They will guide a changing society, but the work of change will be up to the middle aged, their children. Their grandchildren and great-grandchildren will then reap the benefits of a society that supports a diverse, fast-paced, competitive, and fiercely independent way of life, the life of free agents.

Notes

Introduction

2   In 1941, on the eve of America's entry into World War II . . . Lisa Grunwald, "How America Lived the Day Before Disaster," *Life* (Fall 1991), 20.

Chapter 1: The Thrill Is Gone

7   By the early 1990s, over 80 percent . . . "How Deep Is Our Discontent?" *The Public Perspective* (July/August 1992), 91, 93.

9   Most Americans think middle age . . . Eliot Glazer and Cadwell Davis Partners, "Feelings About Age, Part III," cited in *Research Alert* (10 January 1986), 4.

9   So far, few baby boomers have . . . George Gallup, Jr. and Frank Newport, "Baby-boomers Seek More Family Time," *The Gallup Poll Monthly* (April 1991), 37.

Chapter 2: The Birth of the Baby Boom

12 Interestingly, women of that time . . . William F. Pratt, William D. Mosher, Christine A. Bachrach, and Marjorie C. Horn, "Understanding U.S. Fertility: Findings from the National Survey of Family Growth, Cycle III, " *Population Bulletin*, vol 39, no. 5 (1984), 31.

13   The code word for conformity . . . Barbara Ehrenreich, *The Hearts of Men—American Dreams and the Flight From Commitment* (Garden City, NY: Doubleday/Anchor Books, 1983), 17.

13   Marriage was so highly valued . . . Joseph Veroff, Elizabeth Douvan, and Richard A. Kulka, *The Inner American—A Self Portrait from 1957 to 1976* (New York: Basic Books, 1981), 147.

13   As of 1990, more than one-third . . . Arthur J. Norton and Louisa F. Miller, "Marriage, Divorce, and Remarriage in the 1990s," U.S. Bureau of the Census, *Current Population Reports*, series P-23, no. 180 (October 1992), 3.

13   Americans' enthusiasm for big families . . . Richard G. Niemi, John Mueller, and Tom W. Smith, *Trends in Public Opinion—A Compendium of Survey Data* (New York: Greenwood Press, 1989), 269.

13   Today the proportion favoring large . . . George H. Gallup, Jr. and Frank Newport, "Virtually All Adults Want Children, but Many of the Reasons Are Intangible," *The Gallup Poll Monthly* (June 1990), 10.

14   Most American favored laws against . . . Niemi, Mueller, and Smith, *Trends in Public Opinion*, 170–171, 174.

Chapter 3: The Baby Boom Breaks the Rules

15   Though the baby boom is associated . . . Andrew Kohut and Larry Hugick, "Woodstock Remembered—Twenty Years Later, Woodstock Era Gets Mixed Reviews," *The Gallup Report* (August 1989), 25.

16   A glimpse into these facts of life . . . Ira Robinson, Ken Ziss, Bill Ganza, Stuart Katz, and Edward Robinson, "Twenty Years of the Sexual Revolution, 1965–1985: An Update," *Journal of Marriage & the Family*, vol 53, no. 1 (February 1991), 216–220.

16   Americans now in their forties have . . . Tom W. Smith, "Adult Sexual Behavior in 1989: Number of Partners, Frequency of Intercourse and Risk of AIDS," *Family Planning Perspectives*, vol 23, no. 3 (May/June 1991), 103.

16   Only 28 percent of women aged 20 . . . U.S. Bureau of the Census, "Marital Status and Living Arrangements: March 1990," *Current Population Reports*, Series P-20, no. 450 (May 1991), 2.

17 Nearly half of women now in their thirties . . . Kathryn A. London, "Cohabitation, Marriage, Marital Dissolution, and Remarriage: United States, 1988," National Center for Health Statistics *Advance Data*, no. 194 (4 January 1991), 3.

17 People who bought homes in the . . . U.S. Bureau of the Census, 5; and U.S. Bureau of the Census, *Statistical Abstract of the United States: 1991*, 111th edition (Washington, DC: U.S. Government Printing Office, 1991), 732.

18 In fact, men born in 1946 . . . U.S. Bureau of the Census, "Educational Attainment in the United States: March 1991 and 1990," *Current Population Reports*, Series P-20, no. 462 (May 1992), 17.

18 Among people aged 65 or older . . . "The People, the Press and Politics—Campaign '92: 'The Generations Divide,' Survey VIII," Times Mirror Center for the People & the Press, News Release (8 July 1992), 40.

18 When the baby boom came of age . . . U.S. Bureau of the Census, "Projections of the Voting-Age Population, for States: November 1992," *Current Population Reports*, Series P-25, no. 1085 (April 1992), 13.

19 More elementary schools were built . . . "Perspectives on the Baby Boom Generation," Interfunctional Management Program, Rutgers University Graduate School of Management (April 1991), 3.

Chapter 5: The First Free Agent

27 Curt Flood had no inkling . . . Richard Sandomir, "Baseball and N.B.A. Got It, So Does N.F.L." *The New York Times* (7 January 1993), B15.

27 In the 16 seasons between . . . Frederick C. Klein, "One for the Record Books: Twins Inch by Braves," *The Wall Street Journal* (29 October 1991), A20.

28 Sociologists define individualism . . . Norval D. Glenn, "From Communalism to Individualism," *The Public Perspective* (May/June 1990), 3.

28 The "communitarian" movement . . . Peter Steinfels, "A Political Movement Blends Its Ideas from Left and Right," *The New York Times* (24 May 1992), E6.

Chapter 6: Technology and Individualism

31   The dependence of neighbor upon . . . Margaret Mooney Marini, "The Rise of Individualism in Advanced Industrial Societies," paper presented at the Population Association of American Annual Meeting, Toronto (May 1990), 19.

31   In this type of society, says Marini . . . Ibid., 28.

Chapter 7: The First Generation of Free Agents

33   The rise of this individualistic . . . Grunwald "How America Lived," 24.

34   Eighty percent of women college . . . Eric L. Dey, Alexander W. Astin, and William S. Korn, *The American Freshman: Twenty-Five Year Trends* (Los Angeles: Higher Education Research Institute, UCLA, (1991), 92.

34   Among men, these two goals . . . Ibid, 62.

34   By the early 1980s, when the last . . . Ibid., 93.

34   Among men, those citing money-making . . . Ibid., 63.

34   In fact, independence was the single . . . Duane F. Alwin, "Historical Changes in Parental Orientations to Children," *GSS Social Change Report*, No. 28 (Chicago: National Opinion Research Center, 1987), 32.

34   In 1890, just 16 percent of parents . . . Ibid., 30.

35   The parents of 1958 scored . . . Ibid., 32.

35   In 1990, 51 percent of college . . . Dey, Astin, and Korn "The American Freshman," 102–103.

36   Seventy-three percent of 1990 college freshmen . . . Ibid., 112–113.

36   The proportion of freshmen who think . . . Ibid., 122–123.

36   The proportion of college freshmen . . . Ibid., 120–121.

36   The proportion who want to keep up . . . Ibid., 122–123.

36   And the share who plan on marrying . . . Ibid., 120–121.

36   Well over half of today's young . . . "Time/CNN Poll Findings on Post-Boomers," Yankelovich Clancy Shulman, as cited in *Research Alert* (30 November 1990), 6.

36 Americans with college degrees . . . U.S. Bureau of the Census, "What's It Worth? Educational Background and Economic Status: Spring 1990," *Current Population Reports*, Series P-70, no. 32 (January 1993), 5.

37 One in four men and women . . . U.S. Bureau of the Census, "Educational Attainment in the United States: March 1991 and 1990," 7.

Chapter 8: The Next Generation of Free Agents

39 Today's parents rate raising children . . . Alwin "Historical Changes," 32.

40 Over half of new mothers today . . . U.S. Bureau of the Census, "Fertility of American Women: June 1990," *Current Population Reports*, Series P-20, no. 454 (October 1991), 5.

40 Sixty-three percent of children under . . . U.S. Bureau of the Census, "Who's Minding the Kids? Child Care Arrangements: Fall 1988," *Current Population Reports*, Series P-70, no. 30 (August 1992), 6.

40 Only 61 percent of children today . . . National Center for Health Statistics, "Family Structure and Children's Health: United States, 1988," *Vital and Health Statistics*, Series 10, no. 178 (June 1991), 6.

41 Of the twenty-one meals people eat . . . "The Four Faces of the American Family," *Parents*, cited in *Research Alert* (Winter 1991), 6.

41 It is no coincidence that the first . . . James McNeal, "Children as Customers," *American Demographics* (September 1990), 36.

41 Today, children aged 4 to 12 have . . . Valerie Reitman, "Those Little Kids Have Big Pockets," *The Wall Street Journal* (26 August 1992), B1.

41 By the age of 7, most children . . . McNeal "Children as Customers," 39.

42 More than half of 18 to 24 year . . . U.S. Bureau of the Census, "Marital Status and Living Arrangements: March 1991," *Current Population Reports*, Series P-20, no. 461 (April 1992), 11.

42   In fact, those most likely . . . Joyce Munsch, Phyllis Moen, Donna
     Dempster-McClain, Robin M. Williams Jr., "Refilling the Empty
     Nest: Family and Maternal Characteristics as Predictors of
     the Return of Young Adults," presentation at the Population Associ-
     ation of America Annual Meeting, Washington, D.C. (March
     1991).

42   A growing share of students is . . . Joseph Berger, "Dropout Rate
     Down Sharply for New York Schools," *The New York Times* (20 May
     1992), B2.

42   On average, it takes today's college . . . U.S. Bureau of the Census,
     "What's It Worth?" 7; Martha Farnsworth Riche, "The Boomerang
     Age," *American Demographics* (May 1990), 30.

42   Demographers report that there's . . . Arland Thornton, Linda
     Young-DeMarco, and Frances Goldscheider, "Living Arrangements
     During the Transition to Adulthood," paper presented at the Popu-
     lation Association of American Annual Meeting, Washington, DC
     (March 1991), 1.

43   A majority of high school seniors . . . Office of Educational Re-
     search and Improvement, U.S. Department of Education, *Youth
     Indicators 1991—Trends in the Well-Being of American Youth* (Washing-
     ton, DC: U.S. Government Printing Office, 1991), 132.

Chapter 9: Free Agents around the World

45   In Germany, Great Britain, and Italy . . . Alwin, "Historical
     Changes," 38.

46   Surveys in Italy, the United Kingdom . . . Rena Bartos, *Marketing to
     Women Around the World* (Boston: Harvard Business School Press,
     1989), 21.

46   In a British survey . . . Roger Jowell, Sharon Witherspoon, Lindsay
     Brook, *British Social Attitudes: The 5th Report* (London: Social and
     Community Planning Research, Gower Publishing Company Lim-
     ited, 1988), 189.

46   Countries where women's labor . . . Cheryl Russell, "The Post-Wall
     Consumer: Europe's Baby Boom Generation," *Market: Europe*, Spe-
     cial Report (January 1991), 8.

47 In the United States, spending on leisure . . . U.S. Department of Commerce, *Survey of Current Business* (July 1992), 59.

47 In Switzerland, households spend . . . Euromonitor, *European Marketing Data and Statistics 1991*, 25th edition (London, Euromonitor, 1990), 246–247.

47 Nine Western European countries . . . Russell, "Post-Wall Consumer," 8.

Chapter 10: On a Collision Course

50 The average supermarket carries . . . Diane Crispell, "Myths of the 1950s," *American Demographics* (August 1992), 43.

51 Fully 82 percent of mothers . . . Norval D. Glenn, "What Does Family Mean?" *American Demographics* (June 1992), 36.

51 Americans rank having a happy . . . "Personal Values," *Roper Reports 89-1* (New York: The Roper Organization, February 1989), 3.

51 At the same time, a shrinking . . . Norval D. Glenn, "The Recent Trend in Marital Success in the United States," *Journal of Marriage & the Family*, vol. 53, no. 2 (May 1991), 264.

Chapter 11: The Personalized Economy

58 Only six out of ten households owned . . . U.S. Bureau of the Census, *Historical Statistics of the United States, Colonial Times to 1970*, Bicentennial Edition, Part 2 (Washington, DC: U.S. Government Printing Office, 1975), 717.

58 Today, the average American household . . . U.S. Bureau of the Census, *Household and Family Characteristics: March 1991*, Series P-20, no. 458 (February 1992), 5; U.S. Bureau of Labor Statistics, *Consumer Expenditures in 1991*, Report 835 (December 1992), 2.

58 At midcentury, the average grocery . . . Crispell, "Myths," 43.

59 The average American home has 2.6 . . . U.S. Bureau of the Census, *Household and Family Characteristics: March 1991*, 5; U.S. Bureau of the Census, *Statistical Abstract of the United States: 1991* 556.

59 Half of baby boomers are . . . "TV More Pervasive, Viewers More Reflexive," *The Public Pulse* (September 1989), 4.

59   As free agents matured . . . Roper's *The Public Pulse Research Supplement* (September 1989), 2.

59   Television changed the way people . . . John P. Robinson, "I Love My TV," *American Demographics* (September 1990), 24, 26.

60   Forty-six percent say watching TV . . . "Living in the USA," *The Public Pulse* (August 1990), 7.

60   As the number of television . . . "Take Talent Inhouse," *The Marketing Pulse* (31 August, 1992), 1.

60   Over 40 percent of baby boomers . . . Geoffrey Godbey and Alan Graefe, "Rapid Growth in Rushin' Americans," *American Demographics* (April 1993), 26.

61   In one recent survey, researchers . . . Richard F. Hamilton, "Work and Leisure—On The Reporting of Poll Results," *Public Opinion Quarterly*, vol. 55, no. 3 (Fall 1991), 348.

61   But when researchers ask people . . . *The Public Perspective* (May/June 1990), 119.

62   The feeling that they're always . . . "Time's Up: Time Values Survey Reveals Time Has Moved to Top of America's Priority List," Bounceback Weekend press release, 1991 Hilton Time Values Survey, Hilton Hotels & Resorts (12 March 1991), 3; and Time/CNN Poll Findings, "The Simple Life and Police Brutality" (16 May 1991), 1.

Chapter 12: A Preference for Leisure

63   Sixty-six percent of the population . . . U.S. Bureau of Labor Statistics, *Employment and Earnings* (January 1992), 162.

63   Thirty-six percent of Americans . . . Roper's *The Public Pulse Research Supplement* (June 1992), 2.

63   Sixty-eight percent of workers say . . . "Job Dissatisfaction Grows; 'Moonlighting' On the Rise," *The Gallup Poll Monthly* (September 1991), 2.

63   Most Americans now believe . . . "Bring on the Weekend," *The Public Pulse* (April 1991), 1.

63   More than nine out of ten men . . . U.S. Bureau of Labor Statistics, *Employment and Earnings*, 164.

63   Nearly all working men and three . . . Ibid., 202.

64   According to a Roper Poll . . . "Work Ethic Grows Weaker," *The Public Pulse* (June 1992), 2.

64 Just 36 percent of 30 to 49 . . . "Job Dissatisfaction Grows; Moonlighting on the Rise," *The Gallup Poll Monthly*, 13.

64 As baby boomers have children . . . Barbara Dafoe Whitehead and Ralph Whitehead, Jr., "The Birth of a Trend," *Utne Reader* (July/August 1991), 68.

65 The proportion of women who say . . . "Work Ethic Grows Weaker, *The Public Pulse*, 3.

65 Sixty percent of mothers say . . . "Tense Times for Families," *The Public Pulse* (January 1991), 2.

65 In 1990, this proportion . . . *The 1990 Virginia Slims Opinion Poll* (New York: The Roper Organization, Inc., 1990), 67.

65 Among all women, 58 percent . . . U.S. Bureau of Labor Statistics, *Employment and Earnings*, 163.

65 Among women aged 25 to 44 . . . Ibid.: 164; and U.S. Bureau of the Census, *Historical Statistics of the United States, Colonial Times to 1970*, Bicentennial Edition, Part 1 (Washington, DC: U.S. Government Printing Office, 1975), 131.

65 Over half of married women . . . U.S. Bureau of the Census, "Fertility of American Women: June 1990," 4.

66 According to a Gallup poll . . . George Gallup, Jr., and Frank Newport, "Americans Widely Disagree on What Constitutes 'Rich'," *The Gallup Poll Monthly* (July 1990), 28.

66 Since 1987, Americans spend . . . U.S. Department of Commerce, *Survey of Current Business* (July 1990), 52.

66 Americans spent $290 billion . . . U.S. Department of Commerce, *Survey of Current Business* (July 1992), 59.

66 Even in the midst of recession . . . Ibid., 60.

66 One of the most rapidly growing . . . U.S. Bureau of the Census, *Statistical Abstract of the United States: 1991*, 231; and U.S. Department of Commerce, *Survey of Current Business* (July 1992), 59.

68 Retail sales of infant . . . "Retail Sales of Infant/Toddler/Preschool Products Near $19 Billion in 1990," press release from Packaged Facts, Inc., New York (July 1991), 1.

68 On the contrary, households . . . Margaret Ambry and Cheryl Russell, *The Official Guide to the American Marketplace* (Ithaca, NY: New Strategist Publications, 1992), 176–178.

68 Beer, rent, and coin-operated . . . Margaret Ambry, *Consumer Power—How Americans Spend Their Money* (Ithaca, NY: New Strategist, Publications, 1991), 11, 54, 95, 143, 230.

68   By 2000, people aged 35 . . . Ambry and Russell, *Official Guide*, 173–175.

69   As baby boomers face . . . "Is the Public Changing Its Financial Habits?" *The Public Pulse* (December 1989), 6.

69   Consumer installment debt—such as . . . "Baby Boom Debt Likely to Shrink in 1990s," *The Boomer Report* (15 April 1992), 3.

70   Currently, 58 percent of baby boomers . . . *A Rude Awakening from the American Dream*, The Fourth Annual Merrill Lynch Retirement Planning Survey, Merrill Lynch, Pierce, Fenner & Smith, Inc. (June 1992), 13–14.

70   The net worth of households headed by . . . Arthur Kennickell and Janice Shack-Marquez, "Changes in Family Finances from 1983 to 1989: Evidence from the Survey of Consumer Finances," *Federal Reserve Bulletin* (January 1992), 3.

70   Most of the baby boom's wealth . . . Ibid., 9, 11.

70   Forty-four percent had a retirement . . . Ibid., 5, 7.

70   Ninety percent of baby boomers . . . Ibid., 13, 15.

71   In any event, economists predict . . . Nick Ravo, "A Windfall Nears in Inheritances from the Richest Generation," *The New York Times* (22 July 1990), E4.

Chapter 13: The Star System

73   Sixty-one percent of Americans say materialism . . . Survey by the Roper Organization cited in "Popular Tastes: What's In, What's Out," *The Public Perspective* (July/August 1991), 88.

73   A home, a car, and lots of money . . . *Roper Reports 89-1* (1989), 3.

74   The percentage of Americans who strongly . . . Niemi, Mueller, and Smith, *Trends in Public Opinion*, 35.

74   Since over 90 percent of Americans . . . Ibid., 248.

74   Census Bureau statistics show . . . U.S. Bureau of the Census, "Money Income of Households, Families, and Persons in the United States: 1991," *Current Population Reports*, Series P-60, no. 180 (1992), B-3.

74   The proportion of working-age . . . Greg J. Duncan, Timothy M. Smeeding, and Willard Rodgers, "W(h)ither the Middle Class? A Dynamic View," paper prepared for the Levy Institute Conference on Income Inequality, Bard College (18–20 June 1991), 9.

74 The share of income accruing . . . U.S. Bureau of the Census, "Money Income," B-5.

75 This kind of insecurity has been . . . *Life*, 20.

75 Despite these generalized fears . . . "Living Standards: Boomers and Their Parents," *Special Consumer Survey Report*, The Conference Board (May 1992), 1, 2.

76 The proportion of households with . . . U.S. Bureau of the Census, "Money Income," B-3.

76 The proportion of working-age . . . Duncan, Smeeding, and Rodgers, "W(h)ither the Middle Class?" 9.

76 Over half of baby boomers say they . . . "Living Standards: Boomers and Their Parents," 2.

77 Most Americans think the salaries . . . "Sporting Nation: Players' Pay Too High," *The Public Perspective* (September/October 1991), 33.

77 The $10 million advances . . . Meg Cox, "A Tom Clancy Book is Said to Set Record for Biggest Advance," *The Wall Street Journal* (4 August 1992), B6; Patrick M. Reilly, "Magazine Talent is the Talk of the Town," *The Wall Street Journal* (4 August 1992), B1.

77 The average CEO of a major . . . "How CEO Paychecks Got So Unreal," *Business Week* (18 November 1991), 20.

77 Economic researchers describe . . . "Study Looks at Earnings," *The Ithaca Journal* (4 July 1992), 3A.

78 Publishers pay millions of dollars . . . "Is Your Basic Author Contract Up-To-Date?" *The Huenefeld Report* (3 August 1992), 3.

78 Nearly two out of three Americans . . . "Americans Widely Disagree on What Constitutes 'Rich'," *The Gallup Poll Monthly* (July 1990), 36.

79 Even so, 26 percent of households . . . U.S. Bureau of the Census, "Money Income," B-3.

80 Households headed by people . . . Ibid., 1.

80 Forty-six percent of households . . . Fabian Linden, *The Great Income Reshuffle* (New York: The Conference Board, 1991), 20.

80 Married couples are by far . . . U.S. Bureau of the Census, "Money Income," 1.

80 Couples in which both husband . . . Ibid., 80.

80 More than 80 percent of households in . . . Ibid., 7.

80 These richest households received 47 . . . Ibid., B-5.

80 In 1970, the incomes of dual-earner . . . Ibid., B-22.

80   According to the Census Bureau . . . U.S. Bureau of the Census, "Job Creation During the Late 1980's: Dynamic Aspects of Employment Growth," *Current Population Reports*, Series P-70, no. 27 (January 1992), 9.

81   By 2005, 81 percent of all . . . Max L. Carey, James C. Franklin, "Industry Output and Job Growth Continues Slow Into Next Century," *Monthly Labor Review* (November 1991), 46.

81   The share of men who work year-round . . . U.S. Bureau of the Census, "Workers With Low Earnings," *Current Population Reports*, Series P-60, no. 178 (March 1992), 3.

81   The median income of households . . . U.S. Bureau of the Census, "Money Income," 6.

82   By 1991, the median income . . . Ibid.

82   Married couples aged 45 to 64 . . . Ambry and Russell, *Official Guide*, 133.

82   For example, median family income . . . U.S. Bureau of the Census, "Money Income," B-9.

82   The median income of dual-earner . . . Ibid., B-22.

83   On average, the personal incomes . . . Ibid., B-25.

83   By age, men younger than 65 saw . . . Ibid., B-29, B-30.

83   Overall, men had a median personal . . . Ibid., B-25.

83   Narrowing the comparison only . . . Ibid., B-31.

83   Men who went no further than . . . Ambry and Russell, *Official Guide*, 153.

83   Overall, household income fell . . . U.S. Bureau of the Census, "Money Income," xi.

84   The proportion of people with . . . U.S. Bureau of the Census, "Trends in Relative Income: 1964–89," *Current Population Reports*, Series P-60, no. 177 (December 1991), 3.

85   Consequently, lifetime incomes . . . Isabel V. Sawhill and Mark Condon, "Is U.S. Income Inequality Really Growing? Sorting Out the Fairness Question," *Policy Bites*, no. 13, The Urban Institute (June 1992), 3–4.

85   According to an analysis by . . . Norton W. Grubb and Robert H. Wilson, "Trends in Wage and Salary Inequality, 1967–88," *Monthly Labor Review* (June 1992), 35.

85   According to Alan Krueger of . . . Alan B. Krueger, "How Computers Have Changed the Wage Structure: Evidence from Micro-

data, 1984–89," *Working Paper Series*, no. 3858, National Bureau of Economic Research, Inc., 24.

Chapter 14: The Working Family

87   The proportion of workers who . . . "Work Ethic Grows Weaker," *The Public Pulse* (June 1992), 3.
87   Fully three out of four Americans . . . "Majority of Americans Support Employer-Mandated Family Leave," *EBRI News*, Employee Benefit Research Institute (7 January 1993), 1.
88   At least 39 million Americans worked . . . "National Work-at-Home Survey," LINK Resources, New York, cited in "Home Sweet Office: Work-At-Homers Grow in Numbers, Rank and Sophistication," *Research Alert* (21 August 1992), 1.
88   Research conducted by GTE . . . "The Work-At-Home Customer," GTE Telephone Operations, press release (undated), 1.
89   The mistaken belief that people . . . Hamilton "Work and Leisure— On the Reporting of Poll Results," *Public Opinion Quarterly*, vol. 55, no. 3 (Fall 1991), 349–350.
90   Time-use studies show that . . . John P. Robinson, "Time For Work," *American Demographics* (April 1989), 68.
90   Today's workers work twice . . . Ibid., 68.
91   Nearly half of American companies . . . U.S. Bureau of the Census, *Statistical Abstract of the United States: 1991*, 420.
91   Today, about 10 million Americans . . . George Silvestri and John Lukasiewicz, "Occupational Employment Projections," *Monthly Labor Review* (November 1991), 85.
91   According to a Gallup survey . . . "Job Dissatisfaction Grows; 'Moonlighting' On the Rise," *The Gallup Poll Monthly*, 14.
92   Some call the newly emerging business . . . John A. Byrne, "The Virtual Corporation," *Business Week* (18 February 1993), 99.
92   According to business consultant . . . Charles Handy, *The Age of Unreason* (Boston: Harvard Business School Press, 1989), 90–101.
93   The revenue growth of companies . . . "Timothy D. Schellhardt, "Temporary-Help Rebound May Prove to be Permanent," *The Wall Street Journal* (28 July 1992), B4.

93   To prepare for this kind of future . . . Handy, *Age of Unreason*, 183–193.

Chapter 15: The Fight against Obligations

97   Please indicate the importance . . . Dey, Astin, and Korn, *The American Freshman*, 122.

97   In 1966, more than one in four . . . Ibid.

98   Only 7 percent of all Americans . . . *Family Values*, MassMutual American Family Values Program, 1991 American Family Values Study: A Return to Family Values (Springfield, MA: Massachusetts Mutual Life Insurance Company, 1991), 10.

98   Most Americans—including baby . . . *Roper Reports 89-1* (1989), 3.

98   When asked to identify the top . . . *Roper's The Public Pulse Research Supplement* (July 1991), 1.

98   Among the 94 million households . . . U.S. Bureau of the Census, "Household and Family Characteristics: March 1991," 3, 153; U.S. Bureau of the Census, "Households, Families, Marital Status and Living Arrangements: March 1988 (Advance Report)," *Current Population Reports*, P-20, no. 432 (September 1988), 10.

99   Baby boom women married late . . . U.S. Bureau of the Census, "Marital Status: 1990," 2.

99   Baby boomers remained childless . . . U.S. Bureau of the Census, "Fertility of American Women," 13.

99   Baby boomers divorced readily . . . National Center for Health Statistics, "Advance Report of Final Divorce Statistics, 1988," *Monthly Vital Statistics Report*, vol. 39, no. 12, Supplement 2 (21 May 1991), 7.

99   In 1960, Americans could expect . . . David Popenoe, "The Family Transformed," *Family Affairs* (Summer/Fall 1989), 2.

Chapter 16: The Marriage Market

101   According to a survey by . . . *Family Values* (1991), 10.

101 To sociologists, these rankings . . . Glenn, "What Does Family Mean?" 36.

101 The percentage of Americans who say . . . Norval D. Glenn, "The News is Bad, But Not Quite as Bad as First Reported: A Correction," *Journal of Marriage & The Family*, Vol. 55, no. 1 (February 1993), 243.

101 The decline in "very happy" marriages . . . Glenn, "The Recent Trend," *Journal of Marriage & the Family*, 267.

102 Social scientists say today's . . . Glenn, "The Recent Trend," *Journal of Marriage & the Family*, 268–269.

103 The median age at which women . . . U.S. Bureau of the Census, "Marital Status: 1991," 5.

104 The proportion of Americans . . . Larry L. Bumpass, James A. Sweet, and Andrew Cherlin, "The Role of Cohabitation in Declining Rates of Marriage," *Journal of Marriage & the Family*, vol. 53, no. 4 (1991), 916.

104 The proportion grew from 11 percent . . . Bumpass, Sweet, and Cherlin, "Cohabitation," 914.

104 People live together before marriage . . . Bumpass, Sweet, and Cherlin, "Cohabitation," 920, 921.

104 One-fifth of all Swedish . . . Constance Sorrentino, "The Changing Family in International Perspective," *Monthly Labor Review* (March 1990), 48.

104 In the United States, only 5 percent . . . calculations by the author based on U.S. Bureau of the Census, "Marital Status: 1991," 7, 71.

104 Though most cohabitors think . . . Bumpass, Sweet, and Cherlin, "Cohabitation," 920.

105 Over 1 million Americans divorce . . . National Center for Health Statistics, "Advance Report of Final Divorce Statistics, 1988," 7.

105 Because of so much divorce . . . National Center for Health Statistics, "Advance Report of Final Marriage Statistics, 1988," *Monthly Vital Statistics Report*, vol. 40, no. 4, Supplement (26 August 1991), 14.

105 The odds of divorce for couples . . . Norton and Miller, "Marriage, Divorce, and Remarriage" (1992), 5.

106 These were exhaustively documented . . . Nancy Howell, *Demography of the Dobe !Kung* (New York: Academic Press, 1979).

106 Teenage sex is common among . . . Ibid., 175.

106 The proportion of Americans who believe . . . Larry Hugick and

Jennifer Leonard, "Sex in America," *The Gallup Poll Monthly* (October 1991), 69.

106   For the !Kung, there are no formal . . . Howell, 227.

107   While !Kung men and women live . . . Ibid., 230.

107   About half of !Kung marriages end . . . Ibid., 238.

107   The latest projections show . . . Norton and Miller, "Marriage, Divorce, and Remarriage," 5.

107   Demographers project that about . . . Ibid., 7.

107   Among women divorced in the late . . . Kathryn A. London, "Cohabitation, Marriage," 6.

107   In 1970, 58 percent of divorced . . . Bumpass, Sweet, and Cherlin, "Cohabitation," 919.

108   When asked their opinion of men . . . *The 1990 Virginia Slims Opinion Poll*, 54.

108   Yet two-thirds of men describe . . . Roper's *The Public Pulse Research Supplement* (February 1992), 2.

108   Among women who feel resentful . . . *The 1990 Virginia Slims Opinion Poll*, 29–31.

109   Women are much more likely . . . Larry L. Bumpass, "What's Happening to the Family? Interactions Between Demographic and Institutional Change," *Demography*, vol. 27, no. 4 (November 1990), 491.

109   Those most unhappy with the division . . . J. Jill Suitor, "Marital Quality and Satisfaction with the Division of Household Labor Across the Family Life Cycle," *Journal of Marriage & the Family*, vol. 53, no. 1 (February 1991), 224.

109   In the mid-1960s, women spent. . . John P. Robinson, "Who's Doing the Housework?" *American Demographics* (December 1988), 28.

110   In another study of who does . . . Myra Marx Ferree, "The Gender Division of Labor in Two-Earner Marriages: Dimensions of Variability and Change," *Journal of Family Issues*, vol. 12, no. 2 (June 1991), 169.

Chapter 17: The Baby Boom's Children

111   In 1975, fully 25 percent of wives . . . U.S. Bureau of the Census, "Fertility of American Women: June 1990," 14, 17.

112 Twenty-two percent of women born . . . U.S. Bureau of the Census, "Studies in American Fertility," *Current Population Reports*, Series P-23, no. 176 (1991), 3, 7, 8.

112 Today, three out of four baby boom . . . U.S. Bureau of the Census, "Fertility of American Women: June 1990," 17.

112 Overall, 57 percent of Americans . . . Gallup, Jr., and Newport, "Virtually All Adults Want Children," 10.

112 Eighty-eight percent of adults . . . *Speaking of Kids—A National Survey of Children and Parents* (Washington, DC: National Commission on Children, 1991), 9.

113 When asked to list their priorities . . . "American Moms Need a Timeout!" BounceBack Weekend press release, 1991 Hilton Time Values Survey, Hilton Hotels & Resorts (3 June 1991), 7.

113 The results show that for most . . . Ibid., 6.

114 Baby boomers give themselves . . . Gallup, Jr., and Newport, "Virtually All Adults Want Children," (1990), 19.

114 In another survey probing . . . *Speaking of Kids*, 11.

114 With an average monthly mortgage . . . *Statistical Abstract of the United States: 1991*, 732.

114 Most children—whether their . . . *Speaking of Kids*, 14–17.

114 Working fathers hurt family . . . Urie Bronfenbrenner, "What Do Families Do?" *Family Affairs* (Winter/Spring 1991), 5.

115 Integrating all these activities . . . Barbara Dafoe Whitehead, "The Family in an Unfriendly Culture," *Family Affairs* (Spring/Summer 1990), 4.

115 Thirty-eight percent report constantly . . . Godbey and Graefe, "Rapid Growth in Rushin' Americans," 26.

115 Seven out of ten say they want . . . Time/CNN Poll Findings on "The Simple Life and Police Brutality" (16 May 1991), 1.

115 Juggling work and family schedules . . . Bronfenbrenner, "What Do Families Do?" 5.

116 Currently, only six out of ten . . . National Center for Health Statistics, "Family Structure and Children's Health: United States, 1988," 6.

116 The proportion of parents who . . . *Speaking of Kids*, 21.

117 Among children ages 5 to 17 . . . National Center for Health Statistics, "Family Structure and Children's Health: United States, 1988," 28.

117   A minority of children in two-parent . . . Ibid., 32.
117   In Florida, for example, a state . . . Helene Cooper, "Child-Divorce
      Case May Change Thinking," *The Wall Street Journal* (28 September
      1992), B14.
118   The law is slowly beginning . . . Bruce C. Hafen, "Individualism in
      Family Law," in *Rebuilding The Nest—A New Commitment to the
      American Family*, ed. David Blankenhorn, Steven Bayme, and Jean
      Bethke Elshtain (Milwaukee: Family Service America, 1990), 171.
118   "People used to settle affairs . . . Bob Ivry, "Don't Trash Your Ex,"
      Parenting (June/July 1992), 185.
118   In response, the number of lawyers . . . U.S. Bureau of the Census,
      Historical Statistics, 131, 140; Silvestri and Lukasiewicz, "Occupa-
      tional," 69; and Howard N. Fullerton, Jr., "Labor Force Projections:
      The Baby Boom Moves On," *Monthly Labor Review* (November
      1991), 33.

Chapter 18: The Rise of the Matriarchal Family

119   On a scale of 1 to 4, Americans rate . . . Mark Mellman, Edward
      Lazarus, and Allan Rivlin, "Family Time, Family Values," in *Rebuild-
      ing the Nest—A New Commitment to the American Family*, ed. David
      Blankenhorn, Steven Bayme, and Jean Bethke Elshtain (Milwaukee:
      Family Service America, 1990, 76.
119   Seven out of ten Americans say . . . "Living in the USA," *The Public
      Pulse* (August 1990), 7.
119   Sixty-four percent of all Americans . . . Mellman, Lazarus, and
      Rivlin, "Family Time," 75.
119   Americans rank spending time . . . George Gallup, Jr. and Frank
      Newport, "Americans Have Love-Hate Relationship with Their TV
      Sets," *The Gallup Poll Monthly* (October 1990), 10.
120   Married couples with children . . . Cheryl Russell, "On The Baby
      Boom Bandwagon," *American Demographics* (May 1991), 27.
121   The majority of children . . . Judith A. Seltzer, "Relationships Be-
      tween Fathers and Children Who Live Apart: The Father's Role After

Separation," *Journal of Marriage & the Family*, vol. 53, No. 1 (February 1991), 79.

121   It is little wonder that one-fourth . . . Larry Hugick, "Women Play the Leading Role in Keeping Modern Families Close," *The Gallup Report* (July 1989), 28, 30.

121   Fathers complain that they are . . . "Good Family Man, Divorced," letter in *Family Affairs* (Winter/Spring 1991), 19.

121   Fifty-one percent of families . . . U.S. Bureau of the Census, "Money Income," 68,78.

121   Overall, women are the dominant parent . . . author's calculations based on sum of dual-earner families with children and single-parent families headed by women.

123   In a longitudinal study of health . . . U.S. Bureau of the Census, "Health Insurance Coverage: 1987–1990," *Current Population Reports*, Series P-70, no. 29 (May 1992), 1, 2.

124   In the early 1960s, before . . . U.S. Bureau of the Census, "Fertility of American Women," 7.

124   Today, now that free agents . . . National Center for Health Statistics, "Advance Report of Final Natality Statistics, 1989," *Monthly Vital Statistics Report*, vol. 40, no. 8, Supplement (12 December 1991), 31.

124   An even larger proportion of babies . . . U.S. Bureau of the Census, "Fertility of American Women," 7.

124   Over half (52 percent) of women . . . Ibid., 8.

125   Among people aged 18 to 29 . . . "Abortion as a Voting Issue," *The Public Perspective* (January/February 1993), 103.

126   Only one in twenty women under . . . William D. Mosher and William F. Pratt, "Fecundity and Infertility in the United States, 1965-88," *National Center For Health Statistics Advance Data*, no. 192 (4 December 1990), 3.

126   Sperm banks father 65,000 babies . . . John N. Edwards, "New Conceptions: Biosocial Innovations and the Family," *Journal of Marriage & the Family*, vol. 53, no. 2 (May 1991), 351.

126   Egg donation, which started . . . Gina Kolata, "Young Women Offer To Sell Their Eggs To Infertile Couples," *The New York Times* (10 November 1991), 1.

126   They create children who can have . . . Edwards, "New Conceptions," 356.

Chapter 19: Women as Kin Connectors

127 Nine out of ten say they have . . . Hugick, "Women Play The Leading Role," 30.

127 In 1947, when Gallup asked Americans . . . Gallup, Jr., and Newport, "Virtually All Adults Want Children," 11.

128 Social scientists have found . . . Alan L. Otten, "Odds and Ends," *The Wall Street Journal* (4 November 1992), B1.

128 The odds that people will survive . . . Martin Kohli, "The World We Forgot: A Historical Review of the Life Course," in *Later Life—The Social Psychology of Aging*, ed. Victor W. Marshall (Beverly Hills, CA: Sage Publications, Inc., 1986), 278.

128 Four out of ten parents offer . . . David J. Eggebeen, "Patterns of Giving and Receiving in the Later Life Course," presentation at the Population Association of America Annual Meeting, Washington, DC (March 1991), table 1.

128 A quarter of baby boom women talk . . . Hugick, "Women Play the Leading Role," 32.

129 Seventeen percent of Americans move . . . U.S. Bureau of the Census, "Geographical Mobility: March 1990 to March 1991," *Current Populations Reports*, Series P-20, no. 463 (October 1992), viii.

129 Most adult children live near . . . Hugick, "Women Play the Leading Role," 30.

129 Likewise, two out of three parents . . . Peter A. Morrison, "Demographic Factors Reshaping Ties to Family and Place," The Rand Corporation, P-7650 (June 1990), 7.

129 Researchers have found that adult . . . "Survey: Most People Live Near Parents," *The Ithaca Journal* (21 April 1992), 5A.

129 Ninety-six percent of Americans . . . Linda G. Martin, "The Graying of Japan," *Population Bulletin*, vol. 44, no. 2 (July 1989), 16.

129 Eighty-four percent of older Americans . . . Ibid., 17.

130 By the year 2000, one-third of . . . author's calculations based on current percentage of people who have grandchildren under age 18 by age.

130 Among men aged 30 or older . . . Hugick, "Women Play the Leading Role," 29.

130 One-third of Americans now live . . . "Survey Finds Big Changes in Family Life," *The Ithaca Journal* (25 August 1992), 10A.

130 In cities from West (Seattle . . .) "Recognition for Non-traditional Couples," *The Boomer Report* (15 June 1992), 6.

130 Virtually all Americans regard . . . "What Constitutes a Family?" *The Public Perspective* (July/August 1992), 101.

Chapter 20: The Ten Commandments

135 Yoko Ono first attracted John Lennon's . . . Albert Goldman, *The Lives of John Lennon* (New York: William Morrow, 1988), 243–244.

135 Baby boomers and younger generations . . . Marini, "Rise of Individualism," 49.

136 Overall, Americans give the Ten . . . Ibid., tables 3, 5.

138 The proportion of Americans who smoke . . . Ambry and Russell, *Official Guide*, 355; Larry Hugick and Jennifer Leonard, "Despite Increasing Hostility, One in Four Americans Still Smokes," *The Gallup Poll Monthly* (December 1991), 2.

138 Seventeen percent of Americans . . . Ibid., 4, 10.

138 Nearly half (44 percent) of Americans . . . Ibid., 4.

138 Most would ask a guest not . . . George Gallup, Jr. and Frank Newport, "Many Americans Favor Restrictions on Smoking in Public Places," *The Gallup Poll Monthly* (July 1990), 22.

138 A majority of Americans do not . . . Hugick and Leonard, "Despite Increasing Hostility," 8.

138 A near majority of the population . . . Ibid., 8, 5.

138 When asked whether they harbor . . . "Living in the USA," *The Public Pulse* (June 1991), 7.

139 Among those aged 25 to 34 . . . "The Boomer File," *The Boomer Report* (August 1992), 7.

139 Three out of four favor random . . . *The Equifax Report on Consumers in the Information Age* (Atlanta: Equifax, 1990), 9.

139 When the readers of *Child* magazine . . . "Hearts and Minds," *Child* (November 1991), 18.

139 According to a 1990 survey, only . . . Ambry and Russell, *Official Guide*, 357.

140 More than half of baby boomers . . . Kohut and Hugick, "Woodstock Remembered," 25.

140 Eight out of ten baby boomers believe . . . Ibid., 37.

140   Eight out of ten Americans think . . . *The Equifax Report*, 35.

140   By 1990, just one in three Americans . . . Ibid., 9.

140   In that year, fully 11 percent . . . "U-M's annual survey of drug use among American young people has received an $18 million grant to continue to 'Monitor the Future,'" The University of Michigan *News and Information Services* (16 September 1992), 3–4.

140   Over half of Americans think . . . "Outlook on Social Issues," *The Public Perspective* (September/October 1991), 84.

141   Among older baby boomers, 72 percent . . . Larry Hugick and Jennifer Leonard, "Sex in America," *The Gallup Poll Monthly* (October 1991), 64.

141   Free agents in their forties have . . . Smith, "Adult Sexual Behavior," 103.

141   Despite their sexual experience . . . Kohut and Hugick, "Woodstock Remembered," 38.

141   Among baby boom parents with children . . . Hugick and Leonard, "Sex in America," 64.

141   More than one in four baby boomers . . . Ibid., 72.

141   With AIDS now the third . . . Ambry and Russell, *Official Guide*, 405, 363.

141   Seventy percent of Americans . . . Jay Schmiedeskamp, "Magic Johnson's AIDS Announcement Has Dramatic Impact on Young People," *The Gallup Poll Monthly* (November 1991), 2.

141   Between 40 and 50 percent of . . . Eleanor Singer and Theresa F. Rogers, "Trends in Public Opinion About AIDS, 1983 to 1990," *The Public Perspective* (March/April 1991), 13.

142   Forty-eight percent favor it . . . Larry Hugick, "Public Opinion Divided on Gay Rights," *The Gallup Poll Monthly* (June 1992), 3, 4, 6.

142   The proportion of all Americans . . . Alec Gallup and Frank Newport, "Death Penalty Support Remains Strong," *The Gallup Poll Monthly* (June 1991), 40–43.

142   Most Americans think convicted . . . "Get Tough Across the Board," *The Public Perspective* (July/August 1991), 79.

143   They think the Supreme Court . . . "Criticism of the Courts," *The Public Perspective* (July/August 1991), 78.

143   Criminal cases now make up . . . Linda Greenhouse, "The Conservative Majority Solidifies," *The New York Times* (30 June 1991), E1, E3.

Chapter 21: The Rise of Crime

145 The Roper Organization has documented . . . "Living in the USA," *The Public Pulse* (March 1992), 7.

146 In a survey measuring Americans' ethical . . . Marini, "Rise of Individualism," table 5.

147 The violent crime index, which measures . . . Kathleen Maguire and Timothy J. Flanagan, eds., *Sourcebook of Criminal Justice Statistics— 1990*, Bureau of Justice Statistics (Washington, D.C.: U.S. Government Printing Office, 1991), 353.

147 In 1991, 24,000 Americans were . . . "Violent Crime: Rising Costs and Dangerous Trends," *Emerging Issues*, report from the Congressional Clearinghouse on the Future (undated), 1.

148 The percentage of older Americans . . . "Victims," *The Public Perspective* (July/August 1991), 82.

148 In 1964, 31 percent of murder . . . Maguire and Flanagan, *Sourcebook*, 380–381, 384.

148 In the United States, 22 percent . . . U.S. Bureau of the Census, *Poverty in the United States: 1991*, *Current Population Reports*, Series P-60, no. 181 (August 1992), 4.

148 Even those with jobs aren't faring . . . U.S. Bureau of the Census, "Money Income," B-26, B-27.

148 Life Expectancy among black men . . . National Center for Health Statistics, "Advance Report of Final Mortality Statistics, 1989," *Monthly Vital Statistics Report*, vol. 40, no. 8, Supplement 2 (7 January 1992), 420.

148 Firearm mortality for black men . . . Lois A. Fingerhut, Joel C. Kleinman, Elizabeth Godfrey, and Harry Rosenberg, "Firearm Mortality Among Children, Youth, and Young Adults 1–34 Years of Age, Trends and Current Status: United States, 1979–88," National Center for Health Statistics *Monthly Vital Statistics Report*, vol. 39, no. 11, Supplement (14 March 1991), 7.

149 With rates of violent crime taking . . . "Crime, Cops, and Courts," *The Public Perspective* (July/August 1991), 74–75.

149 In 1975, 32 percent of households . . . Maguire and Flanagan, *Sourcebook*, 295.

Chapter 22: The Rise of Tolerance

151   According to University of Texas . . . Glenn, "From Communalism to Individualism," 3.

151   The proportion of Americans who . . . Niemi, Mueller, and Smith, *Trends in Public Opinion*, 170.

152   More Americans now approve than . . . George Gallup, Jr. and Frank Newport, "For First Time, More Americans Approve of Interracial Marriage Than Disapprove," *The Gallup Poll Monthly* (August 1991), 62, 60.

152   The percentage of white Americans . . . Niemi, Mueller, and Smith, *Trends in Public Opinion*, 174.
      As younger generations replace . . . Ibid., 24, 180.

152   In the forty-seven states that report . . . National Center for Health Statistics, "Advance Report of Final Natality Statistics," 1989, 40.

152   Overall, the number of white . . . Ambry and Russell, *Official Guide*, 3.

153   While only about half of all . . . Ibid., 47.

153   The metropolitan area grew by fully 26 percent . . . Ibid., 45, 49, 53, 55.

153   While a majority of whites say . . . Larry Hugick and Leslie McAneny, "White and Black America: Fragile Consensus on Urban Aid," *The Gallup Poll Monthly* (June 1992), 8, 9.

153   Only 12 percent of whites versus . . . "Blacks and Whites Hand Down Opinions," *The Public Perspective* (September/October 1991), 82.

154   The percentage of blacks who "completely" . . . *Times Mirror* (8 July 1992), 21.

Chapter 23: The Rise of Self-Interest

156   French statesman and writer Alexis . . . Alexis de Tocqueville, *Democracy in America*, eds. J. P. Mayer and Max Lerner (New York: Harper & Row, 1966), 477.

156   The proportion who think most . . . Niemi, Mueller, and Smith, *Trends in Public Opinion*, 303; telephone interview with Michael Worley, National Opinion Research Center, University of Chicago (7 October 1992).

156 Between 1973 and 1991, the . . . George Gallup, Jr. and Frank Newport, "Confidence in Major U.S. Institutions at All-Time Low," *The Gallup Poll Monthly* (October 1991), 37.

157 Surveys taken in 1992 reveal . . . "The People, the Press and Politics—Campaign '92: Survey XI," Times Mirror Center for The People and the Press, *News* (17 September 1992), 29.

157 Voter turnout among Americans . . . "The Voters: Gains and Losses in Turnout," *The New York Times* (8 November 1992), E2.

157 Record numbers of Americans registered . . . Jeffrey Schmalt, "Americans Sign Up in Record Numbers to Cast a Ballot," *The New York Times* (19 October 1992), 1.

159 The networks once commanded over . . . "Mass Communications: 'Narrowcasting' And Pluralism," *The Public Perspective*, (September/October 1992), 6.

159 Overall, 70 percent of Americans . . . *Public Pulse Research Supplement* (May 1991), 1.

159 At least 60 percent of those aged . . . Times Mirror (8 July 1992), 48.

159 In a study by the Times Mirror . . . "The Age of Indifference: A Study of Young Americans and How They View The News," Times Mirror Center for the People and the Press (28 June 1990), 7–8.

160 This fact may explain why people . . . "Negative Judgments May Be Automatic, Unconscious," *Standard Story Source*, Stanford University (October 1992), 1.

160 The explosion of the Challenger . . . "Times Mirror News Interest Index September 1992," *News*, Times Mirror Center for the People and the Press (22 September 1992), 20.

161 Americans born in 1946 or later . . . author's calculations based on dates of birth for the CEO's of the thousand most valuable publicly traded U.S. companies, listed in "The Corporate Elite," *Business Week* (12 October 1992), 119–142.

162 Over half of Americans aged 50 . . . Times Mirror (8 July 1992), 25, 26.

162 "Individualism," he wrote, "dams . . ." De Tocqueville, 477.

163 Overall, Americans are less likely . . . Niemi, Mueller, and Smith, "Trends in Public Opinion," 312; telephone interview with Michael Worley (7 October 1992).

163 Fifty-four percent of households . . . *Giving and Volunteering in the United States—Findings from a National Survey*, 1990 ed. (Washington, D.C.: Independent Sector, 1990), 44, 121.

163   The number of volunteer firefighters . . . telephone interview with John Hall, National Fire Protection Association, Quincy, Massachusetts (7 October 1992).

164   The percentage of Americans who belong . . . Niemi, Mueller, and Smith, *Trends in Public Opinion*, 304, 311; telephone interview with Michael Worley (7 October 1992).

164   The trend away from groups is . . . Dey, Astin, and Korn, *The American Freshman*, 120–121.

164   Free agents, spurning organized . . . Times Mirror (8 July 1992), 7.

164   The percentage of Americans belonging . . . Niemi, Mueller, and Smith, *Trends in Public Opinion*, 307, 311; telephone interview with Michael Worley (7 October 1992).

165   When the 1990 census knocked . . . Personal correspondence from Barbara Everitt Bryant, former Director, Bureau of the Census, March 22, 1993; U.S. Bureau of the Census, "Census Bureau Releases Refined 1990 Census Coverage Estimates From Demographic Analysis," *United States Department of Commerce News* (13 June 1991), table 3.

165   More than one-quarter . . . Sar A. Levitan and Frank Gallo, "Workforce Statistics: Do We Know What We Think We Know—And What Should We Know?" paper transmitted to the Joint Economic Committee of the 101st Congress (26 December 1989), 14.

166   When the Census Bureau compares . . . U.S. Bureau of the Census, "Measuring the Effect of Benefits and Taxes on Income and Poverty: 1979 to 1991," *Current Population Reports*, Series P-60, no. 182-RD (August 1992), F2.

166   In the 1960s, the poorest households . . . Susan E. Mayer and Christopher Jencks, "Recent Trends in Economic Inequality in the United States: Income vs. Expenditures vs. Material Well-Being," paper prepared for the Levy Institute Conference on Income Inequality, Bard College (June 18–20, 1991), table 4.

166   Seventy-nine percent of the public . . . *The Equifax Report*, vii, 2.

167   Over 80 percent of Americans younger . . . Ibid., 2.

167   One-third of Americans under . . . Ibid., 14.

167   Most Americans under the age . . . Ibid., 26, 27.

167   Consequently, over 70 percent . . . Ibid., 72.

Chapter 24: Growing Old, but Not Gracefully

172 Two out of three baby boomers say . . . "Fear of Dying," *The Gallup Poll Monthly* (January 1991), 53.
172 Eighty-one percent say they have . . . *A Rude Awakening from the American Dream*, 4.

Chapter 25: The End of Early Retirement

175 Over 70 percent want to retire . . . Gallup, Jr. and Newport, "Baby boomers Seek More Family Time," 32.
176 Today's older Americans have more . . . John P. Robinson, "Quitting Time," *American Demographics* (May 1991), 36.
176 Only 25 percent of people aged 55 . . . Godbey and Graefe, "Rapid Growth in Rushin' Americans," 26.
176 In 1960, 92 percent of men aged . . . Murray Gendell and Jacob S. Siegel, "Trends in Retirement Age by Sex, 1950–2005," *Monthly Labor Review* (July 1992), 24.
177 Today the average age at which . . . Ambry and Russell, *Official Guide*, 321.
177 Today's older women spend one-third . . . Robinson, "Who's Doing the Housework?" 28.

Chapter 26: The Money Supply

179 The proportion of Americans aged 65 or older . . . U.S. Bureau of the Census, "Trends in Relative Income," 8.
180 Among 25- to 44-year-olds, . . . Ibid., 18–19.
180 Between 1967 and 1991, the median . . . U.S. Bureau of the Census, "Money Income," B-7.
181 Retired Americans aged 55 or older . . . Kennickell and Shack-Marquez, "Changes in Family Finances," 3.
181 The savings of Americans aged 45 . . . "Don't Blame Boomers for Decline in Savings Rate," *Maturity Market Perspectives* (January 1992), 9.
182 Over half of baby boomers say . . . "A Rude Awakening From the American Dream," 4.

182 Three out of four baby boomers . . . Ibid., 5.

182 Most free agents would find it . . . U.S. Bureau of the Census, "Money Income," 15, 17, 23.

183 Social Security is the most important . . . personal facsimile transmission of survey results from the National Taxpayers Union Foundation Survey on Retirement Confidence (12 December 1990), question *21h.

183 Yet the average Social Security . . . U.S. Bureau of the Census, "Money Income," 178.

183 Only 15 percent of baby boomers expect . . . "A Rude Awakening From the American Dream," 12.

183 Three out of four Americans . . . National Taxpayers Union Foundation Survey on Retirement Confidence (Washington, DC: Mathew Greenwald & Associates, February 1991), 24.

183 Only 43 percent of 18- to 34 . . . "Confidence in Future of Social Security and Medicare Explored," EBRI News, Employee Benefit Research Institute, Washington, DC (11 June 1991), 1.

184 Thirty percent of baby boomers . . . "A Rude Awakening From The American Dream," 9.

185 This figure is nearly the same . . . personal facsimile transmission of survey results from the National Taxpayers Union Foundation Survey, question *21h.

185 The average elderly private . . . U.S. Bureau of the Census, "Money Income," 178.

185 Already, employer-provided pension . . . Martha Farnsworth Riche, "Men Uncovered," American Demographics (July 1990), 15, 16.

185 But union membership among the . . . Peter Nulty, "Look What the Unions Want Now," Fortune (8 February 1993), 128.

185 Between 1972 and 1988, pension . . . Riche, "Men Uncovered," 15, 16.

185 Forty-two percent of baby boomers . . . "A Rude Awakening From the American Dream," 12.

185 Among the current generation of retirees . . . National Taxpayers Union Foundation Survey, question *21h.

185 The Survey of Consumer Finances shows . . . Kennickell and Shack-Marquez, "Changes in Family Finances," 5, 7.

186 Just 5 percent of all workers expect . . . National Taxpayers Union Foundation Survey, question 21.

186 According to the Urban Institute . . . "Trouble Ahead for Boomers?" *Research Alert* (18 January 1991), 1.

Chapter 27: The Fortunate Few

187 Surveys of pension recipients . . . Martha Farnsworth Riche, "Retirement's Lifestyle Pioneers," *American Demographics* (January 1986), 44.

187 The Census Bureau projects that . . . U.S. Bureau of the Census, "Sixty-Five Plus in America," *Current Population Reports*, Series P-23, no. 178 (August 1992), 5–3, 5–9, 5–10.

188 In 1982, Americans claimed to have . . . "Leisure Creatures? Not Quite," *The Public Pulse* (July 1988), 3.

189 Among the oldest baby boomers . . . Timothy Q. Rounds, "Where In The World Have You Been?" *American Demographics* (May 1988), 32–33.

190 Eighty-six percent of Americans . . . Ibid., 32.

Chapter 28: Old and Alone

191 Marital satisfaction hits . . . Timothy H. Brubaker, "Families in Later Life: A Burgeoning Research Area," *Journal of Marriage & the Family*, vol. 52, no. 4 (November 1990), 962.

192 Social science studies show . . . Ibid., 971.

192 About 15 percent of baby boomers . . . U.S. Bureau of the Census, "Studies in American Fertility," 9.

192 Studies show, however, that childless . . . Brubaker, "Families in Later Life," 968.

192 The unmarried, childless old . . . Ibid.

192 As the number of elderly Americans . . . author's calculations from U.S. Bureau of the Census, "Marital Status and Living Arrangements: March 1990," *Current Population Reports*, Series P-20, no. 450 (May 1991), 13.

193 From the age of 55 on, in fact . . . U.S. Bureau of the Census, "Marital Status: 1990," 13, 17.

193 Only half of women aged 65 . . . Ibid., 12.

193   The chances are seven out of ten . . . Noreen Goldman and Graham
      Lord, "Sex Differences in Life Cycle Measures of Widowhood,"
      Demography, vol. 20, no. 2 (May 1983), 185.

193   According to projections by the Social . . . U.S. Bureau of the
      Census, "Sixty-Five Plus in America," 6-2.

194   Among men aged 65 or older in 2040 . . . Ibid.

194   In 1920, women outlived men . . . Goldman and Lord, 178.

194   In 1920, there were only 1.4 million . . . U.S. Bureau of the Census,
      Historical Statistics, 21; U.S. Bureau of the Census, "Marital Status:
      1990," 17; author's calculations from U.S. Bureau of the Census,
      "Sixty-Five Plus in America," 6-2; U.S. Bureau of the Census, "Popu-
      lation Projections of the United States, by Age, Sex, Race, and
      Hispanic Origin: 1992 to 2050," *Current Population Reports*, Series
      P-25, no. 1092 (November 1992), 52.

194   The number of elderly widowers . . . Ibid.

194   A 65-year-old woman today can . . . Goldman and Lord, "Sex
      Differences," 179.

194   In the 1890s, a woman had only . . . Ibid., 185, 188.

194   According to mortality projections . . . U.S. Bureau of the Census,
      "Sixty-Five Plus in America," 6-3.

Chapter 29: Improving Health

198   Still, this will be an improvement . . . Ambry and Russell, *Official
      Guide*, 412.

198   Three chronic conditions are likely . . . Ibid., 384–387.

199   Among married women born between . . . Mosher and Pratt, "Fe-
      cundity and Infertility," 3.

199   But during the baby boom's lifetime . . . Alan L. Otten, "Charting
      Future Course of Longevity Gains," *The Wall Street Journal* (15
      November 1991), B1.

199   If Americans were to receive Social . . . Marilyn M. McMillen, "Sex-
      Specific Equivalent Retirement Ages: 1940–2050," *Social Security
      Bulletin* (March 1984), 7.

199   In 1990, a newborn boy could expect . . . National Center for Health
      Statistics, "Life Tables," *Vital Statistics of the United States, 1988*, vol.
      II, section 6 (March 1991), 2.

200 At age 40, Americans can expect . . . Ibid., 11; Donald J. Bogue, *The Population of the United States—Historical Trends and Future Projections* (New York: The Free Press, 1985), 212.

200 The healthiest women are not housewives . . . Lois M. Verbrugge and Jennifer H. Madans, "Women's Roles and Health," *American Demographics* (March 1985), 39.

200 While life expectancy at age 65 has grown . . . National Center for Health Statistics, "Life Tables": 2, 11; U.S. Bureau of the Census, "Sixty-Five Plus in America," 3–16.

201 In a study of elderly Canadians . . . Beth J. Soldo and Emily M. Agree, "America's Elderly," *Population Bulletin*, vol. 43, no. 3 (1988), 22.

201 A majority of Americans rate . . . Ambry and Russell, *Official Guide* 352.

201 Four out of five people aged 65 . . . Soldo and Agree, "America's Elderly," 19.

201 The most common chronic condition . . . Ambry and Russell, *Official Guide*, 390–391.

201 Heart disease causes one-third . . . National Center for Health Statistics, "Annual Summary of Births, Marriages, Divorces, and Deaths: United States, 1991," *Monthly Vital Statistics Report*, vol. 40, no. 13 (30 September 1992), 6, 19; U.S. Bureau of the Census, *Statistical Abstract of the United States: 1991*, 79.

201 Four out of ten boomers exercise . . . *The Prevention Index 1992*, Summary Report (Emmaus, PA: Rodale Press, 1992), 5, 11.

202 With heart disease eliminated . . . U.S. Bureau of the Census, "Sixty-Five Plus in America," 3–9.

202 Today, fully 73 percent of people . . . Ibid.

202 The number two killer in the U.S. . . . National Center for Health Statistics, "Annual Summary of Births, Marriages, Divorces, and Deaths: United States, 1991," 6, 19; U.S. Bureau of the Census, *Statistical Abstract of the United States: 1991*, 79.

202 If cancer were entirely eradicated . . . U.S. Bureau of the Census, "Sixty-Five Plus in America," 3–9.

202 The third leading cause of death . . . National Center for Health Statistics, "Annual Summary of Births, Marriages, Divorces, and Deaths: United States, 1991," 6, 19; U.S. Bureau of the Census, *Statistical Abstract of the United States: 1991*, 79.

202 Accidents are the fourth leading . . . Ibid.

203   Lung disease, pneumonia, diabetes . . . National Center for Health
      Statistics, "Annual Summary of Births, Marriages, Divorces, and
      Deaths: United States, 1991," 6.

203   Today, 13 million Americans . . . Mitchell P. LaPlante, Gerry E.
      Hendershot, and Abigail J. Moss, "Assistive Technology Devices and
      Home Accessibility Features: Prevalence, Payment, Need, and
      Trends," *National Center for Health Statistics Advance Data*, no. 217 (16
      September 1992), 6.

204   The number of people using wheelchairs . . . Ibid., 9.

204   Today, 7 million Americans have homes . . . Ibid., 6–7.

204   Today, 16 percent of people aged 65 . . . U.S. Bureau of the Census,
      "The Need for Personal Assistance with Everyday Activities: Recipi-
      ents and Caregivers," *Current Population Reports*, Series P-70, no. 19
      (June 1990), 4.

205   Today, 22 percent of Americans aged . . . U. S. Bureau of the Census,
      "Sixty-Five Plus in America," 6–8.

206   Over half of Americans say people . . . "Fear of Dying," 55, 57.

Chapter 30: Spiritual Therapy

207   The proportion of Americans who think religion . . . Tom W. Smith,
      "Religious Beliefs and Behaviors and the Televangelist Scandals of
      1987–1988," *Public Opinion Quarterly*, vol. 56, no. 3 (Fall 1992), 367.

207   The proportion of Americans who believe in God . . . Niemi,
      Mueller, and Smith, *Trends in Public Opinion*, 253, 261.

207   The proportion who believe in an afterlife . . . Smith, "Religious
      Beliefs," 369, 371, 374.

208   Free agents are less likely than older . . . George Gallup, Jr. and
      Frank Newport, "Baby Boomers Seek More Family Time," 41.

208   According to a survey by Wade . . . Wade Clark Roof, "The Baby
      Boom's Search for God," *American Demographics* (December 1992),
      54, 56.

209   This more personal approach to . . . Peter L. Benson, "Protestants
      in the U.S.: The Next Generation," *The Public Perspective* (November/
      December 1990), 8.

210   *The Road Less Traveled*, a book . . . William Grimes, "Mega-Seller,
      Great Gift," *The New York Times* (8 November 1992), V12.

210   Reincarnation, for example, is believed . . . Roof, "The Baby Boom's Search," 56.

Chapter 31: The Final Judgment

218   Despite all the changes of . . . Niemi, Mueller, and Smith, *Trends in Public Opinion*, 290; and telephone interview with Michael Worley (7 October 1992).

220   And surveys reveal that Americans . . . "Living in the USA," *The Public Pulse* (November 1990), 7.

220   Only 3 percent of Americans say . . . Linda DeStefano, "Pressures of Modern Life Bring Increased Importance to Friendship," *The Gallup Poll Monthly* (March 1990), 24, 25, 31.

222   In 1960, most Americans were high . . . U.S. Bureau of the Census, *Statistical Abstract of the United States: 1991*, 138.

222   Today, 78 percent have a high school . . . U.S. Bureau of the Census, "Educational Attainment," 3.

223   The proportion of Americans currently . . . "Signs Encouraging For an Upsurge in Reading in America," *The Gallup Poll Monthly* (February 1991), 44, 49.

223   In 1941, when the S.A.T. was first . . . Gerald W. Bracey, "The Straight Story About the Education Our Kids Are Getting, *The Washington Post National Weekly Edition* (13–19 May 1991), 23.

223   Between 1980 and 1990, S.A.T. scores . . . Ambry and Russell, *Official Guide*, 334.

223   The ten fastest-growing occupations . . . Silvestri and Lukasiewicz, "Occupational," 81, 82.

225   This point is borne out in . . . K. G. Barnhurst and J. C. Nerone, "Design Trends in U.S. Front Pages, 1885–1985," *Journalism Quarterly*, vol. 68 (1991), 796–804; cited in Diana Mutz, "Impersonal Influence in American Politics," *The Public Perspective* (November/ December 1992), 20.

226   If a house burns down . . . K. G. Barnhurst, "The Great American Newspaper," *The American Scholar*, vol. 60 (1991), 106–112, cited in Mutz, "Impersonal," 20.

228   Nearly eight out of ten Americans . . . Joe Schwartz, "Earth Day Today," *American Demographics* (April 1990), 41.

228   Only 5 percent take public . . . "What We Do and How We Get
       There," *The Washington Post National Weekly Edition* (8-14 June
       1992), 32.
228   Most Americans are not willing to pay . . . Joe Schwartz and
       Thomas Miller, "The Earth's Best Friends," *American Demographics*
       (February 1991), 28, 29.

Index